Richmond PUBLISHING

GM Publications

Sonia

Richmond Publishing
(91) 744 9060 (Spain)
richmondcustomers@
santillana.es

File

INTERMEDIATE

Madeline McHugh

CW01583072

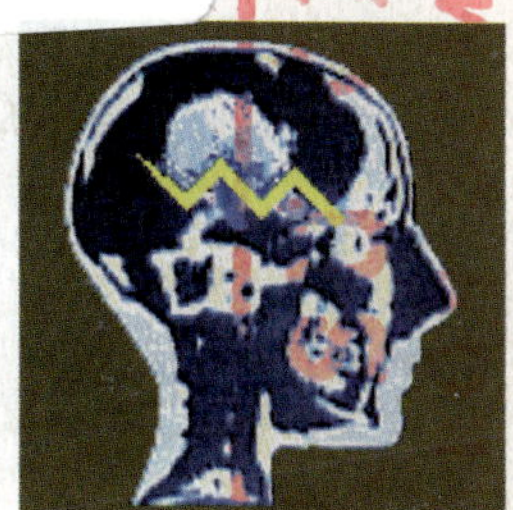

PROHIBIDA LA VENTA
MUESTRA SIN VALOR COMERCIAL

Student's Book

Contents map

© SANTILLANA

SPEAKING	LISTENING	READING	WRITING	CROSS-CURRICULAR
Asking and answering questions using prompts Information gap fill Role play: Travel agents	Following a route on map Following directions Identifying the gist of dialogues Completing dialogues Matching illustrations to stories	Identifying summarising sentences Text completion Matching vocabulary of a similar meaning Interpreting signs and signals Deducing meaning from context	Note taking from full text Writing full text from notes Writing tips to travellers	Acquiring information on different countries Interpreting maps, signs and symbols Using statistical information Presenting information in different formats
Agreeing and disagreeing with opinions Conducting a survey Discussing children's /human rights Controlled dialogue in pairs Relating a children's story	Identifying speakers by age Recording opinions Matching illustrations to text Identifying the topic in a conversation Checking predictions Following a children's story	Text completion with given sentences Giving opinions on a text Predicting the end of a text Interpreting the moral of a story	Recording results of a survey Completing a story from picture prompts	Conducting a survey Making moral decisions
	Transformation		Project: A class survey	
Asking and answering questions from a table Controlled dialogue in pairs Relating past events from: 1 written prompts 2 picture prompts	True/False sentences Note taking and expanding on notes Completing a dialogue	Completing a text with: 1 correct verb tense 2 grammatical words Answering comprehension questions on: 1 a text 2 a table Matching summaries to text	Recounting personal events and experiences Using information in a table to write full text Writing questions for given answers Writing a narrative from prompts	Processing information in different formats Sequencing events chronologically
Re-telling stories and predicting the ending Summarising statements about a text Describing a life history	Checking the accuracy of predictions Description of personal life changes Completing short dialogues	Interpreting meaning from context Descriptions of physical changes to places Description of a political climate	Describing sounds An account of a personal history and life changes	Cross-referencing Looking at historical change
	Error Correction		Project: Heroes	
Telling fact and fiction about yourself Expanding on notes Role play: An interview	Interpreting meaning from intonation Matching dialogues to written notes Drawing up a personal profile from an interview	Jig-saw reading Predicting the end of a story Memorising details from a story Matching written information to pictures Finding specific information from texts Interpreting notes and surveys	Using punctuation A letter of application for a job Survey questions to prepare an interview	Processing different types of information Interpreting information Preparing for a job interview Applying for jobs
Giving instructions for a number puzzle Making statements from statistical tables Summarising written texts from prompts	Following instructions for a number puzzle Making calculations based on information heard	Solving number puzzles Agreeing/disagreeing with points in a text Re-ordering paragraphs	Writing a summary of a text A personal forecast	Logical deduction with numbers Interpreting statistics Memorising information in graphs and tables
	Transformation		Project: Job applications	

© SANTILLANA

Contents map

© SANTILLANA

SPEAKING	LISTENING	READING	WRITING	CROSS-CURRICULAR
Saying appropriate phrases with the correct gesture Agreeing and disagreeing with opinions in text Agreeing and disagreeing with advice	Matching photographs to speakers Summarising speakers' words Identifying specific items of vocabulary	Interpreting signs and symbols Matching letters to responses Following instructions Interpreting opinions presented in a text	Summarising a text: 1 preparing a summary from prompt questions 2 writing the summary Letter to a magazine 'problem page'	Interpreting and using codes and symbols Interpreting human behaviour Discussing questions of literacy
Discussing 'pet hates' Describing objects Describing differences between photographs Describing people and their physical features	Matching pictures to conversations Note taking Identifying objects and processes from sounds Matching descriptions of objects to photographs Identifying specific sentences	Completing a text with grammatical words Understanding mood and atmosphere in text	Describing a person's physical features Describing impressions of a person	Using visual information to draw conclusions Discussing personal characteristics
	Error Correction		Project: Personal problems	
Conducting a survey Giving personal opinions on a text Giving opinions about case studies of crime	Ordering events in a story Matching two parts of spoken sentences	Drawing a conclusion from a story Completing a text according to logical meaning Deducing meaning from context	Note taking from a text Giving advice to people involved in crime	Discussing social and anti-social behaviour Discussing social problems Discussing moral dilemmas
Describing dreams Interpreting dreams Re-telling a story	Jig-saw listening Completing a story with given sentences Making notes on a spoken text Identifying and completing specific statements	Completing a text with given phrases True/False statements in a text Finding specific sentence patterns Matching descriptions to pictures	Descriptions of dreams Summarising people's beliefs and opinions Sentence patterns under specific grammatical headings	Categorising syntactic meaning in language Discussing beliefs and fears
	Transformation		Project: Crime and criminals	
Re-telling a story Telling a story from visual prompts	Ordering pictures according to a sequence of events Completing a story from notes	Summarising events in a chronological order Completing a text with given verbs Completing a text with grammatical words Extracting specific phrases	A description of a famous monument Writing a story from visual prompts	Discussing myths, beliefs and superstitions Putting events into chronological order
Discussing personal language errors	Completing sentences with specific phrases Identifying key/redundant phrases in text Reporting statements and questions Matching complete text to notes and re-ordering	Illustrating a text according to appropriate meaning Analysing poetry	Looking at spelling in relation to pronunciation	Reviewing personal learning strategies International aspects of language
	Error Correction		Project: Famous places	

© SANTILLANA

Take Off!

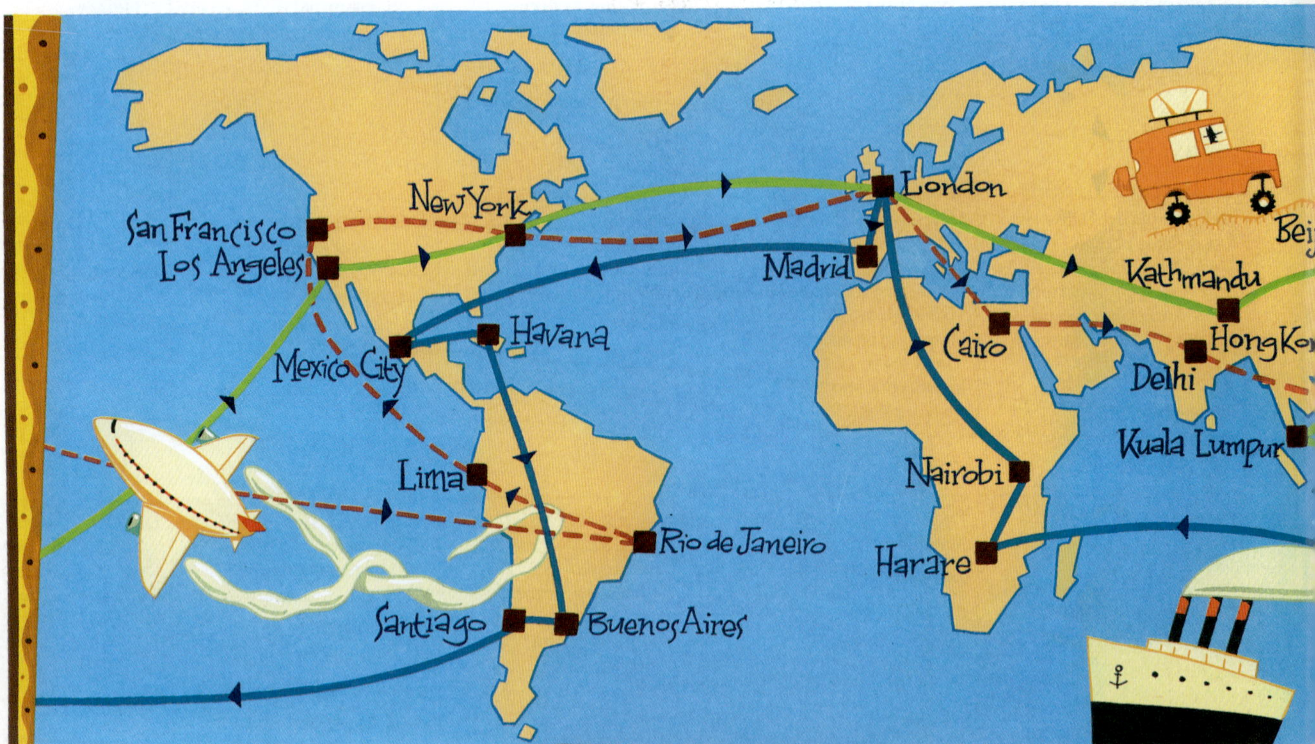

Ticket 1

BRITISH AIRWAYS
PASSENGER TICKET AND BAGGAGE CHECK — FLIGHT COUPON NO1
ORIGIN/DESTINATION LON/LON
BOOKING REFERENCE DIRCLM 3
S/N666666 LONJ21SEP
CONJUNCTION TICKETS 4480-4482
NAME OF PASSENGER SHERIDAN/S MS

		CARRIER	FLIGHT	CLASS	DATE	TIME	STATUS	FARE BASIS
FROM LONDON	LHR	BA	155	M	10OCT	1630	OK	Y1D00N1/1
TO CAIRO	CAI	BA	570	M	15OCT	1015	OK	Y1D00N1/1
FROM DELHI	DEL	BA	4098	M	20OCT	0930	OK	Y1D00N1/1
TO MANILA	MNL	BA	493	M	01DEC	2140	OK	Y1D00N1/
TO TOKYO	NRT							

FORM OF PAYMENT 3551/MLR498
TOTAL GBP1112
3 124 7685444480 3

Passport

United Kingdom of Great Britain and Northern Ireland
Passport Passeport
Type/Type: P
Code of issuing/Code de l'Etat: GBR
Passport No./Passeport No.: C329703E
Surname/Nom (1): SHERIDAN
Given names/Prénoms (2): SUSAN
Nationality/Nationalité (3): BRITISH CITIZEN
Date of birth/Date de naissance (4): 28 MAR/MARS 67
Children/Enfants (5): 0
Sex/Sexe (6): F
Place of birth/Lieu de naissance (7): LONDON
Date of issue/Date de délivrance (8): 15 MAY/MAI93
Authority/Autorité (9): UNITED KINGDOM PASSPORT AGENCY
Date of expiry/Date d'expiration (10): 15 MAY/MAI03
Occupation/Profession (11): COMPUTER OPERATOR
P<GBRSHERIDAN<<SUSAN<<<<<<<<<<

Ticket 2

BRITISH AIRWAYS
S/N666666 LONJ21SEP
CONJUNCTION TICKETS 4480-448
NAME OF PASSENGER SHERIDAN/S MS

		CARRIER	FLIGHT	CLASS	DATE	TIME	STATUS
FROM TOKYO	NRT	BA	155	M	23DEC	1630	OK
TO RIO	GIG	BA	570	M	08JAN	1015	OK
FROM LIMA	LIM	BA	4098	M	15FEB	0930	OK
TO SAN FRANCISCO	SFO	BA	493	M	20FEB	2140	OK
TO NEW YORK	JFK						

TOTAL GBP980
3 124 7685444480 3

Ticket 3

BRITISH AIRWAYS
ORIGIN/DESTINATION LON/LON
BOOKING REFERENCE DIRCLM 365
DATE AND PLACE OF ISSUE 8592310 21SEP3 BRITISH AIRWAYS LONDON SALES SHOP
S/N666666 LONJ21SEP
CONJUNCTION TICKETS 4480-4482
NAME OF PASSENGER SHERIDAN/S MS

		CARRIER	FLIGHT	CLASS	DATE	TIME	STATUS	FARE BASIS	ALLOW
FROM NEW YORK	JFK	BA	178	M	01MAR	1740	OK	Y1D00N1/13M42	23K
TO LONDON	LHR								

FORM OF PAYMENT 3551/MLR49875 VISA
TOTAL GBP300
3 124 7685444482 3
DO NOT MARK OR STAMP IN THE WHITE AREA ABOVE

© SANTILLANA

1 Round the world *Asking questions*

a Look at the ticket and the map. Which route on the map matches the route on the ticket? Which countries would you like to visit on a round-the-world trip?

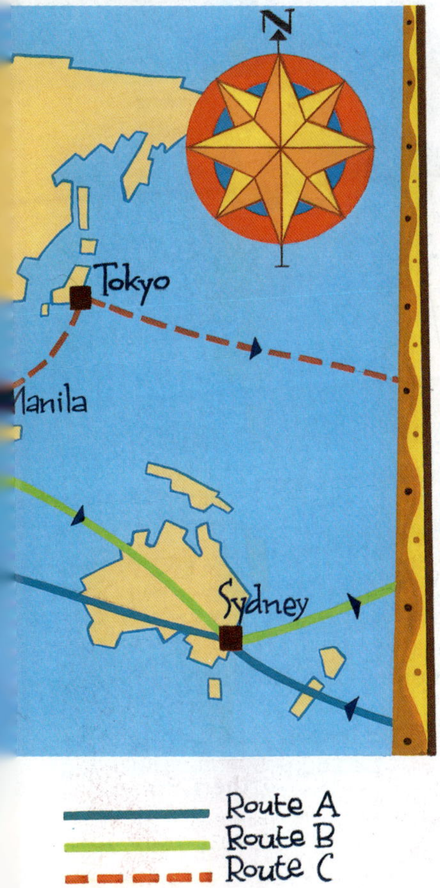

b Look at the ticket and the passport and answer the questions.

1 What is the passenger's name?
2 When is she flying to Tokyo?
3 How long is she staying in San Francisco?
4 How did she pay for the ticket?
5 What does BA stand for?
6 What does she do?
7 Where was she born?
8 How old is she?

c With a partner, ask and answer more questions about the information on the ticket and the passport.

2 Follow the route *Future plans*

a Look at the map and listen to Steve talking about his trip round the world. Which route does he describe?

b Read the sentences below and listen again. Mark the sentences True or False, then correct the false sentences.

1 Steve is going to Latin America.
2 He is travelling with his girlfriend.
3 He is staying in Santiago for a fortnight.
4 His cousin is getting married in Santiago.
5 He is flying direct from Australia to London.
6 He is staying mostly in hotels.

3 What's Australia like? *Describing places*

Work in pairs to complete the information about Australia. Partner A reads the text on this page and partner B reads the text on page 158. Ask questions to complete your text.

EXAMPLE:
What's the population of Australia?
What's the climate in the north of Australia like?

AUSTRALIA is the world's sixth largest country. Although it is large in size, it has a very small population of about ______. About 90% of the people live in towns and cities. The largest city is ______ with a population of over five million, but the capital is ______ with only about 250,000 people.

The climate is varied: in the north it is ______ with summer rains, parts of the south and west are desert lands, while in the southeast there are ______ winters and Mediterranean summers. Australia is rich in metals, oil and coal and the main farming produce is wool, beef and dairy produce such as ______.

The first people in Australia were Aborigines who came from ______ thousands of years ago. Now there are only about ______ Australian Aborigines and approximately 80% of the population is of British origin. The official language is ______ and the currency is the Australian dollar.

© SANTILLANA

4 Last minute reminders for travellers

a Read the text quickly and tick (✓) the pieces of advice that are mentioned.

packing your suitcase	preparing the house before leaving
informing the neighbours	taking phrase books and guide books
visiting the doctor abroad	checking all documents

b Complete the text by putting these words into the correct place.

address book	electricity	check
atlas	luggage	valid
clothes	misfortune	
documents	toothpaste	

A trouble-free trip

Once you're packed and just about ready to leave, double-check all the essentials for your trip.

Make sure you've got an adequate mix of [1]______, but don't take your entire wardrobe with you. Remember to leave a little room in your luggage for presents and souvenirs from your trip, and once everything is packed, ensure your [2]______ is not too heavy to carry.

[3]______ you've made all the necessary arrangements for your own home while you are away. Don't forget to cancel the milk, papers and so on*. If you are away for over a month, you should have your telephone, [4]______ and gas supplies cut off temporarily.

Most important of all, just before you leave, check that you have remembered every one of the various [5]______ you will need. Make sure you have your ticket and passport. Check that your passport is valid for the duration of your journey and that you have all necessary visas attached to your passport. Take your credit cards and check they are up-to-date.

If you are travelling to South America, Asia or Africa, you will probably need up-to-date vaccination certificates. Some of these, such as cholera, are only [6]______ for six months. Don't leave necessary health certificates behind, keep them with your passport – they can be just as important as the passport itself.

It's also worth taking an [7]______ with you on your travels. Not only will you know exactly where you are going (and where you've just been), but you will be able to see exactly which countries you fly over and how many different time-zones you are passing through.

One last vital document to take is your [8]______. Not only will you need this for addresses to send postcards home, but you can also make a note of any useful addresses abroad, such as your embassies or consulates. These addresses may be very helpful in the event of some [9]______, such as a lost passport, stolen money and so on. So don't keep your address book in the same place as your passport and money.

Remember, it costs nothing to check, double-check and check again that you've remembered everything from visas to [10]______. The alternative may be a miserable, or even disastrous holiday.

*NB: This article was written for people travelling from Britain. It is very common in Britain for people to have bottles of milk and newspapers delivered to the front door of the house or flat every morning.

c Find the phrases *such as* and *and so on* in the text. Which phrase means 'other similar things', which means 'for example'? Which pieces of advice do you agree with?

Write them in two columns.

dos	don'ts
Double check …	Don't bring …

d What additional advice would you give?

© SANTILLANA

Pronunciation File

Final consonants

Make sure you pronounce the final consonant of words in English. (Vowels are: a e i o u and consonants are: b c d f g h j k l m n p q r s t v w x y z)

Listen to the pronunciation of these countries. Repeat the word, making sure you pronounce the final consonant.

Brazil	Switzerland	Iran	Poland
Egypt	Iraq	Sweden	Denmark
Pakistan	New Zealand	Spain	Belgium
England	United States	Japan	Thailand

Learning Tips

Classroom language

When we want to know the meaning of words or phrases we ask:

What does ... mean?

When we want to know the meaning of initial letters we ask:

What does ... stand for?

Write the questions and answers for these words and initial letters:

souvenir homesick customs BA USA UK

5 Advice for travellers

a Read the sentences about good travellers. Find one word for each of these phrases.

1 before doing something
2 put too many things in the suitcase
3 a feeling of sadness for your home town/country
4 presents from the places you have visited
5 habits and lifestyles

b Put the list in order of importance (1 = very important, 8 = not important at all). Compare your list with your partner's. Is it the same? Agree on the three most important points.

A good traveller ...

- *plans the journey very carefully beforehand*
- *does not overpack*
- *always arrives at the airport/station in plenty of time*
- *takes lots of photographs*
- *does not get homesick*
- *tries to follow local customs*
- *does not run out of money*
- *brings back lots of souvenirs for family and friends*

6 When in Rome ...

a What does this famous saying mean?
When in Rome do as the Romans do.
Find one sentence in exercise 5 which means the same as this saying.
Do you agree with this saying? Why/Why not?

b What advice would you give to travellers in your country?

Go to ...	Don't go to ...
Travel from ... to ... by ...	Don't travel from ... to ... by ...
Buy ...	Don't buy ...

Give more dos and don'ts about your country.
Talk about these things:

famous places food and drink money
language local customs entertainment
what clothes to wear
souvenirs transport

© SANTILLANA

Grammar File

1 Present simple

On official documents you find these kinds of words: nationality, age, height, etc. But when we speak to people in conversation we do not use these words. Write the questions we would ask in informal language. The final word in each question is given.

1 Nationality: *Where do you come from?/Where are you from?*
2 Age: ______ you?
3 Height: ______ you?
4 Occupation: ______ do?
5 Marital Status: ______ married?
6 Place of residence: ______ live?

Now ask your partner these questions and write down his/her answers.

2 Asking for descriptions

Look at these questions and answers.

What's Australia like?	It's a very big country with a small population. It has a varied climate.
What's the climate in the north like?	It's tropical with a lot of summer rain.
What was your hotel like?	Terrible. It was dirty and the food was awful.

Write questions asking for descriptions of:

a region in your country, the climate of a country, a person, a journey someone made, a film/concert/book someone saw/read, a meal/holiday someone had.

Exchange your questions with a partner. Answer your partner's questions.

3 Present continuous for future plans

a Look at these examples.

When is she flying to Tokyo?
He is staying in Santiago next week.

The verbs are in the present continuous tense, but is the meaning of the sentence present or future? Look at exercise 2 and find more examples like this. Read about when we use the present continuous tense for future meaning in the Grammar Reference on page 138.

b Look at Anna's travel plan. With a partner, complete the questions and ask about Anna's plans.

EXAMPLE:
When is she ______ London?
When is she leaving London?

1 Which airline is she ______ with?
2 What time ______ at New York?
3 How ______ to her hotel?
4 Which hotel ______ in?
5 How long ______?
6 When ______?

c Write the travel plans for Anna Macintosh.

Anna Macintosh [1]______ London [2]______ 4.40 [3]______ 4th July. She [4]______ with British Airways. [5]______ in New York at 9.55 [6]______ morning. [7]______ the bus to her hotel, Hotel President. [8]______ four days. [9]______ 11.30 [10]______ 8th July.

```
Name:      Anna Macintosh
Depart:    London Heathrow 04.40  4/7/95
Flight:    BA137
Arrive:    New York JFK 09.55  4/7/95
Transfer:  Airport bus to hotel
Hotel:     President, 444 62nd Street NY
Stay:      4 days
Depart:    8/7/95 New York JFK 11.30
```


© SANTILLANA

7 Reading the signs *Airport vocabulary*

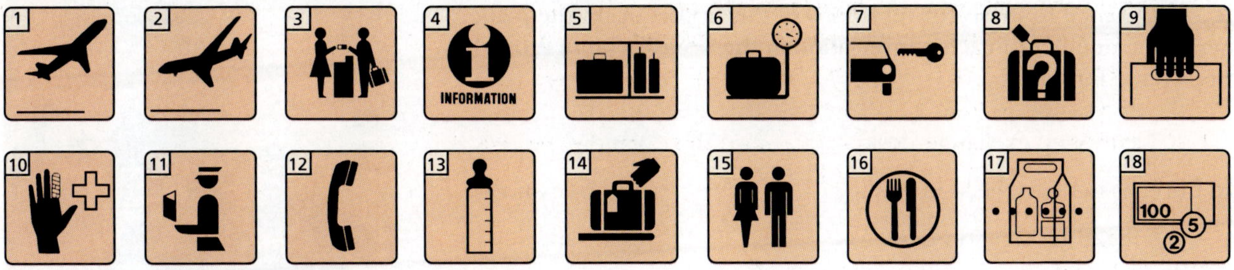

a Look at the pictograms and write the correct numbers in the boxes. The first one has been done for you.

arrivals	2	baggage check-in desk		security check	
car hire desk		currency exchange desk		baggage claim	
departures		duty free shop		customs control	
flight information desk		international telephones		first aid room	
left luggage		lost property office		passenger check-in desk	
restaurant		nursery		toilets	

b Listen and check your answers.

8 Finding your way *Giving directions*

a Listen to these three conversations to find out where these places are:

the currency exchange desk
the nursery
the flight information desk

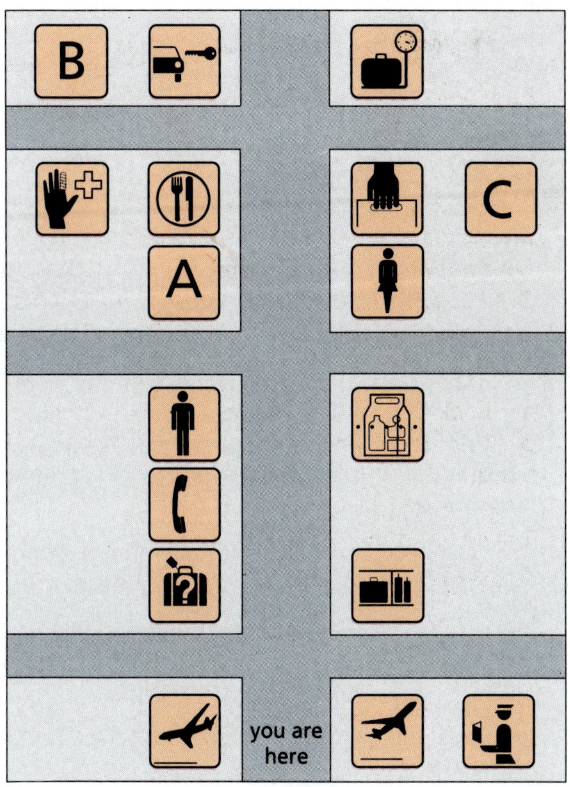

b With a partner, ask for and give directions using these phrases.

Excuse me.	Can you tell me where the … is, Do you know where the … is, Where can I find the … ,	please?

Go	down here. straight on.

Take the	first second third	turning on the	left. right.

Go past the …

It's	next to … opposite	the …

© SANTILLANA

9 Airport language *Revising functions*

a Listen to these conversations in the airport or on the plane. Write the number of each conversation in the boxes. The first one has been done for you.

at the	currency exchange desk	☐	*on* the	plane	☐
	passenger check-in desk	☐	*in* the	duty free shop	1
	flight information desk	☐		restaurant	☐

b Listen to the conversations again and fill in the gaps.

conversation 1

A: [1]______ your boarding card, [2]______.
B: Yes.
A: Sorry, madam. You [3]______ two litres of wine into Italy.
B: Oh, I see. Well. I'll just take these two bottles, then.
A: Right. [4]______ paying?

conversation 2

A: Yes. [1]______?
B: Yes. What [2]______ to San Francisco leave?
A: Let me see. The next one is at 10.45. It [3]______ gate 37.
B: Thanks.
A: [4]______ book a ticket?
B: Yes.
A: [5]______ TWA desk over there. They'll book a seat for you.
B: Thanks [6]______.

conversation 3

A: Just [1]______ please.
B: Right. Oh, [2]______ a pen?
A: Yes. [3]______.

conversation 4

A: [1]______ two teas and three coffees, please.
B: The milk's [2]______.
A: Thanks.
B: [3]______?
A: No thanks.
B: [4]______?
A: No, [5]______.
B: [6]______ £3.25, please.

conversation 5

[1]______ ladies and gentlemen. [2]______ all passengers to fasten their seat-belts and to observe the no-smoking sign? [3]______ in two minutes. We hope [4]______ journey with us. [5]______.

conversation 6

A: Can I see your ticket please?
B: Right.
A: [1]______ to Madrid.
B: [2]______.
A: How much hand [3]______?
B: Just one bag.
A: OK. [4]______ in the smoking or non-smoking section?
B: Non-smoking, please.
A: Would you like a window seat or an aisle seat?

Pronunciation File

Stressed syllables

a Listen to the pronunciation of the words.

departures   telephone   arrivals   restaurant

Look at the stress marks on these words and phrases. Listen again to the stressed syllables.

b Listen to more words and phrases from exercise 7. Mark the stressed syllables in each word and phrase.

passenger	international	information
luggage	nursery	car hire
first aid	check-in	security

c Read the words and phrases with the stress marks. Pronounce them with the correct stress.

© SANTILLANA

10 The 'real' Spain?

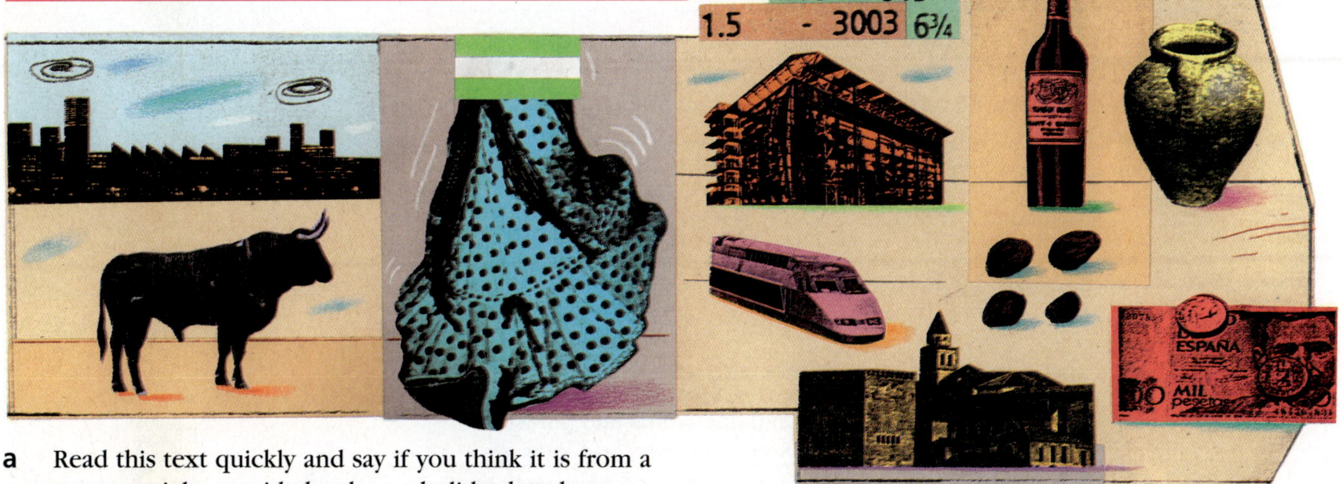

a Read this text quickly and say if you think it is from a newspaper article, a guide book or a holiday brochure.

WELCOME TO SPAIN

It is the largest country in Europe after Russia and France – twice the size of the United Kingdom. It is the world's tenth most important industrial nation, the fifth largest in shipbuilding and one of the biggest wine producers in the world. It produces more olive oil than [1]_____ and is the world's biggest exporter of cement. It has a wide variety of landscapes, cultures and even languages. It is the most popular holiday country in Europe. Do you recognise it? This country is Spain.

And yet, many people think of Spain as the land of guitars and castanets, swirling dresses and stamping feet; a land where donkeys trot through narrow streets of dazzling white houses; a land of Arab horses and [2]_____ . If this is the Spain you are looking for, you can still find it, but mostly in the region of Andalucía.

Andalucía

Andalucía is Spain's largest region. It has nearly 500 miles of coastline – the Mediterranean Costa del Sol and the Atlantic Costa de la Luz. Rising behind the Costa del Sol are the massive Sierra Nevada mountains. The highest mountains of the Sierra Nevada are snow-capped all year round. This means that you can ski in the morning and sunbathe on the warm, sandy beaches of the Costa del Sol [3]_____.

If you are [4]_____, there is plenty to see in Andalucía – the lace, fans and tapestry of Guadix, the leatherwork of Ubrique, the dolls and ceramics of Chiclana and the gold and silver work of Córdoba. What also makes Andalucía so fascinating is the fantastic architecture of the Moors, such as the famous Alhambra palace in Granada. The Moors came from north Africa and brought to Spain sugar cane, rice, cotton and several fruits, [5]_____. They established wool and silk industries in Andalucía and introduced paper to Europe through their university at Córdoba. It is also thanks to the Moors that Europe has the number system it still uses today.

Andalucía is rich in culture but if you visit Sevilla, remember to take a look at the numerous orange trees. But only look and smell, [6]_____! Sevilla oranges are usually much too bitter to eat and the whole crop goes into marmalade – the marmalade we find on millions of breakfast tables all over Britain.

Local fiestas – February: Masked dancing, fireworks, bullfighting ...

b Read the text again and put these phrases into the correct place in the text.

interested in handicrafts
any other country
don't eat them
in the afternoon
such as peaches and apricots
fighting bulls

c Look at the second paragraph and find the words *swirling*, *trot*, and *dazzling*. Imagine the picture to help you guess the meaning.

swirling	describes the movement of the women's dresses while dancing
trot	is the verb for the way donkeys walk
dazzling	describes how white houses look in bright sunshine

Can you now guess the meaning of these words? Find other words that you can guess the meaning of before you look them up in a dictionary.

© SANTILLANA

Learning Tips

Guessing the meaning of new words

When you read a text you will see many words you have never seen before. Try to guess the meaning of the word or phrase before you use your dictionary. It is sometimes possible to do this by reading and imagining what the text is describing. If you can work out the meaning for yourself, you will probably remember the word or phrase better.

Vocabulary File

1 Exact and approximate numbers and sizes

a Look back at the text about Spain and find words and phrases which use numbers and describe size. Some numbers and sizes are exact and some are approximate. Write the words and phrases in the appropriate column.

exact number/size	approximate numbers/size
twice the size of	a wide variety of
the world's tenth most	one of the biggest

b Choose a popular tourist region in your country. Write a few sentences to describe:

the size of the region, the numbers of visitors, hotels, beaches/mountains/lakes, restaurants, important food/exports

If you do not know the exact numbers and sizes, give these details approximately.

2 Word groups

Build up collections of words and group them into word spiders.

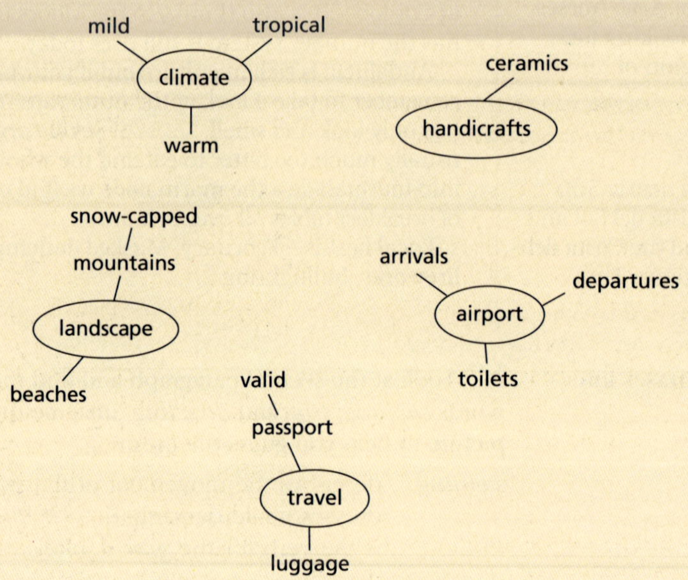

Complete the word spiders with words from this unit and other words you know.

© SANTILLANA

11 Funny but true

a You are going to listen to an air stewardess and a travel agent telling four true stories. Before you listen, look at the cartoons and match them with an appropriate caption.

1 Do I need a passport for him?
2 When is this plane taking off?
3 Excuse me. Can you open the window, please?
4 Have you got a light, please?

b Say what you think each story is about.

c Now listen to the stories and see if you were correct.

A

B

C

D

12 Role play *Language round-up*

Work with a partner and act out the conversation in the travel agent's office. Partner A is the passenger. Partner B is the travel agent and gives the information to the passenger.

Only partner A reads this.

You are taking a round-the-world trip for three months next year. You are travelling with one child, aged 12. You are stopping first in London and then flying to the USA, stopping in Miami, Dallas and San Francisco. You do not know the exact route you want to take, but you are definitely going to Manila, in the Philippines, for two weeks.

You would like to get the cheapest ticket possible and you need to find out about:

1 the cost of the tickets
2 how much it costs from Heathrow airport to the centre of London
3 how long it takes from Heathrow airport to the centre of London
4 if you need a visa for the Philippines
5 what language people speak there
6 if there is a train from Manila airport to the centre

Partner B reads the information on page 158.

© SANTILLANA

A Child's World

1 Through the ages *Making resolutions*

I'm going to …

- get a job abroad.
- save up for a new bike.
- finish with my boyfriend.
- stop sucking my thumb.
- learn how to get dressed by myself.
- lose weight and get fit.
- be the best swimmer in my class.
- make a lot of mess.
- pass all my maths exams.
- learn to talk.

a Match the phrases in the speech bubbles with the people in the picture. Give your answers like this:

The baby says she's going to make a lot of mess.
The toddler says he's going to …

b Listen and check your answers.

© SANTILLANA

2 Resolutions

a Work in groups.
Each person in the group chooses a famous person (for example, the president of your country, a TV personality, a sports personality, a musician, etc) and writes down three resolutions for him/her. Do not say the name of the person. Put all the resolutions on the desk in the middle of the group. One person takes a piece of paper from the desk and reads out the resolution. The group tries to guess whose resolution it is.

b Decide whose resolution you think is the best and then give your opinion.

EXAMPLE:
... says ... is going to ... . I think this is the best resolution because ...

3 Bringing up children *Making promises*

a This couple wrote a contract for bringing up their child. They made different promises in the contract. Read this part of the contract and complete it with the phrases below.

smack him
do his share of the housework when he is old enough
give him a good education
watch television

b Work in pairs. Tell your partner which promises in the contract you agree or disagree with.

They say they are (never) going to ...

I think this is	*an excellent* *a good* *not a bad* *a ridiculous*	*idea because ...*

Agree or disagree with your partner like this:

Yes, I agree.
No, I don't agree with you there.
Yes, I think that's true.
No, I don't think that's true.

c What do you think about making a parent child contract?
I think it's a (n)... idea because ...

Pronunciation File

/tʃ/, /ʃ/ and /s/

a Listen to this sentence.

Children shouldn't suffer discrimination.

Listen to the sounds in these words then repeat the words.

ch/tʃ/	sh/ʃ/	s/s/
children	shouldn't	suffer
chose	show	so
cheap	she	see
chips	fish	socks
cheese	delicious	soup

b Listen and write down the words you hear.

c Listen and repeat this menu.

Cheese and biscuits. Cheese and biscuits.
Chocolate ice-cream. Chocolate ice-cream.
Fish and chips. Fish and chips.
Soup. Soup.

Parent/Child Contract

We, Patrick and Helen Barclay
make these promises on bringing up our son, Daniel

We are going to: share all responsibility for looking after him
1 ____

We are never going to: tell him a lie
2 ____

We are not going to let him: eat sweets or any unhealthy food
play with guns
3 ____

We are going to make him:
4 ____

4 Children's rights

a What do you think are the three most important rights for children and adolescents (people under 18 years old)? Complete these sentences.

All children and adolescents should …
Adults should not …
Governments should never …

b Now read the text and see how many of your ideas are similar to the ideas in the text.

RIGHTS OF THE CHILD

1979 was the International Year of the Child. The United Nations established a special group to produce a declaration on human rights for children. Ten years later, on 20th November 1989, the Convention on the Rights of the Child was adopted by the United Nations. In this Convention, the word 'child' means any person under the age of 18. The Convention on the Rights of the Child has 54 points. This is a summary of some of the main points:

- children should have enough food and clean water
- children have the right to good health and necessary medical care
- children should have a decent standard of living
- children have the right to be with their family or those who can take care of them best
- children should never suffer physical, psychological or sexual abuse
- children should have special protection during a war
- children should never suffer discrimination because of their race, religion, sex, nationality, culture, beliefs, language or family background
- children should never do any work which damages their health, education or development
- disabled children should have special care and training
- children have the right to play
- children should have a decent education
- children have the right to express their opinions
- children should always have their own particular name and nationality
- children should know what their rights are

The European Community is now writing its own Charter of Children's Rights which is going to be used in all EC member countries.

c Are there any rights which you disagree with or think should be added?

d Can you think of some situations where children or adolescents do not have these rights?

© SANTILLANA

5 Parent power *Conducting a survey*

a In pairs, ask and answer the questions in the survey. Write down your partner's answers.

Should parents:	Yes	No	Not sure	*At what age should children:*	Age
smack their children?	☐	☐	☐	have their own pocket money?	☐
let their children watch TV every day?	☐	☐	☐	choose their own clothes?	☐
let their children eat sweets?	☐	☐	☐	go out by themselves?	☐
buy expensive toys for their children?	☐	☐	☐	start school?	☐
let children play with toy guns?	☐	☐	☐	learn a foreign language?	☐
make children help with the housework	☐	☐	☐		
treat boys and girls the same?	☐	☐	☐		

b Report back what you and your partner think.

We think *I think* *My partner thinks*	*parents should/shouldn't …* *children should … when they are about …*

c In groups, discuss some of the things your parents let you do/didn't let you do, or made you do/didn't make you do when you were a child.

EXAMPLE:

My parents made me do my homework before I watched TV in the evening.

d Find three differences between yourself and other members of the group.

6 What is going to happen? *Making predictions*

a When children play, they often use their imagination to predict what is going to happen. Look at this picture from a children's book. What do you think is going to happen?

b Listen to what these children predict. Match the pictures below with each child's prediction.

© SANTILLANA

Grammar File

1 *Going to …*

a Read the Grammar Reference on page 139 about *going to*.

b Look at Sue's list of things she plans to do this week. There are plans for herself and plans made with her boyfriend, Bob. Write out the plans in full.

EXAMPLE:

She is going to write a letter to her dad.

They are going to buy a wedding present for Tom and Alison.

Me	Me and Bob
write a letter to my dad	buy a wedding present for Tom and Alison
clean my car	take Bob's nephew to the zoo
mend my black dress	
send a birthday card to my sister	book our holidays get our passports

c Read the information in these sentences and then make a prediction.

1 There are lots of black clouds overhead and the sky is very dark. It's ______.

2 It's five minutes before the end of the match and the score at the moment is Italy 4, Switzerland 1. Italy ______.

3 Your brother has not done any work for his exams next week. He ______ not ______.

4 Two cars are travelling towards each other. They are both going very fast and there is no time to move out of the way. They ______.

5 You and your friend are in a traffic jam in the city centre. Your train leaves in four minutes and you are a kilometre from the station. We ______ not ______.

d Write down three resolutions for yourself.
I am (not) …

2 *Should*

a Look at these examples of:

1 asking a question
2 giving a negative answer
3 making a negative statement

with the verb *should*.

Should parents let their children eat a lot of sweets?
– No, they shouldn't.
Children shouldn't watch too much television.

Notice how *should* is used in questions and negatives. There is no *do/does*.

Should is called a modal verb. There are several other modal verbs in English, for example *can, must, might, may, would* are all modal verbs.

b Look at examples of *should* in the texts in exercises 4 and 5. Write down three questions and answers about what children/parents should do, and three things that children/parents shouldn't do.

3 *Make/let* (someone) do (something)

Look at these examples:

My parents	let me don't let me	stay out late.
	let me didn't let me	stay out late (when I was young).

Does Did	your teacher	make your do a test	every month? when you were at school?

What is the past tense of the verb *let*?

Write down examples of:

what your	parents sister/brother teacher boss	let(s) don't/doesn't let make(s) don't/doesn't make	you do.
what	they	let didn't let made didn't make	you do.

© SANTILLANA

7 Sitting ducks

This is an extract from a children's book called *The Magic Finger* by Roald Dahl. In this story, the Gregg family are always shooting animals. One day, they wake up to find they have become birds and a family of ducks has moved into their house.

a The first sentence of each paragraph is missing. Read the story and put the sentences 1–5 into the correct place.

1 At last the morning came and with it the warm sun.
2 So they flew off to an apple tree.
3 On the ground below them stood the four enormous ducks, as tall as men, and three of them were holding guns in their hands.
4 'Look at that one holding my lovely gun!' shouted Mr Gregg.
5 That night, while Mr and Mrs Gregg and Philip and William were trying to get some sleep up in the high nest, a great wind began to blow.

A ... 'One of them is lying in my bed!' yelled William, looking into a top window.

'And one of them is playing with my electric train!' cried Philip.

'Oh, dear! Oh, dear! Oh, dear!' said Mrs Gregg. 'They have taken over our whole house! We shall never get it back. And what are we going to eat?'

'I will not eat worms,' said Philip. 'I would rather die.'

'Or slugs,' said William.

Mrs Gregg took the two boys under her wings and hugged them. 'Don't worry,' she said. 'I can mince it all up very fine and you won't even know the difference. Lovely slugburgers. Delicious wormburgers.'

'Oh no!' cried William.

'Never!' said Philip.

'Disgusting!' said Mr Gregg. 'Just because we have wings, we don't have to eat bird food. We shall eat apples instead. Our trees are full of them. Come on!'

B ... But to eat an apple without holding it in your hands is not at all easy. Every time you try to get your teeth into it, it just pushes away. In the end they were able to get a few small bites each. And then it began to get dark, so they all flew back to the nest and lay down to sleep.

60

C ... The tree rocked from side to side, and everyone, even Mr Gregg, was afraid that the nest would fall down. Then came the rain. It rained and rained, and the water ran into the nest and they all got as wet as could be – and oh, it was a bad, bad night!

D ... 'Well!' said Mrs Gregg. 'Thank goodness that's over! I never want to sleep in a nest again!' She got up and looked over the side...

'Help!' she cried.

'Look! Look down there!'

'What is it my love?' said Mr Gregg. He stood up and peeped over the side.

He got the surprise of his life!

E ... One had Mr Gregg's gun, one had Philip's gun and one had William's gun.

The guns were all pointing right up at the nest.

'No! No! No!' called out Mr and Mrs Gregg, both together. 'Don't shoot! Please don't shoot!'

'Why not?' said one of the ducks. It was the one who wasn't holding a gun. 'You are always shooting at *us*.'

'Oh, but that's not the same!' said Mr Gregg. We are *allowed* to shoot at ducks!'

'Who allows you?' asked the duck.

'We allow each other,' said Mr Gregg.

'Very nice,' said the duck. 'And now *we* are going to allow each other to shoot you.'

61

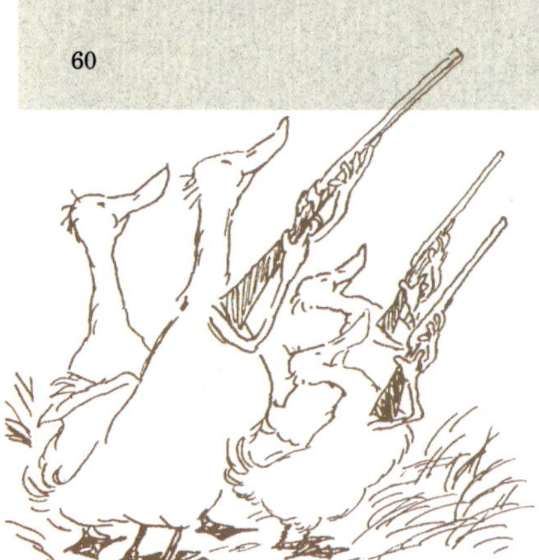

b What do you think is going to happen next? How do you think the story is going to end?

c What do you think the moral of this story is?

You shouldn't shoot ducks.
You shouldn't kill animals for sport.
Human beings shouldn't pretend to be animals.

d Can you remember a children's story with a moral?

© SANTILLANA

Vocabulary File

1 Speaking verbs

There are five different speaking verbs used in the text in exercise 7. One of them is the word *said* (past tense of the verb to *say*). Find and write down the other four. One of the speaking verbs in the text is a verb phrase and consists of two words.

2 Cognates

a Cognates are words which are the same, or almost the same, in your own language. Look at exercise 4 and find the words *ideas, physical* and *psychological.* Are these words the same, or almost the same, in your language? Read the text and check that the words have the same meaning in your language.

Write down all the cognates you can find in exercises 3, 4 and 7. Is the spelling exactly the same or a little different? Learn the spelling in English.

b These words are missing from the sentences below. Put them into the correct place in the sentences.

enormous physical psychological stadium theory

1 Exercise helps to keep us in good ______ condition, but it also helps us feel more relaxed and less stressed.
2 It was a good idea in ______, but it just didn't work in practice.
3 Losing a parent can cause serious ______ damage to a young child.
4 When the pizza came, it was absolutely ______. I could only eat half of it.
5 The Maracana is the most famous football ______ in Brazil.

3 Using your dictionary

Look at this extract from the dictionary.

> **enormous** /ɪˈnɔːməs/. 1 Something that is **enormous** is extremely large in size or amount. EG *There was an enormous cat crouching on the counter eating fish... There is an enormous amount of hard work in child care.* ADJ QUALIT = massive

Notice the phonetic script beside the word. (If you are not sure how to read this phonetic script, look at the list of phonetic symbols on page 148.) Read the phonetic script for the word *enormous* and say the word aloud. Then check you know the correct pronunciation for all the cognates you wrote down in part 2. Look up the words in the dictionary and read the phonetic script for the correct pronunciation. Make sure you learn the correct pronunciation of any new words you learn.

*For glossary of dictionary terms see page 160

4 *Each other*

a Look at this example from the Sitting ducks text on page 21.

We allow each other.

Give examples of how you can use *each other* with these verbs.

like love hate know look at meet see help

EXAMPLE: *They are sisters, but they don't like each other very much.*

b The words in these sentences are in the wrong order. Unjumble the words and write the sentences in the correct order.

1 know we each No, don't other.
2 and other. Jane hate brother each her
3 see these other much We days. don't each very
4 the other can. students to they All each try when help

© SANTILLANA

8 Fairy story – Part 1

a Do you know this famous children's story? It is called *Cinderella* in English.

What can you remember about this story?

b These words are often used in fairy stories to describe good and bad characters. Put the adjectives into the correct column.

cruel wicked beautiful ugly kind
gentle bad-tempered mean stupid
good-natured handsome nasty charming
good-looking ridiculous

good characters	bad characters

c Listen to these children telling the story of *Cinderella*. Check your lists of good and bad characters. Can you add any more words to the lists?

d In pairs, look at the pictures and say what happens next.

9 Fairy story – Part 2

a Listen to the children telling the rest of the story. Check if you told the story correctly.

b Listen again to part 2 of *Cinderella*. The children use these phrases when they cannot remember the correct word or phrase to use.

A what-do-you-call-it? What's its name?

A what's it called? What's that word?

© SANTILLANA

10 A good read *Likes and preferences*

a Put these kinds of books into the correct column.

travel books historical novels detective novels
short stories biographies science fiction novels
cookery books love stories books about art
books about nature

fiction	non-fiction
historical novels	travel books

Can you think of any other kinds of books to add to the lists?

b Listen to these three conversations and say which kinds of books people talk about in each conversation.

c Listen to the conversations again. Listen for these phrases and complete the phrases you hear.

What kind of … ?
I'm not so keen on …
I'd rather …
I like … best.
I'm quite keen on …
How about … ?
I can't stand …
Would you rather … ?

d In pairs, ask and answer similar questions about books. Use some of the phrases in part C.

Pronunciation File

Sentence stress

a Listen to this sentence.

We like each other.

Look at the stress marks in this sentence and listen again.

b Listen and put the stress marks over the stressed syllables.

They hate each other.

We saw each other.

They help each other.

We don't know each other.

We never see each other.

Did they look at each other?

c Listen and repeat the sentences with the correct stress and rhythm.

Do you like each other – or do you hate each other?

Yes, we like each other, we don't hate each other.

But we never see each other, so we can't help each other.

Learning Tips

What's that word?

a If you cannot remember, or do not know a word when you are speaking, you can use one of the words or phrases in exercise 9.

EXAMPLE: *I haven't got a what's it called.*
I need a what's its name.

People use these words and phrases when they forget a word. It is better to use a word or phrase like this than to remain silent, because then people know how to help you find the word or phrase you want.

b You can also try to get other people to help you find the word you want.

EXAMPLE:
I don't know what it's called, but it's a kind of …
We use it for …
It's got …
What's that word?

c You can always try using a cognate too. You never know, it could be the correct word!

© SANTILLANA

11 Telling a story *Language round-up*

a Work in pairs. Partner A reads the first part of the story aloud.

The Three Little Pigs

One day the three little pigs have to leave home. The mother pig waves goodbye and tells them to be careful of the big bad wolf.

The first little pig, who is quite lazy and not too keen on hard work, sees a pile of straw.

'I'm going to build my house with this straw,' he says.

So he builds his house in a few hours and settles down to watch TV. After a few minutes, along comes the wolf and knocks on the door.

'Let me come in,' cries the wolf. 'It's cold out here and I can't stand the cold.'

'Go away,' says the first little pig. 'Come back tomorrow.'

'I'd rather come in now. I'm cold and hungry.'

'No,' says the little pig, 'You can't.'

'Then I'm going to blow your house down,' the wolf calls out. So he blows and blows and the little straw house falls down in a few seconds.

'And now I'm going to eat you up,' the wolf says. And he eats the little pig up in one bite.

b Partner B looks at the pictures and tells story of the second little pig.

c Look at the final pictures of the story together. What do you think is going to happen? Tell the rest of the story.

1 Personal information and plans

Claudia Wilding dropped her bag on the train. These were the contents of her bag.

a Write down questions about:

1 her personal details
2 her family
3 her social and work plans

EXAMPLE:
How old is she?
What is she doing on ...?

Then ask and answer the questions with a partner.

b Write two short paragraphs. One giving personal information about Claudia, the other giving details about her future plans.

2 A fresh start

a Read this information about Jason. Write the words *should* or *shouldn't* in the sentences.

Jason is in prison for robbery. He has another two months in prison before his release. Prison officers and social workers have given him a lot of advice about what to do and what not to do when he finally leaves prison. This is some of the advice they have given him:

1 You _____ go back to where you lived before, you _____ try to have a fresh start in life.
2 You _____ meet all your old friends, they might get you into trouble again.
3 You _____ try to make new friends once you have found a place to live.
4 You _____ spend time planning your future before you leave prison.
5 You _____ start a job training scheme as soon as you leave prison.
6 You _____ just let things happen to you, make your own decisions now.

b Jason agrees with this advice and is already starting to make plans. Write down four resolutions you think Jason makes.

EXAMPLE:
I am going to have a fresh start in life.
I am not going to go back to where I lived before.

© SANTILLANA

3 Powerful words – *make* and *get*

a Look at the text in exercise 4, unit 1, and find these phrases.

make sure   make arrangements   make a note of

Unit 2 also has these expressions with the word *make*.

make a mess   make a resolution   make a promise

Look at the reading text in exercise 7, unit 2 and find these phrases.

get some sleep   get (something) back
get dark   get wet   get up   get a surprise

The words *make* and *get* are used in several expressions in English.

b Write your own sentences using each of the expressions with *make* and *get*. You can use the verbs in different verb tenses.

EXAMPLE:
I made sure I wrote those five new words in my notebook.

Make a note of any more expressions in the rest of the book using *make* or *get*.

4 Dictionary work

a The following words all appear as nouns in units 1 and 2. Use your dictionary to find the verbs.

EXAMPLE:

1 education *educate*
2 discrimination ________
3 production ________
4 entertainment ________
5 protection ________
6 information ________
7 advice ________
8 preparation ________
9 description ________
10 explanation ________

b Notice how the stress changes on these words.

education   educate

Check the pronunciation of the words in your dictionary and mark the stress on the words.

c Look these words and decide which are cognates and which are false friends (words that look similar to words in your language, but have a different meaning in English). Use your dictionary to help you.

1 sensible
2 carpet
3 temperature
4 embarrassed
5 educated
6 punctual
7 deceived
8 sympathetic

5 Transformation

Rewrite the following sentences without changing the meaning. Use the word or phrase in brackets.

EXAMPLE:

1 What is your age? (old) *How old are you?*
2 What's your nationality? (from)
3 What's her occupation? (do)
4 What's his date of birth? (born)
5 How many people live in Canada? (population)
6 What is the meaning of the letters BA? (stand for)
7 Do they intend to have a big wedding? (going to)
8 It is wrong for children to start work before they are 16 years old. (should)
9 She doesn't speak to him, and he doesn't speak to her anymore. (other)
10 Her parents do not allow her to stay out past 11 o'clock. (let)

6 Project

a Ask questions to other students in the class to collect the information for the table.

EXAMPLE:
What do you do?
Do you have any special interests or hobbies?

Complete the table for as many students as you can.

Class questionnaire

Name:					
Age:					
Address:					
Occupation:					
Special interests:					
Reasons for learning English:					
Personal resolution for 199… :					

b Use the information you have collected in part A to write a report on your class. Include the following information:

how many people were interviewed
the average age of the class
where most students live
the most common reason for learning English
the most original personal resolution

It is a good idea to keep a special file for the projects you do in this course. At the end of the course you will have lots of information and you can see how much you have learned.

© SANTILLANA

Pushing the Body to the Limit

1 The human body *Choosing the correct tense*

a Read the texts and match each paragraph with one of the pictures.

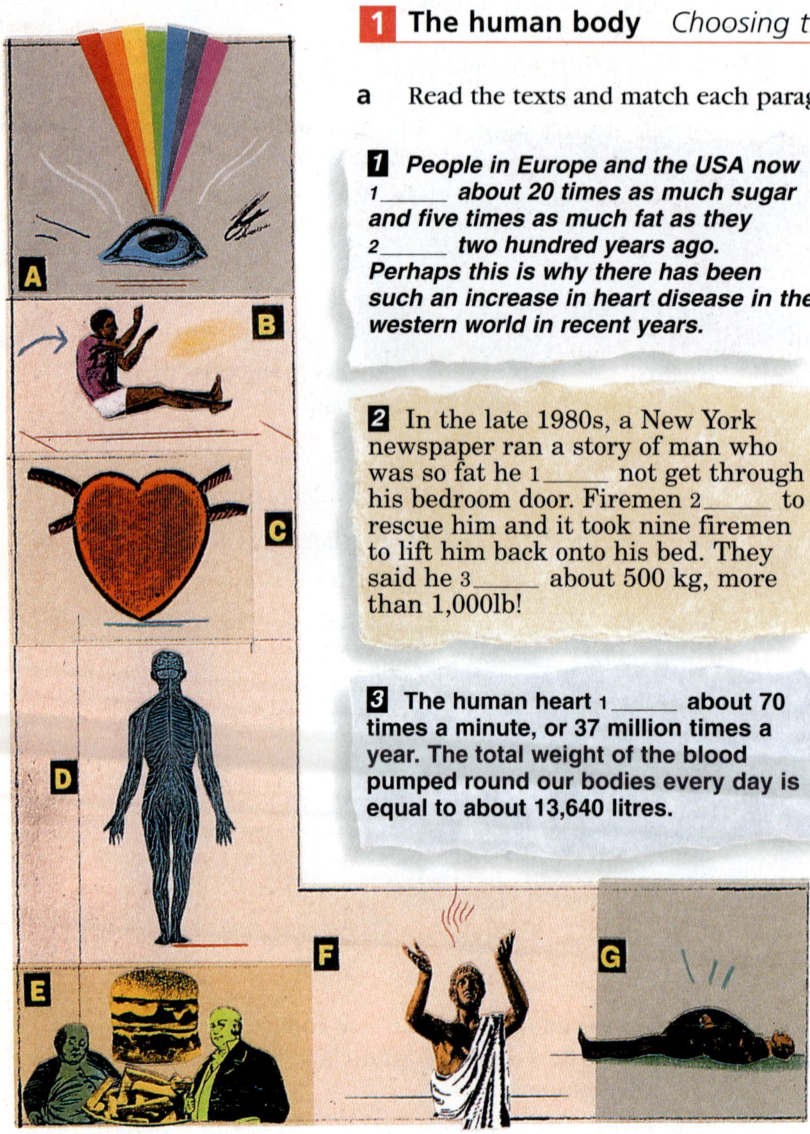

***1** People in Europe and the USA now 1 _____ about 20 times as much sugar and five times as much fat as they 2 _____ two hundred years ago. Perhaps this is why there has been such an increase in heart disease in the western world in recent years.*

2 In the late 1980s, a New York newspaper ran a story of man who was so fat he 1 _____ not get through his bedroom door. Firemen 2 _____ to rescue him and it took nine firemen to lift him back onto his bed. They said he 3 _____ about 500 kg, more than 1,000lb!

3 The human heart 1 _____ about 70 times a minute, or 37 million times a year. The total weight of the blood pumped round our bodies every day is equal to about 13,640 litres.

4 In 1896, the 1,500 metre race was won in a time of 4 minutes 33·2 seconds and the long jump record 1 _____ 6.4 metres. Since then athletes have broken these records many times. Several modern athletes have run 1,500 metres in just over 3 minutes and have jumped approximately 9 metres in the long jump.

5 Our nerve cells 1 _____ messages from the brain to the rest of our body. An adult brain 2 _____ about 12 billion nerve cells. But after the body has stopped growing, thousands of these nerve cells are lost every day and never replaced.

6 Human colour vision is so sensitive that some people can distinguish as many as 300,000 different shades. The human ear 1 _____ distinguish more than 1,500 different musical notes.

***7** The original Olympic Games 1 _____ as early as 776 BC. At that time athletes ran races, 2 _____ in boxing matches, jumped in long jump competitions and 3 _____ the discus and javelin. There were also poetry reading competitions. However, when the Romans conquered Greece in 394 AD they 4 _____ the games. The Olympic Games did not reappear until 1896 when it was held in Greece once again.*

b Put the verbs below into the correct places in the texts. Use the correct form of the present or past simple.

carry begin eat throw can fight
end eat be come weigh have
can beat

c Do you think people's eating habits are getting better or worse in your country?

d Do you think the human body is going to change in the next few thousand years because of our modern lifestyle?

EXAMPLE:

I think our legs are going to get smaller and thinner because we don't walk so much.

© SANTILLANA

2 Everyday figures *Saying numbers*

a How do you say these different numbers?

the 1980s   31st January 1900   tel: 081 802 2911   6.4m   1,050lb
$50,000   Holland 7 – San Marino 0

b Listen and check if you were correct. Now listen again and find four different ways of saying '0'.

c Listen and write down the numbers you hear.
Listen again. Then look at the numbers and say the complete sentence for each number you have written down.

d Work in pairs.
Write down three important dates in the past (for example, birthdays or historical dates). Then write down what happened on those dates. Do not show your partner the information. Read out the three dates and then say the three things that happened, but in the wrong order. Your partner must match the correct dates to the three different events.

Pronunciation File

/iː/ and /ɪ/

a Listen to the pronunciation of these two dates.

1918   1980

Notice the short sound of eighty and the long sound of eighteen.

Now listen and write down the numbers you hear.

b Listen to the difference between these pairs of words.

eat	it
feet	fit
Jean	gin
cheap	chip
leave	live
beat	bit
teen	tin

Now listen and write down the words you hear.

c Listen to this verse and repeat it.

I eat cheese. I eat fish.
I eat beans. I eat fish.
I'm fit, fit, fit
And I'm quick on my feet.

3 Marathon man

a Read these sentences about John, a marathon runner. Then listen to the interview with the runner and mark each sentence True or False.

1 John was an amateur runner ten years ago, but now he is too old.
2 He ran hundreds of marathons ten years ago.
3 He ran a race in Scotland two years ago.
4 He was 70 years old at the time.
5 After 11 miles of the race he suddenly stopped.
6 He did not finish the race.
7 He met the old man a second time.
8 The old man did not overtake him this time.
9 He saw the man many times after that.
10 John has often beaten him in races.

b Listen again and correct the false sentences.

© SANTILLANA

4 Wrestling Japanese style

a Read the text and complete it with the words below. You can use a word more than once.

a the and but or is are he in on at by of to with

SUMO

The rules 1_____ very simple. The two wrestlers fight inside a ring of rope. The loser is 2_____ first fighter to leave the ring or to touch the floor inside the ring with any part of the body except the soles of the feet. 3_____ course, punching, poking in the eyes, hair pulling and so 4_____ are not allowed.

The secret 5_____ the sumo diet is a stew called *chanko-nabe*. *Chanko* means whatever is available. There 6_____ no set recipe; it usually has about a dozen ingredients, most 7_____ them fresh vegetables plus chicken, pork 8_____ fish. Everything is cut up very small and then cooked 9_____ water for about fifteen minutes. There 10_____ many popular chanko restaurants in the sumo district 11_____ Tokyo. *Chanko* itself is not very fattening, 12_____ the amount the wrestlers eat is enormous. It is also served 13_____ dozens of bowls of rice for each wrestler 14_____ washed down with litres of beer and *sake* (Japanese rice wine). All meals are followed 15_____ short sleeps which help convert the calories to flesh. 16_____ wrestlers also eat large quantities 17_____ noodles between meals and the younger ones take frequent snacks 18_____ the local fried chicken or burger fast food stores.

Sumo wrestling is a tough sport that involves a lot of training, 19_____ although they are overweight, sumo wrestlers 20_____ very fit. Most wrestlers retire 21_____ their early 30s. There is 22_____ retirement ceremony where the sumo wrestler's topknot of hair is cut off. When a sumo wrestler has retired, 23_____ is often invited 24_____ attend prestigious dinner parties where the wrestler eats well, sometimes sings 25_____ has his photograph taken with everyone in the room. For this service 26_____ receives a payment of about £500 in cash. This is not taxable and 27_____ called *kuruma-dai*, or 'car-fare'. Once they have retired, the wrestlers lose most of their extra weight 28_____ several have suffered from heart disease, diabetes and bad knee joints 29_____ later life.

The Wolf

Age 34. 6ft (1.80m) 265lbs (120kg). Has fought 1,000 times in the top division and has won well over 700 fights. He was grand champion for nine years. Not one of the heavyweights, but his skill and power made him difficult to beat.

b Read the completed text and answer these questions.

1 What are the rules of sumo wrestling?
2 What do sumo wrestlers eat?
3 What happens at their retirement ceremony?
4 How do some retired wrestlers earn extra money?
5 What can happen to wrestlers in later life?
6 How long was 'The Wolf' grand champion? Give as many details as you can about him.

© SANTILLANA

5 Mr Universe *Past and present*

J.J. Marsh started body building in 1980, after his mother bought him his first set of weights. Since that time he has worked very hard to become Mr Universe. The table below shows his progress from 1979.

a Look at these questions and answers about J.J. Marsh.

When did his mother buy him his first weights? In 1979.
Did he start weight training straight away? No, he didn't.
How long has he done weight training? Since 1980/ For the last 15 years.

Complete these questions using information from the table.

1 Did he ______ in Arizona in 1980? No, he didn't.
2 Where did ______? In Los Angeles.
3 How long has ______ in Arizona? Since 1986/For the last ______ years.

b In pairs, ask and answer more questions using information from the table.

c Write an account of J.J.'s career so far. When you describe something that happened at a date in the past, use the past simple tense. When you describe something that continues from the past to the present, use the present perfect tense (*has/have* + past participle).

EXAMPLE:
He entered his first body building competition in 1980 and he has entered hundreds of competitions since then.

1979	1980	1982	1986	1989	1992	Now
mother bought his first set of weights	started weight training			(do) weight training →		
		entered first body building competition		(enter) hundreds of competitions →		
lived in Los Angeles →		moved to Arizona		(live) in Arizona →		
				met girlfriend Michelle	(help) him a lot →	
					got married (be) married →	
					started aerobic training (do) aerobic training →	
					changed his diet (have) new diet →	
During this time		(go) all around the world → (take) his mother to Tokyo and Madrid →				

© SANTILLANA

Grammar File

1 Present simple/past simple/present perfect

a Look at this example from exercise 1.

People in Europe and the USA now eat about 20 times as much sugar and five times as much fat as they ate two hundred years ago. Perhaps this is why there has been such an increase in heart disease in the western world in recent years.

Find the verbs in each sentence. Underline them.

Which verb is:
1 in the past simple tense?
2 in the present perfect tense?
3 in the present simple tense?

Look at these time phrases:
two hundred years ago
now
in recent years

Which ones are connected to the present simple tense, the past simple tense, the present perfect tense?

b Find more examples of time phrases in the texts in this unit. Write them in the correct column.

past simple tense	present perfect tense
at that time	since that time

2 Forms of the verb

a The present perfect tense is made with *have/has* + the past participle of the main verb. When you learn a new verb, make sure you know the three forms of the verb: present simple, past simple and present perfect, for all irregular verbs.

present simple	past simple	present perfect
eat/eats	ate	(have/has) eaten
run/runs	ran	run

b Check in your dictionary to see if the verb is regular or irregular. Look at these examples from the dictionary. Which verb is regular, which is irregular? Add both verbs to the table above. Can you add any more verbs?

complain /kə'pleɪn/, **complains, complaining, complained**. If you **complain**, 1 you tell someone about a situation affecting you that you think is wrong or unsatisfactory and should be dealt with. EG *They complained to me about the noise.... He's always complaining... Women complain of pressure cn them to get jobs... He complained that the office was not 'businesslike'.* — V OR V + REPORT-CL/QUOTE : IF + PREP THEN *to/about/of* ⇑ protest = grumble, moan

understand /ʌndəstænd/, **understands, understanding, understood**. 1 If you **understand** someone or **understand** what they are telling you, you know what they mean when they are telling you something. EG *She understood him perfectly... Did I understand you correctly?... I don't understand what you mean.* — V + O, V + WH, OR V : NO CONT = comprehend, get

c Put the verb in brackets into the correct form and correct tense: present simple, past simple or present perfect.

1 We usually ______ (go) to France for our holidays, but last year we ______ (go) to Greece.
2 ______ you (see) him yesterday?
– No. I ______ (not see) him since last week.
3 How much ______ he (weigh) now?
– About 100kg. He ______ (lose) 20kg since January.
4 A Japanese man ______ (climb) Mount Fuji when he ______ (be) ninety years old.
5 He usually ______ (run) in the London Marathon, but he ______ (not run) last year because he ______ (be) injured.
6 I ______ (live) here for the last ten years.
– Where ______ you (live) before that?
– In Bristol.
7 They ______ (be) married for twenty years. It ______ (be) their anniversary yesterday.
8 ______ you ever (eat) Japanese fish stew?
– No. I ______ never (eat) Japanese food.

3 Life experiences

We use the present perfect tense to talk about experiences in our life or our career where there is no specific time given. Look at this example from exercise 4.

(The Wolf) has fought 1,000 times in the top division and has won well over 700 fights.
(= during his lifetime/career)

For this reason the present perfect tense is often used with the words *ever* and *never*.

EXAMPLE:
I have never eaten frogs' legs.
Have you ever run in a marathon race?
(= during my/your lifetime)

4 *For* and *since*

Look at the examples.

He has lived here *for* ten years.
He has lived here *since* 1985.

Write *for* or *since* next to each time phrase.

______	three months	______	Christmas
______	1990	______	three hours
______	12 o'clock	______	a long time
______	two weeks	______	several years
______	that time	______	1967

© SANTILLANA

6 The psychic surgeon

Many stories about a Brazilian man, called José Arigo, appeared in newspapers and magazines in the 1950s and 1960s. People said he had special powers to cure the sick.

a Read the text about José Arigo and match each of the summaries to the correct paragraph.

1 Lawyers decide to test Arigo's powers.
2 Arigo becomes a famous psychic doctor after the sick woman is cured.
3 Arigo performs his first 'operation' on a sick woman.
4 Arigo dies in car crash.
5 People begin to believe in Arigo's powers but he gets in trouble with the authorities.

Arigo: Surgeon Extraordinary

A In the small town of Congonhas do Campo, Brazil, a woman was dying of cancer. Relatives and friends had gathered in the house, candles were lit at her bedside and everyone was waiting for her death. Suddenly, one of the men in the room rushed out to the kitchen and returned a few seconds later, with a large breadknife. He ordered everyone to stand back. He made a cut in the woman's body with the knife and put his hand into the cut. The man pulled out a large tumour, as big as a grapefruit. He dropped the knife and the tumour into the kitchen sink, sat down on a chair and began to sob. The man's name was José Arigo.

B A relative rushed off to fetch a doctor. The other people in the room remained silent, astonished at what they had just seen. The woman said she did not feel any pain during the 'operation', and the doctor said that the object in the sink was, indeed, a tumour. The woman recovered completely. Afterwards, José Arigo said he could remember nothing of the strange 'operation', but from that day he became famous throughout Brazil.

C He started his own clinic and when the doors of the clinic opened at seven o'clock each morning there were usually hundreds of people queueing outside. The people who came were from all walks of life, rich and poor alike. José Arigo never accepted any money or gifts for his services. People say that he cured thousands of patients over several years. However, in 1964, he was imprisoned for practising as a doctor without any medical qualifications. By this time, Arigo was extremely well-known both in Brazil and around the world and the authorities decided to let him out of prison after a couple of months.

D Two lawyers decided to go to Arigo's town and watch his 'operations'. There was a woman who was nearly blind because of cataracts on her eye. Arigo asked the lawyers to hold the woman's head and watch the 'operation'. This is what one of the lawyers said afterwards. 'I saw him pick up what looked like a pair of nail scissors. He wiped them on his sport shirt and used no disinfectant of any kind. Then I saw him cut straight into the woman's eye. She did not flinch although she was fully conscious. The cataract was out in a couple of seconds. I was speechless, amazed. She was cured.'

E Arigo himself said that he had the spirit of Dr Adolphus Fritz, a German doctor who had died in 1918. Many of his patients said that when Arigo did the 'operations' he went into a trance and spoke with a German accent. Arigo claimed he could never remember doing any of the 'operations'. He was finally killed in a car crash in 1971, after telling dozens of his friends that he would never see them again.

b Try to guess the meaning of the *gathered*.

EXAMPLE:

A woman was dying of cancer. Relatives and friends had gathered in the house.

Because the woman was dying, her friends and relatives had probably come to stay with her at her death. So everyone came to the house and stayed there together.

Can you now translate *gathered* into your own language?

c Translate these words and phrases into your own language. Check that the translations have a logical meaning in each of the sentences.

candles (line 3)	from all walks of life (line 30)
rushed (line 6)	alike (line 30)
sink (line 13)	gifts (line 31)
sob (line 14)	flinch (line 55)
recovered (line 22)	speechless (line 57)
throughout (line 25)	trance (line 61)
queueing (line 29)	

© SANTILLANA

7 The best and the worst *Talking about experiences*

a Look at the table below and match the adjectives, nouns and verbs to make correct questions. Change the verb in brackets to the past participle.

EXAMPLE:

Who's the strangest person you've ever met?
What's the most beautiful place you've ever been to?

	adjective	noun		verb
Who's What's	the best the worst the strangest the most interesting the most boring the most exciting the most beautiful	film meal place book person restaurant food/drink piece of music musician athlete	you've ever	(meet)? (go) to? (hear)? (see)? (eat)? (taste)? (have)? (read)? (read) about?

b Listen to these people talking about experiences. Complete the sentences for each conversation.

A: _____ the _____ _____ you've ever _____?
B: Erm ... Let me see. Probably _____. Have you ever _____?
A: No, _____. / Yes, I have. I've _____ _____ times/once/once or twice.

c In pairs, ask and answer similar questions.

Learning Tips

Guessing the meaning from context

1 When you see a word or phrase you do not know, try to guess the logical meaning. Read the complete sentence before you try to guess. The meaning of the sentence will help you guess individual words. Sometimes you also need to read the sentences before and after the one with the new word or phrase.

Look first to see if you think the word should be a verb, an adjective or a noun. This will also help you guess the meaning. It is not always possible to guess the exact meaning from the sentence, but it is often possible to guess the approximate meaning.

Try to guess the approximate meaning first and then use a dictionary to check the exact meaning.

2 When you learn a new verb or see a verb you know, make sure you learn the preposition(s) that go with the verb. Many verbs can take more than one preposition depending on the meaning or the context.

Make up sentences to help you remember the verb and the preposition.

EXAMPLE:

A: Have you heard the news about Mandy Smith?
B: Who's Mandy Smith? I've never heard of her.

Pronunciation File

Sentence stress and intonation

a Listen to this question and mark the stressed syllables.

Where did you go?

Notice the falling line above the sentence. Listen to the question again and notice how the voice falls like the line.

b Listen to these questions and mark the stress.

Who did you see?

Why do you ask?

When did you leave?

What do you think?

Listen again and notice how the voice rises and falls in the same way as the first question.

This rising and falling is called intonation. The intonation for questions beginning with *Wh* is often like this.

c Listen and repeat this verse.

Where did she go?
Who did she see?
Why do you ask?
Don't ask me.

© SANTILLANA

8 Mind over matter *Questions in the past*

A

B

C

D

E

F

a Look at the picture story. What do you think is the correct order for the pictures?

b Listen to 72 year-old John Archer telling the story. Check if your order is correct.

c Listen again and write one of these question words or phrases in the appropriate question. Use each word or phrase only once.

Did How How long How many What When Where Why Which Who Whose

Now complete the questions with the past tense of the verbs below. Some verbs can be used twice.

be break escape happen see squeeze take try

EXAMPLE:

	Question	Answer
1	*When did this happen?*	In November 1943.
2	_____ _____ it _____?	Over the Indian Ocean.
3	_____ _____ he _____ from the plane?	He squeezed through the small look-out hole.
4	_____ _____ he in the sea?	About two hours.
5	_____ _____ he _____ coming towards him?	Two sailors from a nearby ship.
6	_____ hospital _____ the ship _____ him to?	To a local military hospital.
7	_____ bones _____ he _____?	Just a couple of bones in his right arm.
8	_____ plane _____ they _____ him to see?	His friend's, which was the same model of plane.
9	_____ _____ he so surprised?	Because the look-out hole was so small.
10	_____ _____ he _____ to do?	He tried to squeeze through the look-out hole.
11	_____ he _____ through the hole?	No, he couldn't do it. It was impossible!

d Look at the questions and answers above. Tell the story in your own words.

© SANTILLANA

9 Sayings

Which of these sayings describes the cartoon best?

If at first you don't succeed, try, try again.
Where there's a will* there's a way.
Look before you leap.*

Which saying best fits the story in exercise 8?

*a will = a desire or strong wish to do something
*to leap = to jump

Vocabulary File

1 Approximate numbers

Here are some more examples of approximate numbers from this unit.

a couple of   dozens of *   several

* (a dozen = 12)

Find more examples in this unit and add them to the list in unit 1 (page 14). Then use the phrases to describe:

How many
- friends you have
- English books you have read
- cities/countries you have been to
- American films you have seen
- places you have lived in
- exams you have taken
- strange people you have met
- Latin American writers you have heard of

Write five sentences using the phrases.

2 Questions ending in prepositions

a Certain verbs are often used with prepositions.

ask for something
go with someone
pay for | *wait for* — *someone/something*
dream about someone/something
go to | *arrive at* — *a place*
work for a company
work with people
hear of a famous person
(i.e. you know his/her name)
hear about something that happened

When you ask a question with *who*, *what* or *which*, remember to put the preposition after the verb.
EXAMPLE: *Who are you waiting for?*

b Put one of the verbs and prepositions from the list in part A into these sentences. Put the verb into the correct form where necessary. Notice when you put the preposition after the verb, you sometimes have two prepositions next to each other in the sentence.

1 Which station does the train ______?
2 Which company does he ______?
3 When you got the bill, how many people did you ______?
4 When you went to France, who did you ______?
5 Which American jazz musicians have you ______ from the ones on this CD?
6 What did you ______ while you were asleep?
7 Which bus are you ______?
8 What are you going to ______ for your birthday?
9 Which cities did you ______ in Italy?
10 Which news stories did you ______ while you were away?
11 Who do you ______ in your office?

3 Word spiders

Complete these word spiders with vocabulary from this unit.

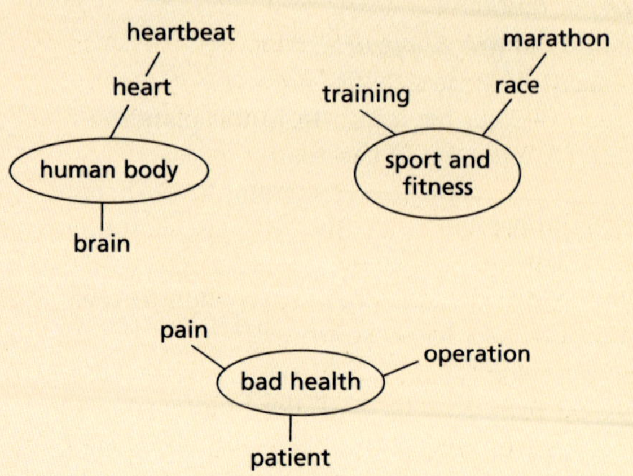

© SANTILLANA

10 Describing past experiences *Language round-up*

a Look at these two picture stories. The pictures are in the correct order. Tell the stories from the pictures.

b Listen to the two stories to see if you were correct.

c Listen again and then tell the stories in your own words. Use the prompts below.

story 1

on holiday/the seaside. /about twelve. Suddenly/brilliant idea. /some water/bucket/over my cousin. My cousin/fifteen/time. /yelled/me. laughed/away, but/a bit scared. Anyway, I/ towards/wall/of the beach. This wall/the same height/me. /about 1m 50cm. Well, I/right over the wall. When/round/at the wall/shocked. I/how/over it. I/to jump/it/day, but/not. We/back/place every year/then. /always tried/the wall but/never/again. I/never/that wall/day. It/experience/had.

story 2

One day the doctor/father that he/gallstones. /to send/hospital/operation, but my father/want/ hospital. He/like the idea of surgery. He/try to cure the gallstones himself. So/special diet. /eat anything/weeks. He only/water with lemon. He/that smoking/also bad for gallstones so/ smoking, as well. Anyway, after/cured. He/never/ gallstones from that/this and /never/another cigarette/life. I think/hardest/ever/. I really/for it.

d Ask questions about the two stories, using the question words and phrases from exercise 8.

e Has anything like this ever happened to you, your friends or your relatives? Can you tell the story?

f Read these prompts and write the story of John the marathon runner. You heard his story in exercise 3.

I/hundreds of races in my life, but I remember one race/ago in Scotland. I met a runner who/70. When he ran/little noises like a steam engine. 'Cheeha-cheeha', like that. Anyway I passed him and everything was OK. But/eleven miles/stopped. I/run. Then suddenly/this noise 'Cheeha-cheeha' coming up behind me/him, the old man. He/me and I/next to last in that race and the old man/before me. Then about two weeks/him again/race. I was just at the top of a hill when/again 'Cheeha-cheeha'. I/'No'. 'It's him again.' I/let him pass me again so/a bit faster. This time my legs were OK and/third. But really I should thank him because/he made me run faster. I/often/about him since that day but/never/him again. But now, every time/tired I/him and it makes me run a little bit faster.

© SANTILLANA

Making Changes

1 Down in the dumps

a Read the two letters and match the pictures with the letters.

Sorry I haven't written before, but I've been a bit down in the dumps in the last few weeks. It's my flat that's getting me down. Just the other night for example, I was cooking dinner in the kitchen, the usual din was coming from the family downstairs – the baby was screaming, the dog was barking, the TV was blaring out. And then there was the noise outside! Trains were clattering past, making my windows rattle, cars were hooting in the street below and, as if that wasn't enough, a police siren started wailing. Honestly, I just sat down at the kitchen table and burst into tears. I thought, 'Why am I living here? I hate this flat.' In fact, I've never really liked it so I've decided I'm going to

A

B

It's rained here non-stop for the past three days. I'm really fed up! Last night we were so cold we got into our sleeping bags at eight o'clock. We were both shivering. (Dave has caught a cold and he was coughing and sneezing all the time.) So we were lying there in our sleeping bags – I was reading a book and Dave was scribbling a letter to his mum and dad. Outside it was pouring with rain. The wind was howling round the tent and then it started thundering and lightning. All of a sudden, I slammed my book shut and I thought, 'I've had enough of this! What sort of holiday is this?' So, this afternoon I'm going to

b Read the letters again. Try to guess the meaning, or approximate meaning, of these words and phrases. Do not use a dictionary at the moment.

letter 1	letter 2
down in the dumps	fed up
din	sleeping bags
screaming	shivering
barking	coughing
blaring out	sneezing
clattering	scribbling
rattle	pouring with rain
hooting	howling
wailing	slammed
burst into tears	

c The letters are not finished. What do you think the writer of each letter is going to do next?

© SANTILLANA

2 Nightmare hotel *Describing past events*

a Look at the illustration of the guest at the hotel. What do you think the hotel is like?

b Read the extracts from this letter about a guest's experience in the hotel. What were the problems? What do you think happened in the end?

> *I was sitting in the hotel bedroom and it was terrible. Outside in the street ... Next door to my bedroom ... Upstairs there was a children's disco and ... So I went downstairs and told the manager I couldn't stand the noise. Fortunately he ...*

c Listen to the complete story and see if you were right.

d Listen to the noises in the hotel bedroom. Describe the noises you heard.

EXAMPLE:

Cars and taxis were hooting.
A police siren was wailing.

e Listen again and add any noises that you missed.

3 Sudden changes

a Read these extracts from three different stories. Match each extract with one of the pictures. Each picture shows what was happening just before.

1 ... All of a sudden, someone tapped me on the shoulder. I nearly jumped out of my skin.
2 ... when suddenly people started screaming. Everyone ran back to the beach.
3 ... The next minute we heard a loud bang in the garden and we both rushed out.

In pairs, ask and answer the questions below. Imagine what was happening beforehand in each of the three extracts.

Where did the incident take place?
What was the weather like?
What time of day was it?
What were people doing/thinking/feeling at the time?

b Now listen to these three people saying what was happening beforehand in each story. Match the extracts 1-3 above with the three stories you hear. You will hear the stories in a different order.

c In pairs, re-tell each story and predict what actually happened in the end of each story. Answer these questions.

story 1 Who was the person who tapped him on the shoulder? What did s/he want?
story 2 Why did people suddenly start screaming and run back to the beach?
story 3 What did they see when they rushed out to the garden?

© SANTILLANA

4 Changing places *Describing changes*

a Look at the photographs of Benidorm, on the Costa Blanca of Spain, and Tangier, on the north coast of Morocco. How do you think they have changed in the last thirty years?

b The texts are extracts from two guide books. Read the texts about some of the changes to Benidorm and Tangier.

Benidorm
Only thirty years ago, Benidorm used to be a small village on a rocky peninsula. The old part of the village is still there, but it is now overshadowed by miles of towering concrete. If you want hordes of British and Scandinavian sunseekers, scores of 'English' pubs, at least seventy discos and bacon and eggs for breakfast, this is the place to come. The beach – nearly 6km of it, mostly created with imported Moroccan sand! – is impressive, when you can see it through the roasting flesh. Surprisingly, except in August, you can usually find a room in Benidorm. The cheaper places are all near the centre and away from the sea, but out of season many of the giant hotels and apartment blocks slash their prices drastically.

Tangier
For the first five decades of this century Tangier was one of the stylish resorts of the Mediterranean, with its own separate laws, administration and a large community of expatriates and refugees. It used to be a free port with very few taxes, over seventy banks and about 4,000 finance companies. Tangier was also the world's first and most famous gay resort.

When Morocco became independent in 1956, however, Tangier's special status was abolished. Almost overnight the finance and banking businesses moved to Switzerland and Spain. Most of the expatriates left. The new national government took control of the administration of the city and ordered a clean-up of the city. Brothels* – previously numbering almost a hundred – were banned and the gay bars were closed.

These days, it is halfway to becoming a mainstream tourist resort – increasingly popular with holidaying Moroccans.

*places for prostitutes

c Find an example in each text of, *Benidorm/Tangier used to be …*
Used to be means: it was in the past, but it is different now. Use the information below to make statements about Benidorm and Tangier in the past.

Benidorm Tangier	used to didn't use to	be have	(a lot of/a few/any) tourists/sunseekers/refugees a stylish resort/a small village very quiet/famous/busy/cosmopolitan (a lot of/a few/any) gay bars/discos/pubs/brothels banks/concrete buildings/large hotels

Pronunciation File

The schwa /ə/1

a The most important sound in English is called a schwa. It is written like this /ə/ in the phonetic alphabet. We often use this sound in English.

Listen to this sentence.

I'm happi<u>er</u> th<u>an</u> I used <u>to</u> be.

The schwa sound is in all the syllables underlined. Listen again.

b Listen to these sentences. Underline all the syllables with the schwa sound. The correct number of schwa sounds is written beside each sentence.

I'm taller than I used to be. (3)
We used to go to Italy for our holidays when I was a child. (6)
The sun was shining and the birds were singing when I arrived at school. (7)
It was eight o'clock when I arrived at the station and the train was leaving. (9)

© SANTILLANA

5 A change for the better

a Listen to Christina and Birgit talking about changes in their lives and answer the questions.

1 Whose life changed because of a personal decision?
2 Whose life changed because of an unexpected event?

b Listen again and answer the questions about Christina and Birgit.

1 What was happening in her life beforehand?
2 Why did her life change?
3 What did she do about the new situation?

c Listen to the second part of the conversations with Christina and Birgit. Make true statements from the information below.

		happier			
		busier			
		kinder			
Christina is		easier			
Christina's life is	slightly	financially better off	than	she	used to be.
Birgit is	much	financially worse off		it	
Birgit's life is		more difficult			
		more exciting			
		more enjoyable			
		more interesting			

d Read these two expressions. Can you guess what they mean?

You take things for granted. (Christina)
I don't want to turn the clock back. (Birgit)

e Do you know anyone whose life has changed dramatically? Describe how and why his/her life changed and how his/her life is different now from how it used to be.

f Write a short account of someone whose life has changed. Write about someone you know or about Christina or Birgit.

Learning Tips

Using a dictionary

Look at this example from a monolingual dictionary.

There are several definitions given for the word *gay*. Look back at exercise 4. Which definition is the correct one for the text?
As you can see, the possible meanings for the word are very different.

When you look up a word in a dictionary, be sure to read all the possible definitions and find the best one for each context.

gay /geɪ/, **gays; gayer, gayest**. 1 A person who is **gay** is homosexual; used especially by homosexuals themselves or by people who support them. EG *I've told them I'm gay...* ▸ used of organizations and magazines for homosexuals. EG *They have an active Gay Group.* ▸ used as a noun. EG *...a holiday spot for gays... Many gays were worried about the new system.* ◇ **gayness**. EG *He wasn't ashamed of his gayness.*
2 In slightly more old-fashioned English, a person who is **gay** is 2.1 lively and enjoyable to be with. EG *...gay, innocent Annabel... Sonny was gayer, more cheerful... Well, he's not the gayest of companions.*
2.2 free from all worries and fears. EG *...the image of the gay bachelor... ...a gay, carefree young woman.*

ADJ CLASSIF : USU PRED
▸ ADJ CLASSIF : USU ATTRIB
▸ N COUNT
◇ N UNCOUNT ⇑ homosexuality
ADJ QUALIT ⇑ happy
ADJ CLASSIF : ATTRIB

You can double-check you have the correct meaning by looking up the English word in a bilingual dictionary. When you see the word in your own language, check that it is the correct meaning for the context.

© SANTILLANA

Grammar File

1 Past continuous

a Look at these examples from exercise 1.

I was cooking dinner in the kitchen …
The baby was screaming, the dog was barking …

The verbs in these sentences are in the past continuous tense. This tense is often used to describe the surroundings – what people were doing, what the place looked like, the noises, the atmosphere, etc at the time.

Find more examples of the past continuous in this unit. Write down five different examples.

b Write the correct form of the verb in brackets in these sentences.

1 When I *left* (leave) home, the sun *was shining* (shine) and the birds *were singing* (sing).
2 The baby _____ (cry) and the dog _____ (bark), so I _____ (run) into the garden and put my hands over my ears.
3 In the first restaurant we _____ (go) to, waiters _____ (run) around, a lot of people _____ (shout) and loud music _____ (blare) out, so we _____ (decide) to find another restaurant.
4 I _____ (watch) some stupid programme on TV and I _____ (feel) really fed up, so I _____ (turn) off the TV and _____ (go) out for a walk to think about everything.
5 We _____ (lie) on the beach, Ann _____ (read) and I _____ (sunbathe) when suddenly we _____ (hear) someone call out for help.
6 I was so angry when I _____ (get) home. The kids _____ (listen) to music upstairs and Jim _____ (talk) to someone on the phone. Everything was in a mess so I just _____ (scream) at them all.
7 I _____ (dream) about my summer holiday as I _____ (walk) down the street the other day when suddenly I _____ (meet) my old friend, Christine.

c Describe the scene as you walked into the school building today. Describe the weather, what people in the street were doing, the noises you heard. Write a short paragraph.

Begin like this:
I was walking into school today, the sun…

End like this:
Just as I came through the door, I met…

2 *Used to*

a Look at these examples.

Benidorm used to be a small village.
It didn't use to have many tourists, but now it has thousands of tourists.
Did it use to be much quieter than it is now?

What do you think is emphasised when we say *used to be* and *used to do*, instead of *was* and *did*?

Do we say *used to* to describe one single action or event in the past, or something that was true for a long period of time?

b In these sentences the verbs underlined are in the past tense. In some sentences we can write *used to, didn't use to* or *did … use to?* In other sentences this is not possible. Change only the sentences where it is possible to write a form of *used to*.

1 He <u>was</u> a revolutionary student, but now he is a respectable businessman.
2 Mark <u>was</u> here yesterday.
3 I <u>went</u> to Portugal for my holidays last year.
4 When I <u>was</u> a child, we <u>went</u> to Portugal for our summer holidays every year.
5 We <u>didn't live</u> in a big city before, but now we live right in the centre of Madrid.
6 They <u>didn't do</u> their homework last week.
7 I <u>didn't like</u> salad, but now I do.
8 What kind of food <u>did you hate</u> when you were a child?
– Vegetables. I never <u>ate</u> vegetables.
9 <u>Were you</u> thinner than you are now?

3 Comparisons with adjectives

a Check in the Grammar Reference on page 141 to remind yourself how to make comparisons with short adjectives and long adjectives.

Write the comparative form of these adjectives.

hot	_____	easy	_____	cheap	_____
cold	_____	difficult	_____	expensive	_____

b Write sentences using the comparative form of the adjectives above.

EXAMPLE: *The north of Argentina is hotter than the south.*

c Write some examples about yourself and your town, comparing the past with the present.

EXAMPLE: *My town used to be quieter than it is now.*

© SANTILLANA

6 What does 'change' mean? *Using a word in different contexts*

a Look at these dictionary definitions of the word *change*. Listen to the conversations and match each conversation with one of the definitions.

A **change** /tʃeɪndʒ/, **changes, changing, changed**. 1 If there is a **change** in something, it becomes different in some way. EG ...*a radical change in attitudes... ...a change of pace... He was shaken by the changes that had taken place since he had left China...* N COUNT/ UNCOUNT ↑ difference = alteration

B 3 If you say that something is happening **for a change**, you mean that it is better or more enjoyable than the thing that usually happens. EG *They were more than glad to leave their cars parked and walk for a change... It's nice to see you with your books for a change.* PHR : USED AS AN A = for once ≠ as usual

C 5 To **change** something also means **5.1** to replace it or to use, have, or get something of a similar kind instead of the thing you previously used or had. EG *I changed the bulb... It was his doctor who advised that he change his job... I took the saucepan back and changed it for a non-stick one.* V+O : IF+PREP THEN *for*

D 7 When you **change** or **change** your clothes, you take off some or all of your clothes and put on different ones. EG *I went to my dressing room to change... She changed into the working clothes she had brought with her... I want to change my socks.* V OR V+O : IF V+ PREP THEN *into/ out of*

E 11 If you **change** or if you **change** buses or trains, you get off one bus or train and on to another in order to continue your journey. EG *Change at Crewe... In Albany you'll change for Ohio...* V OR V+O ↑ transfer = switch, connect

F 16 **Change** is **16.1** the money that you receive when you pay for something with more money than it costs because you do not have exactly the right amount of money. EG *As he took the change, Rudolph had an impulse to buy another ticket...* N UNCOUNT

G 17 When you **change** money, **17.1** you give someone an amount of money in smaller coins or notes in exchange for the same amount of money in larger coins or notes. EG *Can anyone change a ten pound note?* V+O

H 7.10 If you **change your mind**, you change a decision you have made or an opinion that you had, especially so that you do or think the opposite. EG *All of a sudden I changed my mind and decided not to go anywhere... I'm not going to change my mind about the divorce.* PHR : VB INFLECTS = have second thoughts

b Listen again and write out the complete conversations.

conversation 1

A: 1____ decided 2____ stay in this job 3____ more year.
B: I thought you 4____ another job.
A: Well. Yes, I was going 5____, but 6____ my mind.

conversation 2

A: 1____ me. 2____ a five pound note?
B: Er ... I 3____. Yes. 4____. 5____ one-pound coins. 6____?
A: 7____. Thanks 8____.

conversation 3

A: 1____ Glasgow, please.
B: Right. A single, return or day-return?
A: 2____ please.
B: Standard class? First class?
A: 3____ please. What time 4____?
B: The next one's 5____, from platform 6____.
A: 7____. Do I have 8____?
B: No. 9____ Glasgow.

conversation 4

A: Guess what! I saw Paul Morgan yesterday.
B: 1____?
A: 2____ really 3____.
B: 4____?
A: 5____. And he's going bald.
B: No!

conversation 5

A: Hi! 1____ too early?
B: Hi! No, 2____ fine. 3____. Make yourself at home.
A: Thanks.
B: I'm just 4____. 5____ minute.

conversation 6

A: 1____, please.
B: 2____.
A: Thank 3____. 4____.

conversation 7

A: I 1____, but I'm afraid 2____.
B: 3____. Oh yes. Er ... 4____ receipt, please?
A: Yes.
B: Right. 5____. Just take a seat for a moment.

conversation 8

A: I thought you were going to France on holiday.
B: Well I was, but I decided to go Italy for 1____.

c Does the word *change* have the same meanings in your language as it does in English? Which meanings are the same and which are different?

d Complete the sentences using one of these expressions with the word *change*.

changed his mind
a change is as good as a rest
really changed her tune

1 She used to say she thought he was wonderful, but now she can't stand him. She's ____.
2 He was going to buy a new car, but he's ____.
3 It's so much better now I've moved to my new office. It's true what they say, ____.

© SANTILLANA

7 Changes for the worse

a The text below is an extract from a book called *Wild Swans* by Jung Chang. She is a Chinese writer who has lived in London for the past fifteen years. Look at the photograph and say what you think the book is about.

Read the introduction and the extract from the book. Then answer the questions.

1 How was she feeling the night the Red Guards came to the house?
2 What was she doing when they arrived at the house?
3 What did she do when they came?

In the 1960s in China, many teenagers formed groups called the Red Guards. The job of the Red Guards was to make sure that all adults followed the teachings of the leader of China, Mao Zedong. The Red Guard had to denounce any adults who were not following his teachings. Many teachers were put in prison because of denunciations by Red Guard members, some teachers killed themselves and some were even killed by their students. Some Red Guard members even denounced other members of their family, including their parents. The writer, Jung Chang, was a teenager at this time in China. This is part of her story.

Wild Swans

Starting from June 1966 there was no schooling. No school meant no control. But what could we do with our freedom? There were virtually no books, no music, no films, no theatre, no museums, no teahouses, almost no way of keeping oneself occupied – except cards. Naturally "Red Guardship" became many youngsters' full-time occupation. The only way they could release their energy and frustration were in violent denunciations.

One day one of my friends told us that her parents, both actors, had committed suicide, unable to stand the denunciations. Not long after, news came that the brother of another girl had killed himself. Someone had denounced him for trying to organise an anti-Mao party. He threw himself out of a third-floor window when the police came to arrest him. Tragedies like this were part of our everyday life.

To occupy myself I began writing poetry. The first poem was written on my sixteenth birthday, 25th March 1968. There was no birthday celebration. Both my parents were in detention. That night, as I lay in bed listening to the gunshots and the loudspeakers blaring out, I reached a turning point. I had always been told that I was living in a paradise on earth. Now I asked myself: If this is paradise, what then is hell?

It was in this mood that I composed my poem. I described my bewilderment at the new world, at not knowing what and how to think. I wrote the poem down. I was lying in bed, going over it in my head, when I heard banging on the door. From the sound I knew it was a house raid. When the pounding on the door began, I quickly ran to the toilet and locked the door while my grandmother answered. My hands were trembling but I managed to tear the poem into tiny pieces, throw them into the bowl and flush the toilet. I searched the floor carefully to make sure no pieces had fallen out. But the paper did not disappear the first time. I had to wait and flush again. By now the Red Guard were banging on the door of the toilet. They were ordering me to come out immediately. I did not answer.

b Read the text again. Find the words or phrases you do not know. See how many of the words and phrases you can guess before you look them up in a dictionary.

These clues will help you to guess the meaning of the words underlined.

1. The words teachings and schooling come from the words teach and school? (introduction and line 1)
2. 'There were virtually no books.' Probably people could only read books by Mao Zedong, but no other books. (line 3)
3. The word loudspeaker is made from two words: loud and speak. She could hear the loudspeakers outside her bedroom window. (line 17)
4. The loudspeakers were blaring out in the street. This is what loudspeakers usually do. (line 17)
5. She described what she was thinking and feeling. Then, in this mood, she wrote her poem. (line 21)
6. The word bewilderment is followed by the phrase, 'not knowing what and how to think.' (line 22)
7. The Red Guards came suddenly, banging on the door to check what she and her family were doing. This was a house raid. (line 25)
8. The Red Guards were banging or pounding on the door. (line 25)
9. Her hands were trembling as she tried to tear the paper. Imagine yourself in this situation. Would your hands tremble? (line 27)
10. She threw the pieces of paper into the toilet bowl and tried to flush the toilet. She wanted the pieces of paper to disappear. (line 28)

c The writer is describing a period of terror and horror in China. Write down as many words and phrases which give the feeling of terror or horror.

EXAMPLE:

no control
violent denunciations
committed suicide

d Can you think of a situation in another country which is/was similar to the situation in China at this time? How is/was it similar?

Vocabulary File

1 Word endings

a Look at this example from the text on page 44.
I described my bewilderment.

The ending *-ment* is used with several nouns which describe feelings, thoughts or actions.
adjective = *bewildered* noun = *bewilderment*
EXAMPLE: *She felt bewildered.*
She experienced a feeling of bewilderment.

These adjectives follow the same rule.
excited astonished amazed contented

These verbs follow the same rule.
state punish agree disagree

b Look at these examples from the text.

To occupy myself, I began writing poetry.
Red Guardship became many youngsters' full-time occupation.

The ending *-ation* is used with several nouns which come from verbs.
verb = *occupy* noun = *occupation*
Can you find any other examples like this in the text?
These verbs also follow the same rule.
invite concentrate examine inform educate

Make two lists of nouns, one with the ending *-ment*, one with the ending *-ation*. Write the words given here and any other examples you know. If you are not sure of the correct spelling, check in a dictionary. Do these words have similar endings in your language?

2 Reflexive verbs

a Look at these examples from the text.
To occupy myself …
He threw himself out of a third-floor window …
… some teachers killed themselves …

Put the correct ending on these reflexive pronouns, *-self* or *-selves*.
my- your- (singular) him- her- our-
your- (plural) them-

b These verbs are often used with reflexive pronouns.
enjoy hurt burn cut look after
take care of control blame behave

Choose a suitable verb from the list above to complete these sentences. Put the verb into the correct tense. Put the correct reflexive pronoun after the verb.
EXAMPLE: *The concert was great! I really enjoyed myself.*

1 He ______ while he was shaving this morning.
2 You mustn't ______. It wasn't your fault.
3 She is very independent. She has ______ since she was eighteen. She has no family.

Write more examples using the other verbs in the list.

c These verbs are NOT used with a reflexive pronoun.
wake up wash dress shave comb brush
get up stand up sit down feel relax

It is possible to say:
In the morning, I wash, shave, dress, etc.

But it is more usual to say:
I get dressed.
I have a wash/shave/bath/shower/my breakfast.
I brush my teeth/my hair/comb my hair.

In pairs, say the order you do everything in the morning. Remember, do not use reflexive pronouns!
EXAMPLE:
I wake up about seven, I …

Pronunciation File

The schwa /ə/ 2

a Listen to this conversation again and underline the schwa sounds you hear.
A: A ticket to Glasgow, please.
B: Right. A single, return or day-return?
A: Return, please.
B: Standard class? First class?
A: Standard, please. What time does the next one leave?
B: The next one's at ten fifty, from platform three.
A: Right thanks. Do I have to change anywhere?
B: No. It's direct to Glasgow.

b Notice how the word *is* usually contracts to *'s* in normal spoken English. In pairs, practise the conversation in part A using the schwa sounds and contractions where necessary.

c Listen to this long sentence. Repeat it and then underline the schwa sounds.
We arrive at the station at seven o'clock, at the cinema at eight o'clock and at the station again at eleven.

How many schwa sounds did you find?

© SANTILLANA

8 A dramatic change *Language round-up*

a Twenty years ago Edison Ortega had a dramatic change in his life. Look at the photographs. Can you guess what happened in his life?

b Listen to his story and answer the questions.

1 What did his life use to be like?
2 Why did he leave Chile?
3 What was he doing at the time of the military coup?
4 What was he doing when he heard the news of the coup?
5 What did he do?
6 How long has he lived in Scotland?
7 What has happened to him since he came to Scotland?
8 When did he go back to visit Chile?
9 What is Santiago like now compared to how it used to be?
10 What is he going to do for the next few years?

c In pairs, tell Edison's life story. Begin each part of his story like this:

He used to …
At the time of the military coup, he was …
When he heard the news he was …
Then he …
Since he came to Scotland, he has …
Two years ago, he …
He found Santiago different from how it used to be.
Now it is …
For the next few years, he is …

d Do you know anyone whose life has changed in some way? Write a short paragraph, giving some details about this person's life.

© SANTILLANA

1 Biography of a president

Full name:	Nelson _____ Mandela
Date of birth:	_____, 1918
Place of birth:	Transkei, Cape Province, South Africa
Education:	University of Fort Hare. He was expelled for _____.
First job:	lawyer in Johannesburg
Entered politics:	in 1944 as _____ . He campaigned for equal rights for all South Africans. became _____ in 1991
Married:	married Winnie Mandela in _____
Imprisoned:	on _____ in 1964. In 1988, he was put under _____.
Released:	_____, after world-wide campaigns for his release
Present job:	President of South Africa since _____.

a In pairs, ask and answer questions to complete the information on Nelson Mandela. Partner A reads this information. Partner B reads the information on page 158.

b Look at the completed notes and write the life story of Nelson Mandela.

2 It used to be peaceful

50 years ago

now

a Write a description of what the village used to be like 50 years ago and how it has changed in the last 50 years. Describe the village, the people, the population of the village, the houses and transport in the village.

b Say if you would prefer to live in the village as it used to be or as it is now. Give your reasons. Compare what you have written with a partner to see if you agree or disagree.

© SANTILLANA

3 Powerful words – *go*

a Look at these sentences and choose the correct definition for the phrasal verbs with *go* underlined.

1 What a terrible smell! The milk has gone off.
2 I've gone without a cigarette for three days now.
3 They've been going out for over two years.
4 He went on with his job for three years, even though he hated it.
5 Could you go over it just one more time? I'm not sure I understand.
6 That shirt doesn't go with that tie.

a repeat
b to be boyfriend/girlfriend with someone
c become sour/rotten
d match
e manage not to have
f continue

b Rewrite the sentences using one of the phrasal verbs with *go* from part A.

1 Is it clear or do you want me to repeat it again?
2 Will you continue telling the story? It's really interesting.
3 That jersey looks good with your shirt.
4 Humans cannot survive without water for more than three days.
5 If you don't keep yoghurt in the fridge, it becomes rotten within a day.
6 He was her boyfriend for six months, but it didn't work.

c Write your own sentences for each of the phrasal verbs with *go*.

4 Dictionary work

a Look at this list of verbs. Write *R* after the verb if it is regular and *IR* if it is irregular, then write the past tense form of all the irregular verbs. Check your answers in your dictionary.

pay	__	________	arrive	__	________
agree	__	________	fight	__	________
wait	__	________	listen	__	________
speak	__	________	need	__	________

b Write down the preposition which usually follows each verb.

EXAMPLE:
pay *for*

c Write sentences in the past tense with each verb and preposition.

EXAMPLE:
I paid for the cinema tickets with my credit card.

5 Error correction

There is one mistake in each of these sentences. Find the mistake and rewrite the sentences correctly.

1 *What time does the train arrive to Swindon?*
2 *What's the strangest thing you have ever ate?*
3 *She usually went skiing at Easter, but she can't go this year because she has broken her wrist.*
4 *Wolverhampton Wanderers use to be a great football team.*
5 *This exercise is more difficult that the last one.*
6 *You can't talk to him in the mornings, he's always in such a bad humour.*
7 *I find it hard to relax myself when I am worried about work.*
8 *How did you came here?*
9 *I haven't seen them since three years.*
10 *I had this terrible dream with a snake last night.*

6 Project

a Who are your heroes? Think about who you admire and why you admire them. Is it because of what the person has achieved, her/his character or a particular thing the person has done?

b In groups, discuss people you admire and why you admire them. Try to agree on a list of ten people who you all admire. Compare your list with other groups in the class. Which people do you most admire as a class?

c Choose someone from your list who you particularly admire. Find out as much information about this person as you can and write a description about her/his life. Include the following information:

1 her/his childhood, school and family
2 a particular event or action which demonstrates why you admire the person
3 personal characteristics which you admire in her/him

Keep this project in your file with the project from Review Unit 1-2.

REVIEW UNITS 3-4

© SANTILLANA

Jobs with a Difference

1 Sounds different

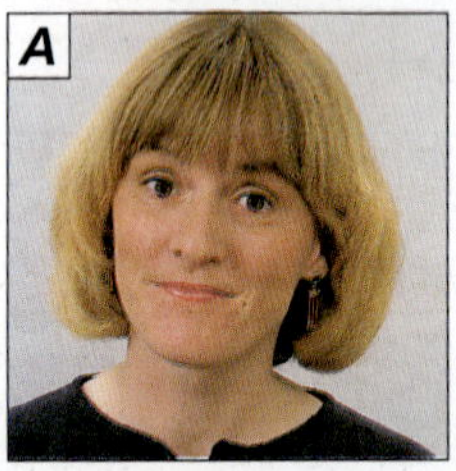

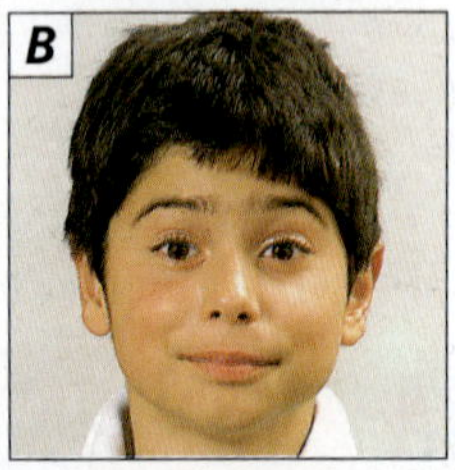

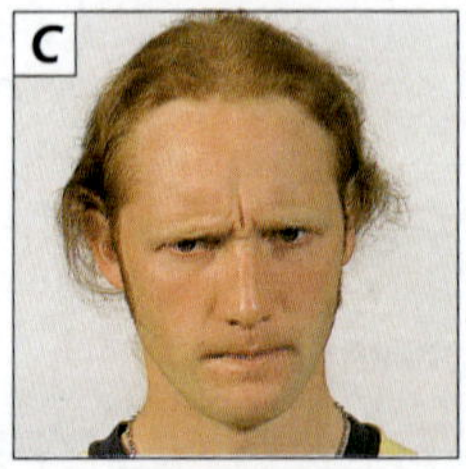

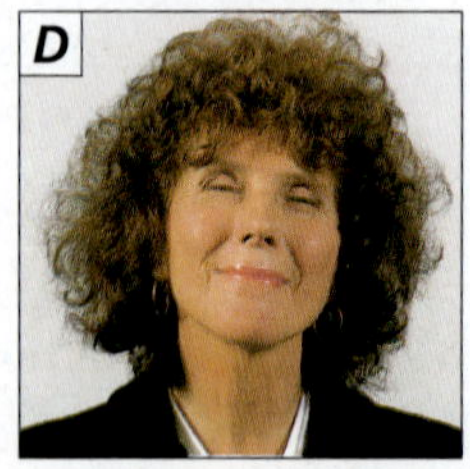

a Listen to these five people. They are all saying, 'Mmm-mm'. Match each 'Mmm-mm' with one of the meanings below.

1 Yes. 2 No. 3 I don't know.
4 Really? 5 Delicious!

Look at the faces in the photographs. Match each of the meanings 1–5 with a face.

b Listen to the phrases 1–5 and try to say the word 'Mmm-mm' to match each phrase you hear. Now listen again and say the phrase to match the 'Mmm-mm' you hear.

2 Ways of speaking

a Listen and match the words in speech marks (' ') in column A with the speaking verbs in column B. The first one has been done for you.

	A	B
1	'Ha-ha!'	he shouted.
2	'Sh-sh!'	she sighed.
3	'Mmmm!'	he muttered.
4	'Oh, no!'	she screamed.
5	'Ow!'	he laughed.
6	'Um-erm,'	she whispered.
7	'Aaa-aah!'	he groaned.

b Look at the cartoon and write a word from column A in each of the speech bubbles.

c Listen to people saying the sentences below. Complete the sentences with one of the speaking verbs in column B. The first one has been done for you.

1 Hey Stop he *shouted*.
2 It's a rat she _____.
3 Be careful he _____.
4 Oh dear What is it now she _____.
5 Oh, no I've got the answer wrong again he _____.
6 Well, I don't know. I'm sorry I can't help you he _____.
7 How stupid she _____.

d Now punctuate the sentences. Put speech marks (' ') around the spoken words. Put an exclamation mark (!), a question mark (?) or a comma (,) at the end of the spoken words.

EXAMPLE:
'Hey! Stop!' he shouted.

© SANTILLANA

3 The Little Old Lady from Cricket Creek

a Look at the picture of the Little Old Lady from Cricket Creek. What do you think the story is about?

Some of the story is missing. The missing paragraphs are on page 159, but they are not in the correct order. Put the paragraphs into the correct order in the story where you see ***.

b What do you think the end of the story is?

Art Bowen and I were trying to work out some figures when Penny Thorpe, my secretary, walked into the office.

'Yeah, Penny. What's up?'

'Mr Cummings, there's a woman out in the lobby. She's applying for the clerk's job.' Penny walked over and laid the application form on my desk.

'Good. Good. I hope she's ...' I stopped, staring at the form. 'Age sixty-five!'

Penny remained standing in front of my desk, tapping her pencil. 'Well?' she asked haughtily.

'OK, Penny. Send Mrs Jumpstone in.'

1 ***

'This is a very interesting application, Mabel. It says you were born in Cricket Creek California.'

'That's right young man.'

Art bent over. 'Let me see that application, Ralph.' He grabbed it from the desk and took a few minutes to study it. Mabel and I sat and watched each other. Every once in a while she winked. I tried to look at the ceiling.

Art glanced up and asked 'You worked at California Insurance for ten years. Why did you quit?'

2 ***

'Mabel,' I said, 'the job we have involves quite a bit of work, you know, in an office this size.'

'Really?'

'Really. It even requires a bit of typing. You *can* type?'

'Oh, good heavens, yes. Would you like me to take a test?'

'Er ... yes, that might be a good idea. Let's go find a typewriter.' We walked out of the office. Art whispered in my ear. 'About ten words a minute would be my guess.'

3 ***

Within two months, Mabel Jumpstone was the most popular employee in the building. Whenever someone had a birthday, she brought in a cake for the afternoon break. People went to her with their problems. She arrived early each morning and stayed late. She never missed a day off work. Not one.

4 ***

'You're kidding. You've got to be *kidding*, Art.'

He shook his head. 'The money and Harvey's car are gone. So is Mabel.'

I stared at him. 'I can't believe it.'

'It's true. Every word. What are we going to do?'

I snapped my fingers. 'The application! Come on.'

We ran to the filing cabinets and opened the file named *Employees*. The application form was gone, of course. There was a single sheet inside the folder. It was typed very neatly. *I resign. Yours sincerely, Mabel.* The name was typed, too. There was no handwritten signature. Mabel had always typed everything.

5 ***

I finally got home to my apartment late that evening. I opened a can of beer and then walked into one of the bedrooms ...

c Find the words or phrases in the story which mean:

1 calculate (line 1)
2 What is it? (line 4)
3 entrance hall (line 5)
4 looking with surprise (line 8)
5 with her nose in the air (line 11)
6 took it quickly (line 17)
7 closed one eye (line 19)
8 looked up quickly (line 21)
9 finish (line 22)
10 needs (line 26)
11 Yes, of course (line 28)
12 joking (line 42)
13 am leaving the company (line 51)

d Write down the words and phrases in the text which are connected to office work. Put the words under one of these three headings.

people	stationery	equipment
secretary	application form	typewriter

© SANTILLANA

4 What did she say? *Reporting speech*

a How much can you remember from the story in exercise 3? In pairs, ask and answer these questions about Mabel without looking back at the story. There are three answers given, but only one is correct.

1 What's Mabel's surname?
 a Jumpstone b Thorpe c Bowen
2 How old is she?
 a 60 b 65 c 70
3 Where does she come from?
 a Washington b New York c California
4 Where did she work before?
 a Cummings International
 b California Insurance
 c the Bank of California
5 How long did she work there?
 a 5 years b 10 years c 20 years
6 Why did she leave her home town?
 a because the weather was so bad
 b because she lost her job
 c because she had been in prison
7 How well can she type?
 a quite slowly but accurately
 b very fast and very accurately
 c fast but with a lot of mistakes
8 Is she married?
 a she was married, but her husband died
 b she is still married
 c she has never been married

b Mabel gave a lot of information about herself, but we do not know if it was all true. Make statements about Mabel's information and say if it was true or not.

EXAMPLE:

She said her surname was …	*but we don't know if that was true.*
	and that was true.

5 Who's speaking? *Giving personal information*

a Look at the photographs of these four people. Then look at their personal information and match the people to the photographs.

A

B

C

D
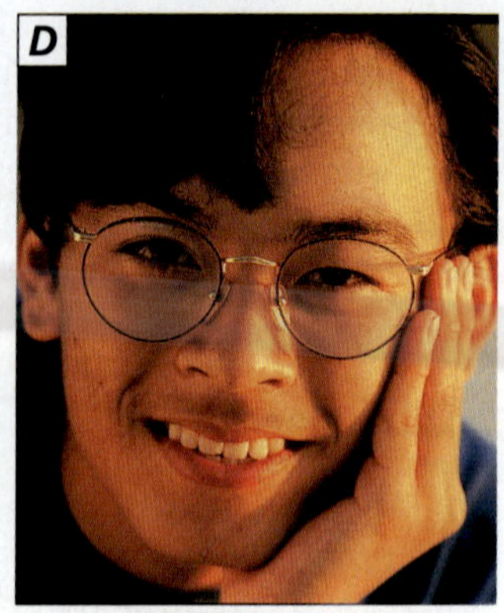

Name:	Jim Daley	Samantha Forsythe	Chi Hung	Kim Sharp
Nationality:	American	British	British	Australian
Age:	35	25	22	19
Children:	two children	one daughter	no children	no children
Job:	mechanic	computer analyst	designer	nanny
	15 years	2 years	9 months	3 months
Languages:	English only	English, Spanish and Italian (excellent) French (quite good)	bilingual Chinese and English German (school)	English and a little Italian and Greek

© SANTILLANA

b Listen to the four people being interviewed and find out which one is speaking. In pairs, ask and answer questions like this:

Who was the first speaker? *It was …*

How do you know? *Because s/he*	*said*	*s/he*	*was …*
	told us		*came from …*
			had …
			had been …
			could …

6 Fact or fantasy

Work in pairs. Tell your partner three facts about yourself, two are true and one is false. Use some of these phrases.

I like … *I am …* *I have been to …* *I can …*
I was … *I have never …* *I've got …*

Listen to your partner's facts then tell the class which ones you think are true or not true.

EXAMPLE:

He said he liked … and I think this is true.
She told me she was …, but I don't think this is true.

Ask the class if they think it is true or not. Then ask your partner, 'Is it true or false?'

Pronunciation File

Pronunciation of *-ed*

a Listen to the past tense of these verbs.

laughed screamed shouted

There are three different ways of pronouncing the *-ed* ending of the verb.

/t/	/d/	/ɪd/

Listen to the three verbs again. Write each verb in the correct column, according to the pronunciation of *-ed*.

b Say these verbs aloud.
Write each verb in the correct column, according to the pronunciation of *-ed*.

ordered	typed	whispered	demanded
groaned	explained	translated	decided
clapped	winked	responded	sighed
watched	danced	suggested	

There are three groups of verbs.

1 verbs ending in a /t/ or /d/ sound in the infinitive
2 verbs ending in a /k/, /f/, /p/, /s/, /x/, /ʃ/ or /tʃ/ sound in the infinitive
3 verbs with any other sound ending in the infinitive

Look at the groups of verbs above. Can you see when *-ed* is pronounced /t/, /d/ and /ɪd/?

c Now listen to see if you were right.

d Listen to these verbs in the infinitive and say the correct past tense.

© SANTILLANA

Grammar File

1 *Say* and *tell*

a Look at these examples.

She told	*me/you/him/etc* *the company* *Mr Bowen*	*(that) her surname was Jumpstone.*

She said (that) her name was Jumpstone.

What do you need to say after the word *told*? Is it the same after the word *said*?
The word *that* is in brackets because we can say it here, but it is not necessary.

b Look at this example.

'I am sixty-five,' Mabel said.
She said that she was sixty-five.
She said she was sixty-five.
She told him that she was sixty-five.
She told him she was sixty-five.

All four sentences are possible.
Write these two sentences in four possible ways.

1 'I am from Cricket Creek,' Mabel said.
2 'I am very good at typing,' Mabel said.

2 Indirect speech

a When we change from direct to indirect speech, we often need to change the verb tense. Look at these examples.

'My name is Kim,' she said.
'I come from Britain,' he said.

She *He*	*said* *told us*	*(that)*	*her name was Kim.* *he came from Britain.*

Change these sentences from direct to indirect speech. Remember to change *I* to *she* or *he*, *you* to *me/us* and *my* to *his* or *her* etc.

1 'I have got one daughter,' she said.
2 'I have never been to America,' he said.
3 'We are going to Italy for our holidays next year,' they said.
4 'I can type well, but I can't speak French,' she said.
5 'I work for an insurance company,' he said, 'And I've worked there for over ten years.'
6 'My mother is coming tomorrow, so I can't meet you,' she said.
7 'I speak French and Italian and I'm learning German,' he said.
8 'They're arriving this morning,' she said, 'And they hope to meet you tomorrow.'

b Look at this example.

'I'm coming tomorrow,' he said.
He said that he was coming the next day.

Look how the time phrases change from direct to indirect speech.

Direct speech		→	Indirect speech		
today		→	that day		
this	morning afternoon	→	that	morning afternoon	
tomorrow		→	the	next following	day
next	week month year	→	the	next following	week month year

Look back at the exercise in part A. Check that you have changed the time phrases correctly.

3 Present perfect continuous

a Look at these examples.

How long have you been working as a designer?
– For about nine months.

I've been learning French since last year.

The present perfect continuous is used to stress that something has continued, without a break, from a time in the past until now. It is often used with verbs of habit, such as *live*, *work*, *learn*, *study*, *save* (money) and *play* (a sport or a musical instrument).

It is also used with these verbs, *wait for*, *say*, *tell*, *try* and *ask for*, to express impatience with something that has been going on for a long time.

EXAMPLE:
I've been saying that for years, but nobody ever listens to me.

b Think of examples from your own life of things you have been doing over a period of time. Write down five examples, then ask your partner.

EXAMPLE:
Where do you live?
How long have you been living there?

© SANTILLANA

7 Jobs with a difference

a **Match the photographs with the job categories.**

construction work   tourism   teaching   conservation   farmwork

A

B

C

D

E

b **In groups, find out:**

1 how many people have worked abroad.
2 which is the most popular job from the jobs shown here.
3 if anyone in the group would like to work abroad.
4 where they would like to work.

Ask questions, like this:

Have you ever ...?
Would you like to do one of these jobs?
Would you like to ...?
Where would you ...?

© SANTILLANA

8 Jobshop

1

Claude Sirejol Le Castagné, 46170 St Paul de Loubressac, Montrutier, France 65 21 90 81 (recorded message)
A small number of volunteers interested in agriculture, organic farming, and tourism are needed to help with general farmwork throughout the year. Tasks include looking after livestock, crops and vegetables, and training in bread and yoghurt making. No experience necessary. Applicants under 18 must have parental consent. Full board and lodging in farmhouse or campsite and a small payment at the end of the work provided. Volunteers pay own travel and insurance costs.

2

Kids Klub, The Hall, Great Finborough, near Stowmarket, Suffolk IP14 3EF, UK
✆ Stowmarket (0449) 675907
Provides activity holidays for 6–15 year olds at a country house. Staff are needed to organise and play with the children, creating a happy family atmosphere and holiday of a lifetime. Activities are many and varied. Staff are chosen for their enthusiasm and love of children. Knowledge of European languages an asset but not essential. 48 hour week during Easter, and beginning July – end August. Ages 18+. Wages negotiable; full board accommodation provided. Participants pay own travel and insurance costs.

3

Santa Cruz Seaside Co. Employment Office, 400 Beach Road, Santa Cruz, California 95060 ✆ Santa Cruz (408) 427 1777
Santa Cruz Beach Boardwalk opened in 1907 and is classed as a State Historic Landmark. It is California's only seaside amusement park and features a variety of arcades, rides and food stops. Paid summer positions available in ride operations, food service, merchandise, arcades and ticket sales. Training given for all positions. Ages 18+. Applicants must speak English and be cheerful, co-operative, enjoy working with people in a tourist environment, and preferably have experience of customer service. May-September. 35 hour, 5– 6 day week, Limited amount of dormitory accommodation available, cost approx. $50– $60 per week. Staff must pay own travel costs and organise own visa/work permit through an approved scheme operator. *Application forms available at beginning of year, to be returned by 1 April.*

4

GENESIS II – TALAMANCA CLOUD FOREST
Apdo 655, 7.050 Cartago, Costa Rica
Volunteers are needed to help with new trail routing, construction, maintenance and upgrade work on existing trails, in a rare tropical white oak cloud forest in the mountains of Costa Rica. The forest is situated at a height of 2360m and is being preserved for academic research and recreational activities such as bird-watching.
Ages 21+. Experience preferred, but not essential as training can be given. All nationalities welcome; some knowledge of Spanish helpful. 30 hour week, for 4+ weeks, all year. Volunteers contribute US$100 per week to cover dormitory style accommodation, all meals and laundry facilities, but make own travel and insurance arrangements. *Only fully fit and dedicated people need apply; competition for places is strong.*

5

Bangladesh Work Camps Association (BWCA) 289/2 Work Camps Road, North Shahjahanpur, Dhaka 17, Bangladesh
Promotes international development and peace through voluntary activities, and organises workcamps in urban and rural areas of Bangladesh. Projects include afforestation, construction work, digging water tanks, health education and community work. Working language is English. Ages 16 – 45. 30 hour week, 1 – 6 weeks, October – April. Volunteers pay own insurance and travel. Participation fee US$30 per day. Apply at least 3 months in advance enclosing US$25 application fee.

a Read the texts quickly and match each job description with one of the photographs on page 55.

b In pairs, ask and answer the questions.

1 Which jobs can you do if you are under 18?
2 In which jobs do you pay for your own accommodation?
3 In which jobs do you receive any pay?
4 Which job has the best pay and conditions?
5 Which job has the worst pay and conditions?
6 For which jobs do you need to speak particular languages?

Write three more questions like these and ask your partner to answer.

c Choose one of the jobs. Write a short letter applying for this job. Follow this format:

1 Write your address, today's date and *Dear Sir/Madam,*.
2 Say where you saw the advertisement.
3 Give a few details about yourself, your education, qualifications, interests, etc.
4 Say why the job interests you.
5 Say: *I am available for interview any time in May/June/July … or from the end of May/June … to the beginning/middle of … .*
6 End the letter with this sentence: *I look forward to hearing from you.*
7 Write: *Yours faithfully,* and then sign your name.

© SANTILLANA

9 Right for the job?

a Kim Sharp applied for one of the jobs on page 56. This is her interview form, with parts A and B completed. She was offered one of the jobs. Read the form and say which job you think it was.

	Kim Sharp	your partner
A *Has the candidate had any experience of:*		
living away from home	☑ ✓	☐
working abroad	☑ ✓	☐
working with children	☑ ✓	☐
dealing with the public	☒	☐
farmwork	☒	☐
office work	☒	☐
catering	☒	☐
heavy manual work	☒	☐
B *Does the candidate:*		
play any sports	☑ ✓ tennis swimming + scuba	☐
play a musical instrument	☒	☐
speak any foreign languages	☑ ✓	☐
have a driving licence	☒	☐
have any medical problems	☒	☐
have any physical disabilities	☑ ✓ deaf in one ear	☐
C *Do you think the candidate is:*		
hard-working	☐	☐
quick-thinking	☐	☐
out-going	☐	☐
easy-going	☐	☐
broad-minded	☐	☐
self-confident	☐	☐
even-tempered	☐	☐

b In her interview, Kim had to talk about herself for two minutes. These are the notes one of the interviewers made as Kim talked. Work out what Kim said by looking at the notes.

Kim S
19
Aus
→ school last yr
→ Eng → a nanny – 3mths
→ Aus → teacher

children, swim, tennis, scuba
langs? Italian Greek
Eng ✓ new friends
→ 1yr Eng → Aus
friends + family

Now listen to Kim talking about herself and see if you guessed correctly.

c Look at the notes and say what Kim said about herself.

EXAMPLE:
She told us she was nineteen. She said she came from Australia.

d Read part C of the form. Can you work out what some of these words mean? You can use a dictionary to help you.

Listen to Kim again and tick (✓) any words in part C which you think describe Kim.

e Work in pairs and ask a partner the questions on the form. Remember to change the questions.

EXAMPLE:
Have you had any experience of …?
Do you …?
Are you …?

Are you/Is your partner suitable for any of the jobs?

© SANTILLANA

10 What else can I say? *Conversation fillers*

a When Kim wasn't sure what to say next, she said:
'Er …'
'Let me see …'
'Let's think …'
'Well …'
'What else can I say?'

Listen to the tape again and repeat the phrases after Kim.

b Work in groups.
Speak for one minute about yourself. If you are not sure what to say, use one of the phrases in part A so that you speak for one minute without stopping.

Other people in the group take notes. When one person has spoken for one minute, others in the group look at their notes and report what the person said.

EXAMPLE:
S/he told us that she … *S/he said she …*

11 Just the job! *Colloquial sayings*

a Match the sayings in italics in column A with the meanings in column B.

A	B
It's a good job I took my credit card because we spent all our money.	work too hard for not enough money
I can't get a job there, *it's jobs for the boys* in that place.	thank goodness
I'm overworked and underpaid.	exactly what we need
They *are workshy.*	depends if you know someone in the company
That's *just the job.*	don't like work

b Which of the expressions in part A best describes the cartoon?

Learning Tips

Natural speech

1
Go into a room by yourself. Practise reading the story in exercise 3 aloud. When you read, try to say the spoken sentences in a dramatic way. For example, sound surprised, amused, angry, pleased, etc and whisper, shout, mutter, etc where necessary.

You can also record yourself when you read aloud. Then listen to see if you really sound surprised, angry, etc.

Try this with other reading texts you find in English.

2
When you learn new vocabulary, write down definitions and a sentence using the new vocabulary. This can help you to remember the new vocabulary better than just writing the translation in your own language.

Pronunciation File

Stress and the schwa

a Read these sentences aloud and mark the stressed syllables. Then read them again and underline the schwa sounds.

She said she was from Australia.

He told us that he had never been to Italy before.

They said they wanted to interview the candidates after June 1st.

She said she couldn't speak Spanish very well, but she was much better at Italian.

He said that he didn't want to tell us the answer to question seven.

She told me she was going to Canada the following year.

b Now listen to see if you were correct.

© SANTILLANA

Vocabulary File

1 Speaking verbs

Look back at exercises 1, 2 and the reading text in exercise 3. Find as many different words as you can for ways of speaking. Write down the words and give a definition and an example for each word.

EXAMPLE:

Groan: How people speak when they realise they have made a mistake.
'Oh no! I've got all the answers wrong again,' she groaned.

2 Compound words

Look at these words.

easy-going out-going broad-minded quick-thinking even-tempered self-confident hard-working

Words like this are very common in English. They are called compound words and are made by joining two words together to make a new word. Make more words like this by joining a word in column A to one in column B.

A	B
well	tempered
narrow	centred
quick	educated
self	minded

In pairs, explain what the new words mean. Check with a dictionary if necessary.

3 Job vocabulary

a You have seen or heard this job vocabulary in this unit.

application form apply for (a job) employee company pay conditions insurance candidates interview experience education training available staff

Complete the sentences with an appropriate word. Only use eight from the list.

1 I am ______ for interview any time in July and August.
2 I had ______ of looking after children when I worked in Milan as an au pair.
3 If you are interested in this job please send for an ______ from this address.
4 We are going to interview all ______ in May.
5 Experience is not essential because we offer three weeks ______ to all applicants.
6 Send us details of your ______: schools attended, examinations passed and so on.
7 All employees in this ______ get very good pay and conditions.
8 I have seen an interesting job in Mexico. I'm going to ______ it next week.

b Write your own sentences for the other six words in the list above.

12 A job interview *Language round-up*

PROBLEMS *Unlimited*
86 Alexandra Road, Windsor, Berkshire SL4 1HU & Windsor (0753) 830101
Can place au pairs mainly in the southeast of England; also Scotland and Wales. Ages 18–27. Basic conversational English and some experience in housework and childcare essential. Weekly pocket money £35.

CAMP AMERICA
Dept. Antric, 37A Queens Gate, London SW7 5HR
An Exchange Visitor Programme enabling young people to spend the summer in the US. Openings at the summer camps in the US on the Campower programme, working with automatic washing and drying machines in the laundry; helping with food preparation, serving, dish and pot washing in the kitchen; dining room service; indoor and outdoor work, grass cutting, painting, moving and clearing rubbish, cleaning and general repair work; driving camp vehicles; and secretarial work. Experienced cooks and bakers also required.
10+ hour day. Students aged 18+.
Pocket money $300.
The programmes include return flight from London, plus full board and lodging. Applicants must be willing to work hard, be fit, with a doctor's certificate of good health, and speak good English.
Apply September – May

Work in pairs.
Prepare questions to ask a candidate who is applying for one of these jobs. Write the questions down in a list, like the ones on page 57. Remember to leave a space beside the questions to record the candidate's answers.

Work with another pair.
Pair A are the interviewers. Pair B are the candidates. Interview each other for one of the jobs. Decide if each candidate is suitable for the job.

EXAMPLE:

I think/don't think ... is suitable for the job because s/he said (that) ...
told us (that) ...

© SANTILLANA

Facts and figures

1 Magic numbers?

a Look at the pictures. Read the mathematical calculations.

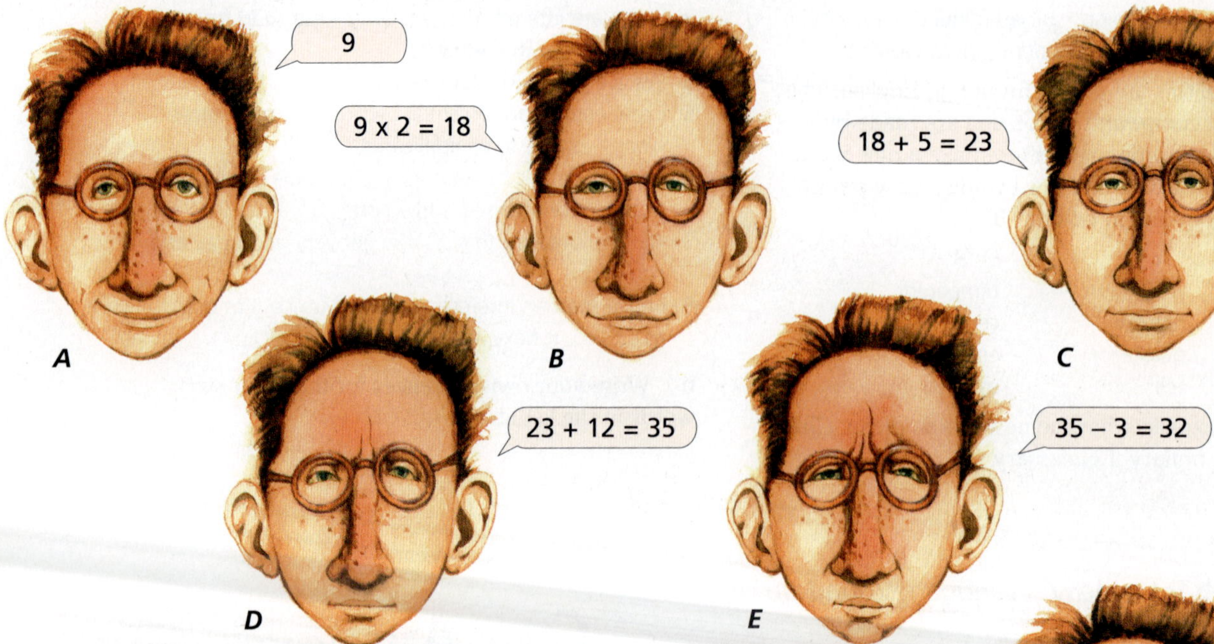

b Listen to two people doing the mathematical puzzle. What do these phrases mean?

Double it.
Subtract 3.
Take away the number you first thought of.

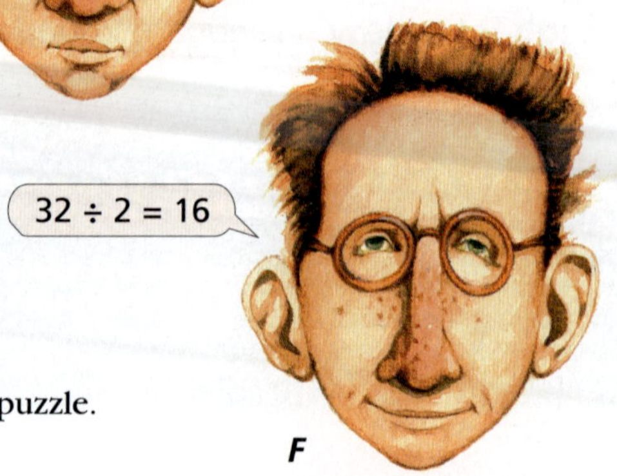

c Listen again and write down the instructions for the puzzle.

EXAMPLE:
Think of … . Double it. Add 5.

Now do the puzzle in pairs. Partner A gives the instructions, partner B does the calculations.
Partner A gives the final answer like this:
The answer will be …

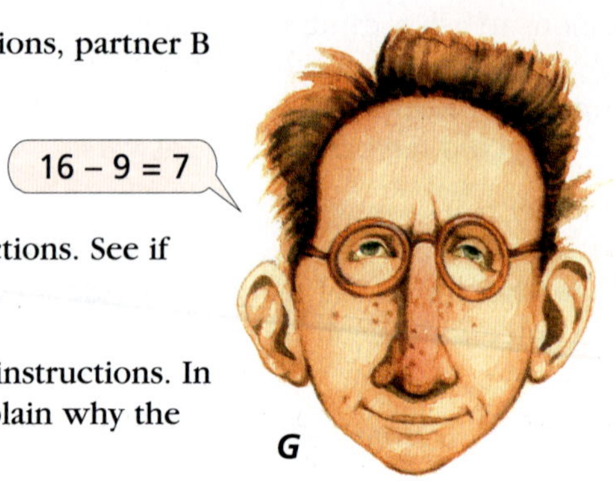

d Listen to another puzzle and follow the instructions. See if your final answer is the same as the answer on the tape.

e Listen again and memorise or write down the instructions. In pairs, give the instructions to your partner. Can you explain why the answer is always the same number?

© SANTILLANA

2 Number puzzles *Giving instructions*

a Read and solve this puzzle.

Tony and Anna are friends. They each have a bag of sweets. Tony says to Anna, 'If you give me one of your sweets, we'll both have the same number.' Anna replies, 'Well, if you give me one of your sweets, I'll have twice as many as you.'

How many sweets do they each have in their bags?
If you can't work it out your teacher will give you the answer.

b In groups, discuss any puzzles you know. (They can be word puzzles, number puzzles, shape puzzles, etc.) Prepare the instructions for the puzzle. Give the instructions to another group and see if they can work out the answer.

3 Looking at statistics *Making comparisons*

a Look at the graph of the world's top ten oil consumers, then look at the phrases below. Which phrases can be used to compare which countries?

1 … about ten times as much as …
2 … nearly as much as …
3 … slightly more than …
4 … slightly less than …
5 … about as much as …
6 … much more than …

b Listen to this interview about oil consumers and complete the phrases above.

c Look at the pictographs of wine and beer producers. In groups, write four true statements, and four false statements about the different countries. Mark each statement True or False.

EXAMPLE:

Argentina produces much less wine than Italy. T
Japan produces about twice as much beer as Germany. F

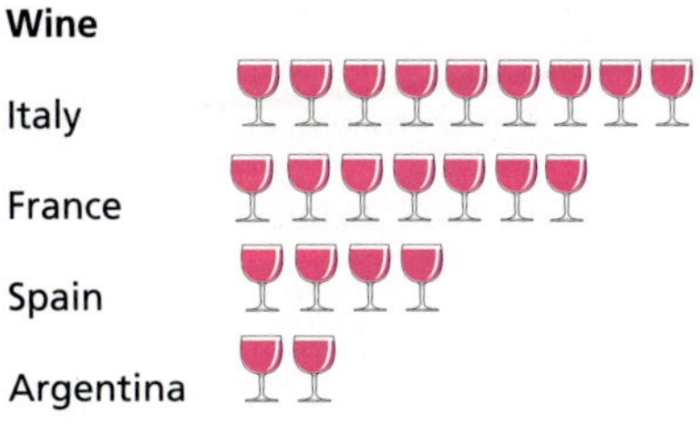

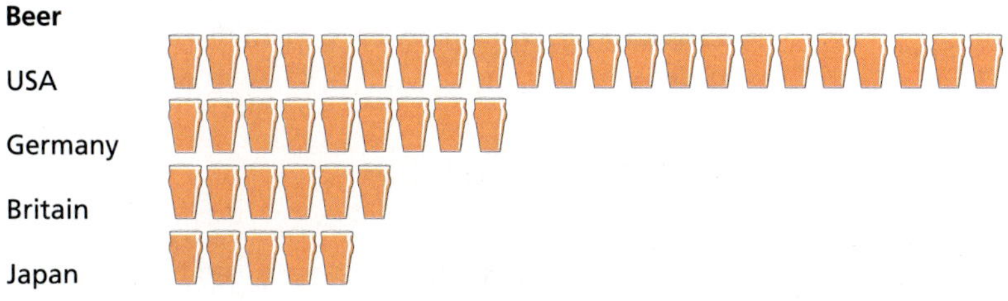

d Try to remember as much information as you can about the pictographs. Close your books. Each group reads out a statement. Other groups say if it is true or false.

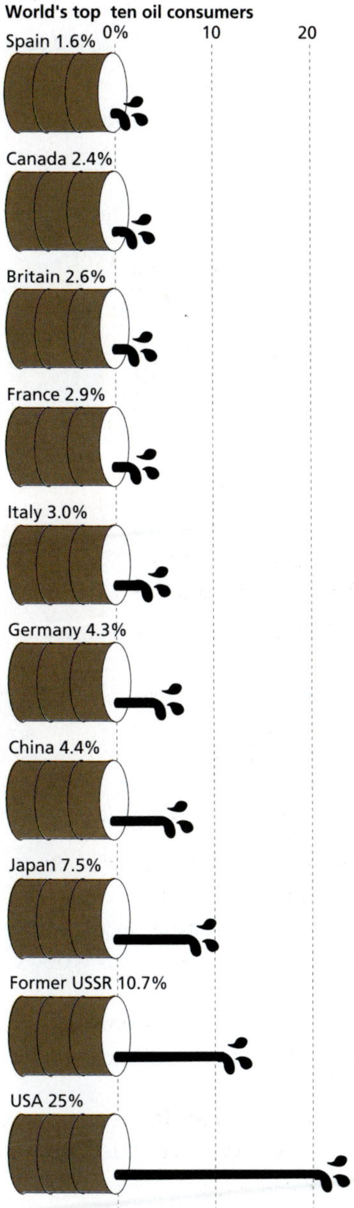

© SANTILLANA

4 Reading the signs *Describing consequences*

a Look at the pictures. What do you think the symbols are telling us?

Join the phrases below to make sentences about each symbol.

If you	give the plant a little water	(or) it will go yellow and die.
Don't	put the plant in direct sunlight	it will grow well.
If you	give the plant too much water	(or) it will go brown and die.
Don't	give the plant a little shade	it won't die.

EXAMPLE:
If you put the plant in direct sunlight, it will go brown and die.

b Match these symbols to the prompts below. Then write five sentences saying what each symbol is telling us.

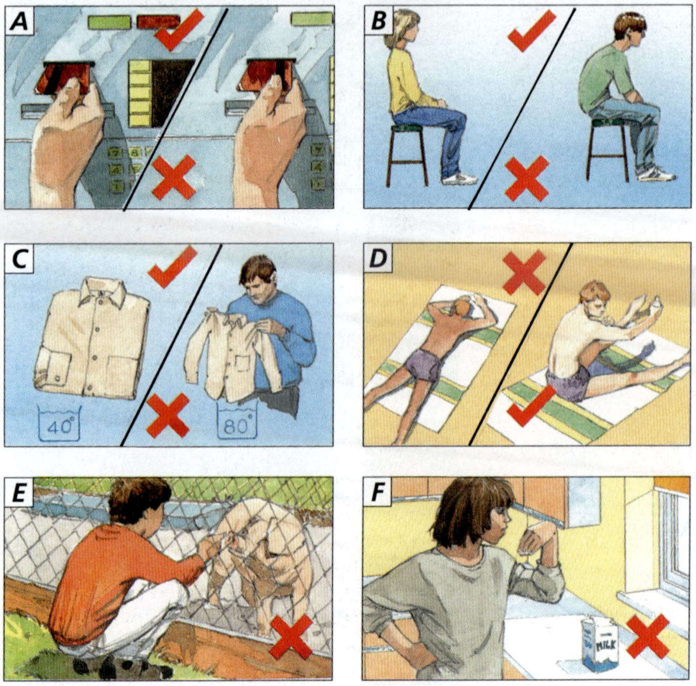

1 shirt in cool water/not shrink
2 card in this way/(not) work
3 finger in the cage/bite it
4 this cream/not get sunburnt
5 like this/(not) get backache
6 not in fridge/go off

EXAMPLE:
1-C *If you wash the shirt in cool water, it will not shrink.*

Pronunciation File

/b/ and /v/

a How do you pronounce these two sounds?
/b/ /v/
Say these words.

cover covered cupboard

Does each word sound different?
What sounds are different between:
1 cover and covered?
2 covered and cupboard?
3 cover and cupboard?

Listen and check if you were correct.

b Listen to the pronunciation of these words and repeat them.

give divide five driven deliver vision
club subtract buy ribbon double bishop

c Read these pairs of words aloud. Listen to the words and write them down in the order you hear them.

bet vet vote boat
berry very bat vat
best vest

d Listen to these sentences and then say them aloud several times.

Five bottles of your very best beer, please.
I've been to Boston, but I've never been to Vienna.

© SANTILLANA

5 Getting your facts right

a What special preparations do you make before an exam? Think about:

when to start revising.
the best way to revise.
personal habits/superstitions.

b This article is from a teenage magazine called *Check It Out!* Read the text and pick out any words you do not know. See if you can guess the approximate meaning of the words from the context. Then check the meaning in a dictionary.

• THE EXAM SURVIVAL KIT •

Oh no! It's that time of year again. The sun's out and you are trapped inside, revising. Exams are a pain, there's no question about that. But some Check It Out! readers are here to offer their sympathy and top tips.

Brothers can be useful

I'm going to follow my brother's advice. He says, 'Just do your best. If you don't worry too much you'll do much better.' He obviously followed his own advice because now he's at university. . . . . **Tim**

Why?

Why is passing exams so important? There are lots of people with good exam results who can't get jobs. . . . . **Luke**

How can you make those little facts stick in the brain?

I learned the periodic table in chemistry with little sayings like this:

Zinc(Zn)	Iron(Fe)	Sodium(S)	Carbon(C)
Zips	*for*	*snoring*	*camels*

I even drew little pictures as well.

. . . . **Vickie**

If you record the facts onto a tape and listen to the tape before you go to sleep you'll probably remember everything the next morning.. . . . . **Sally**

The best way to remember key words for a test, like French or Geography, is to make the words into a song. . . . . **Laura**

If there are some important facts to remember, write them on Post-it notes and stick them round the house. If you do this you'll see them every day. . . . . . . **Claire**

Too late

Don't leave revision until the last minute in case you run out of time. . . . . . **Gemma**

TOP REVISION TIPS

1 Find a quiet place. If you can work in a quiet room with no distraction, like the TV, you'll concentrate better.. . . . **Clare**

2 Don't worry too much in case you make yourself nervous. . . . . **Laurie**

3 Don't revise different subjects on the same day in case you get muddled. **Rachel**

4 Don't revise everything. Make your own notes and then revise them. Only revise key facts or you'll waste hours and hours. . . . . **Matthew**

5 Set yourself a time when you'll stop revising, say, 10 o'clock, or your brain will be too tired to take anything in. . . . . **Laural**

6 Revise for fifteen minutes. Then stop and recap for five minutes. Revise for fifteen more minutes, and so on. If you do this you'll find you remember things much better. . . . . **Sean**

You'll panic and you won't concentrate properly if you leave everything to the last minute. That's the worst thing you can do. You'll try to cram everything into your brain and you'll probably forget half of it. . . . . **Claire**

Relax

'Exams stop a lot of people giving their best. If you freeze when you walk into an exam you'll know what I mean,' says psychologist Bill Farrell. His job includes helping university students beat exam stress. 'And remember, if you fail it won't be the end of the world. It isn't worth making yourself ill. There are simple ways to relax, like controlling your breathing.'

Parents

Parents shouldn't expect too much of their kids in case it makes them feel under pressure. . . . . **Sean**

My Dad's great. He always says, 'If you do well, I'll buy you something special.' That helps me to try even harder.. **Anna**

Wise words

You have to work hard before the exam if you want to get good marks. Sad but true. . . . . **Shalini**

Cheat

If you cheat you won't learn anything. . . . . **Tom**

I'm not going to cheat again. In a German test I looked at my friend's paper and changed my answer. But my first answer was correct and my friend got it wrong. . . . . **Peter**

c In pairs, discuss the points you agree/disagree with. Write down the points in two columns.

agree	disagree

Report back to the class and see which points everyone agrees/disagrees with.

d Think about what you should do the night before and on the day of the exam itself. Write down three pieces of advice with a reason.

EXAMPLE:
Go to bed early the night before an exam or you will be tired the next day.
Take a rubber, in case you make some mistakes.

© SANTILLANA

Grammar File

1 *Will*

a Look at these three examples.

Don't worry, I'll help you.
When the water reaches 0°c, it will freeze and turn to ice.
I'm afraid you won't pass the exam with this standard of work.

Which of these sentences is:

1 a general truth because it is what usually or always happens?
2 a promise?
3 a warning?

Notice you can write *'ll* instead of *will* and *won't* instead of *will not* in informal language.

b Use *will* or *won't* with the vebs in brackets. If you think the sentence is informal, write *'ll/won't* instead of *will/will not.* If you think it is more formal write *will.* After each sentence write 1, 2 or 3 to match the descriptions in part A.

1 In two months time, he ______ (be) eighteen and then he ______ (be) an adult.
2 I'm sure he ______ (pass) his exams because he has done no work at all.
3 The water ______ (change) to ice because the temperature is higher than 0°C.
4 My boss says I ______ (get) a pay rise next month.
5 Don't eat any more chocolate, or you ______ (eat) your dinner.
6 The sun sets at about half past eight, so it ______ (be) dark at seven o'clock.
7 All these fish ______ (die) because they've been poisoned by polluted water.
8 You don't need to leave yet, I ______ drive you home.

2 Conditional sentences with *if*

a Look at these examples of sentences in the first conditional.

If you sit up straight, you won't get backache.
This plant will die if you give it too much water.

Which verb tense is used in the *if* clause of each sentence?

b Write sentences in the first conditional from these prompts.

EXAMPLE:
I buy you something special – you do well in the exams
I'll buy you something special if you do well in the exams.

1 you touch that heater – burn yourself
2 you get the tickets – I pay for the meal afterwards
3 this watch waterproof, so it (not) break – put it in water
4 we leave now – (not) miss the train
5 always get the answer 0 – you multiply any number by 0
6 you stop smoking – I buy you a new CD player, but you carry a smoking – (not) buy you anything

3 Warnings

Look at these examples.

If you sit like this, you'll get backache
Don't sit like this or you'll get | backache.
in case you get |

Which verb tense is used after *in case*?

Find examples of warnings in exercise 4. Choose three warnings and write three sentences for each, as in the examples above.

© SANTILLANA

6 Numerology

a Look quickly at the text. Can you guess what Numerology is?

b Listen to the Numerology Hotline and calculate your personal numbers.

What do your numbers say about you? Read your forecast.

c Look at these sayings from the Numerology forecast. Match them with the correct illustration.

1 make your point (paragraph 2)
2 people in the know (paragraph 3)
3 keep your head down (paragraph 4)
4 life (will not be) a bed of roses (paragraph 5)
5 caught with their hand in the cookie jar (paragraph 7)
6 on the right lines (paragraph 8)
7 round the corner (paragraph 9)

NUMEROSCOPE

1 You are thinking about the possiblity of a change either at work or at home. You will find it difficult to make the changes you want, but not impossible. So don't delay. You know what you want. Why waste any more time?

2 *You will have an important conversation with your family this week and it won't be very pleasant. Be careful. Make your point clearly and don't criticise too much, or there will be a big misunderstanding.*

3 A lot of good things will happen to you this month, but please, don't be too impatient. Follow the advice of people in the know and you'll soon find yourself in a stronger position.

4 *You will probably find yourself involved in someone else's dramas this week. You will be unwilling to join in, so keep your head down and do not be indiscreet or you will find you are also part of the drama.*

5 Friends and neighbours have been very inactive over the past few weeks. And you feel you have been a workhorse in comparison to them. Soon your work will be appreciated, but not as much as you would like. I'm afraid your life will not be a bed of roses this month.

6 *Someone you respect will be very charming to you this week. This person will tell you that you are 'extremely interesting'. This will bring you good luck in either business or love. Things are looking very rosy for you at the moment.*

7 A person you like will disappoint you soon. I'm afraid they will be caught with their hand in the cookie jar. The question will be whether or not you believe that they are sorry for their dishonesty. Listen carefully to what they tell you and then make up your mind.

8 *At times in the past year you have wondered whether you were really in the right place, with the right person and on the right lines. Throughout this month you will see that you have not made as many mistakes as you think.*

9 Throughout your life you have always had extreme high points and terrible low points. This month will be no different. But if you are strong now success is waiting round the corner and soon things will look much better.

A

B

C

D

E

F
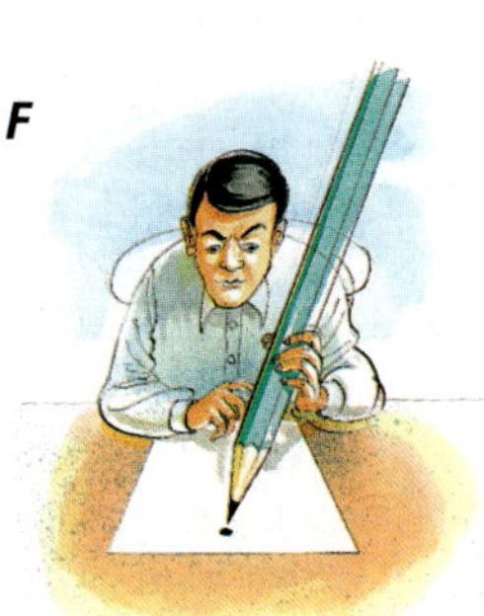

G

With the help of the pictures, read the complete Numerology forecast and interpret the meaning of each saying in part C.

d Do you think your forecast will come true?

© SANTILLANA

7 Millions, trillions and more

a Do you have any idea how long a million seconds is? Is it:

1½ years? 11½ days? 46 hours?

Guess the answer. You will probably be surprised.

b This text is from *The Guardian* newspaper. The paragraphs are not in the correct order. Read the paragraphs A - F and put them into the correct order. This summary of how the text is constructed will help you.

paragraph 1 introduces the topic of big numbers
paragraph 2 gives a definition of big numbers
paragraph 3 gives some examples of big numbers
paragraph 4 introduces the contrast between big numbers and small numbers
paragraph 5 gives an example of multiplying a small number
paragraph 6 sets a problem to test our understanding of big and small numbers

c When you have put the paragraphs in order check the order matches the contruction of the text in part B. Say why you think the order you have is correct.

EXAMPLE:
Because paragraph 1 introduces big numbers when it says …

A
We agree on the definitions, now try to imagine what these numbers describe. Think about a billion in connection with time. If we tried to count a billion seconds, it would take about 33 years. Only one billion minutes and about 3 billion seconds have passed since the birth of Christ. And think about the Government's borrowing again. If, for example, we want to pay off £100 billion of Government debt, and we pay £1 per second, 24 hours a day, 7 days a week, 52 weeks of the year, it will take 3,169 years to pay off the whole debt.

B
Now try another example of multiplying by 2 several times. Imagine that you have a huge sheet of extremely fine paper and you tear the sheet in half, then put the two pieces together and tear them in half again. If you carry on like this, tearing and stacking the paper fifty times, how high will the final stack of paper be? As tall as you? As tall as a house? Will it be a mile high? What do you think? In fact, it will be much more than that. The final stack will be more than 17 million miles high. Now is that high or not?

C
So do we agree? A billion is an amazingly large number. But if you agree that a billion is large, now look at a small number, 2. Think about the extremely large numbers that can be created by multiplying 2 by itself a few times.

D
On a piece of paper draw an upside-down family tree. Put a single person at the bottom of the page and then above him or her put two parents. Above that put the parents' parents and carry on like this for three or four generations. It is obvious that everyone has (or had) two parents, four grandparents, eight great grand-parents and so on. If we assume that a generation is about 30 years and we go back 20 generations, or 600 hundred years, can you guess how many ancestors that will be? The answer is more than one million, 1,048,576 to be precise.

E
We read about big numbers every day. Stories appear in the newspapers about singers and business people being paid millions of pounds. And we read about the Government borrowing tens of billions of pounds each year to pay the difference between the amount which it spends and the amount which it receives in taxation.

F
But just how big are these big numbers? Is it possible to imagine what a million of anything looks like, let alone a billion? To begin with we need to establish exactly what we are talking about. A million is one thousand thousand, or 1,000,000, or 10 x 10 x 10 x 10 x 10 x 10 which we can also write as 10^6. A billion is one thousand million or, 10^9 and a trillion is one million million, or 10^{12}.

© SANTILLANA

d Find the words and phrases in the text which mean the same as these words and phrases.

1 money we borrowed which we must now pay back (line 12)
2 very big (line 14)
3 putting one piece on top of another (line 18)
4 the wrong way round (the top is at the bottom and the bottom is at the top) (line 29)
5 surprisingly (line 24)
6 very (line 27)
7 continue (line 32)
8 clear to see (line 33)
9 parents' grandparents (line 35)
10 our grandparents' grandparents' grandparents (line 38)
11 taking money for a period of time which you will pay back later (line 43)
12 the sum of money (line 45)
13 money people pay to the government to pay for schools, roads, etc. (line 46)
14 never mind (line 49)

8 Summarising a text

Read the text again, with the paragraphs in the correct order then cover it. Write a summary of the text in your own words. Use the prompts below to help you.

We often read about big numbers in the newspapers, for example, business people/singers/governments/taxes. Let's be sure we know what these big numbers are. A million is …

It is difficult to imagine such big numbers, but here are two examples. If we/count/a billion seconds/33 years. If we want /£100 billion debt/take 3,169 years.

So, we/at big numbers, now let's/small/.
The number 2/become a very large number.
Try this experiment. On a piece/draw a family tree/ for about 20 generations/600 years/guess/ancestors?/ 1,048,576 exactly.

Here is another example. If you/huge sheet /tear/ carry on stacking/ 50 times. How high? As high as/ a mile high?/17 million miles high.

© SANTILLANA

Vocabulary File

1 Making opposities with prefixes

a Look at forecast number 1 in exercise 6. Which two letters do you add in front of the word *possible* to make the opposite meaning? This is a prefix.

Look through the numerology forecasts to find the prefixes which make the opposite of:

patient active willing discreet honesty

b Write these words in the correct word spider, depending on how the opposite is formed. Check with your dictionary if you are not sure. The first one has been done for you.

happy successful pleasant believe polite lucky tolerant important dependent

Add as many other words as you can to the word spiders.

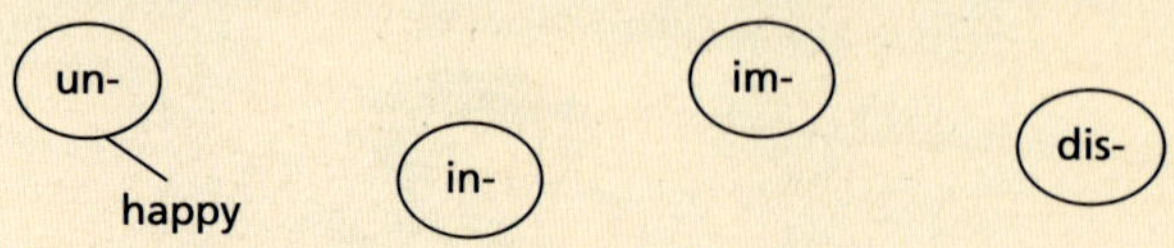

2 Useful phrases

a Find these phrases in the reading text in exercise 6.

either at work *or* at home
waste any more *time*?
follow the advice of
in comparison to them
but *not as much* as you would like
will *bring you* (good) *luck*
whether or not you believe
make up your *mind*
as many mistakes *as* you think
will be *no different*

b Look at the words in italics in each phrase. Write your own sentences for each of the phrases.

EXAMPLE:

I am going to Venezuela either this year or next.

I don't want to waste my time in the weeks before the exams.

3 More time phrases

Look at the reading text in exercise 6 and write down as many of the time phrases as you can find.

EXAMPLE: *this week, this month, in the past few weeks*

Write five sentences using the time phrases that you have found.

4 Exam vocabulary

a Look back at the reading text in exericse 5. Write down as many words as you can which are connected to exams.

EXAMPLE: *revise, pass, results*

b Write four sentences using the exam words that you have found.

EXAMPLE:

I'm revising for my exams now so that I will pass all of them and get better results than last year.

© SANTILLANA

Learning Tips

Techniques for remembering and revising

1
You can use pictures to help you understand the meaning of an expression or remember a word or phrase.

If you want to remember a word, phrase, a piece of information or even an item of grammar, try drawing a simple picture to help you remember.

2
At the end of each unit, look carefully through all the reading texts and pick out as many useful words and phrases as you can. Build your own word spiders and word lists. Write your own sentences using the words and phrases. Do this even when it is not a set exercise in the book.

3
Revise grammar and vocabulary regularly. Do not only revise just before an exam. If you learn things very quickly you will also forget them very quickly. Try to remember a little each day. Fifteen minutes revision each day is much better than three days revision every six months.

Pronunciation File

Rising and falling intonation

a Listen to these pairs of questions.
In which questions does the voice go 1 up or 2 down at the end?

1 Where do you live?
2 Is he coming tomorrow?
3 When is he coming?
4 Do you live near here?
5 Have you ever been to China?
6 Where have you been in Asia?

b Yes/No questions are questions which need the answer 'Yes' or 'No'. Which three questions above are Yes/No questions?

Listen to these Yes/No questions and mark where the voice goes up.

Did he use to be different?

Should we write him a letter?

Do you want a cheese sandwich?

Will the shirt shrink if I wash it in hot water?

Is he going to Canada for his next holiday?

If I give it too much water, will it die?

c Listen again to the first three questions and mark the stressed syllables. The stress pattern of each sentence should be the same.

d Now listen to the next three questions and mark the stressed syllables.
Say each sentence aloud, following the intonation marks and the stress marks.

9 Your future *Language round-up*

a Look at this list of negative adjectives. Decide which one describes you.
impatient inactive indiscreet dishonest
unlucky impolite intolerant

b Work in groups.
Tell the group the adjective that describes you. In groups write forecasts for each adjective chosen. Do not mention the adjective itself in the forecast. Say who the forecast is for.

EXAMPLE:
This is a forecast for ... . You will want to know the results of your exams this month, but do not get ... . Stay calm and wait for the month to finish and you will find out what you want to know.

Other groups have to guess what the adjective is and say a sentence like this:
(name of student) ... is sometimes impatient.

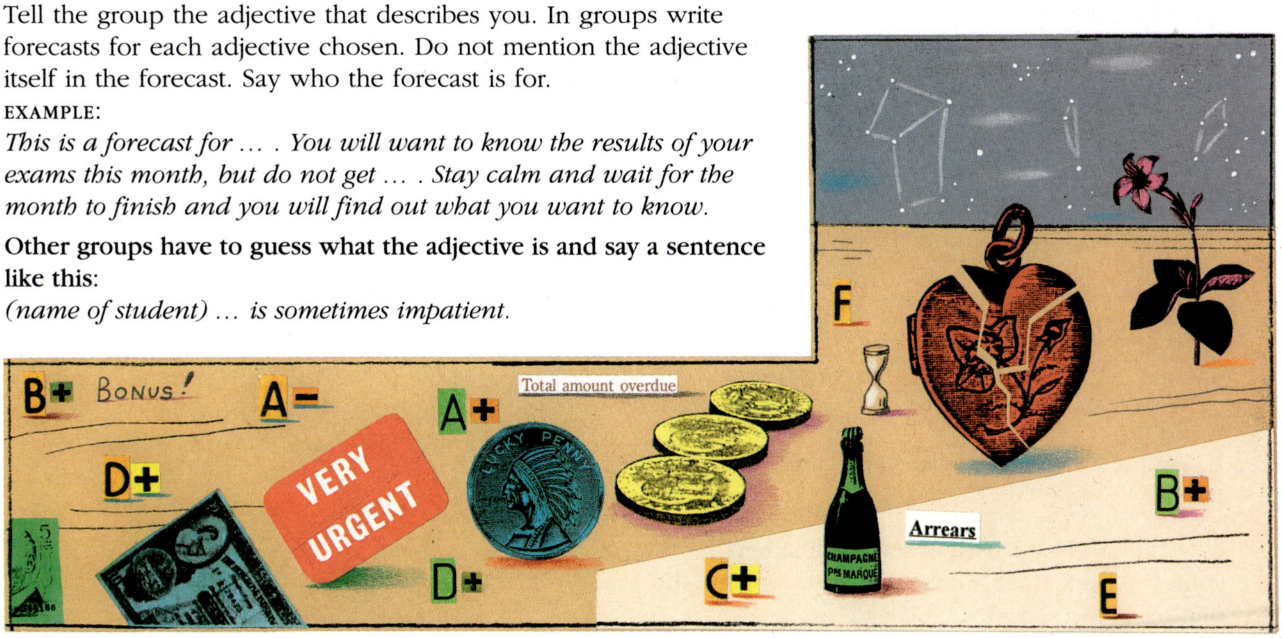

© SANTILLANA

1 From then until now

Peter Hess met his wife, Gabriella, in Switzerland. Peter is Swiss, but his wife is from Argentina. They decided to move to Argentina in 1988. This table shows what has happened to him since then.

1988	■ moved to Buenos Aires, Argentina ■ Gabriella got a job as a journalist
1989	■ bought a flat in Buenos Aires ■ Peter got a job in a Swiss bank
1990	■ had a son called Nicholas ■ Gabriella started to work freelance from home ■ Peter started to learn English
1991	■ had a daughter called Emilia ■ Peter got a job in an American bank
1992	■ Peter became International Manager at the American bank ■ went back to Switzerland for a holiday
1993	■ bought a house in the outskirts of Buenos Aires ■ Gabriella wrote her first book
1994	■ went back to Switzerland for a holiday ■ Gabriella wrote her second book
1995	■ Nicholas started school

a Read the Grammar Reference on page 142 on *How long ...?* and *How many ...?* Ask and answer ten questions about Peter and Gabriella's life.

Study the table and notice which activities continue to the present time. In pairs, ask and answer questions.

EXAMPLE:
How long has Peter been working for the American bank?
How many children have Gabriella and Peter had?

b Write down ten statements about their life.

EXAMPLE:
Peter has lived in Argentina for seven years.
Peter worked at the Swiss bank for two years.

2 Looking at the future

a Read the Grammar Reference on using future tenses with *going to* on page 139 and *will/won't* on page 142. In groups, make predictions about these things:

the next exams you have
the future episodes of a well-known TV soap opera
something which is in the news at the moment
the future careers of people in the group
a big sporting occasion which is taking place soon

b Compare your predictions with other groups in the class. Which predictions do you think are the most accurate?

3 Powerful words – *speaking verbs*

a Look at these definitions.

speak = the physical action
talk = communicate by speech with others
say and tell = report information to others

Look back at unit 5 for the difference between *say* and *tell*.

Put one of the verbs *speak, talk, say* or *tell* in these sentences. Put the verb into the correct form.

1 She _____ she was from Canada.
2 We _____ for hours when we met at the party.
3 I can't _____. I've just been to the dentist.
4 He _____ us that he was leaving at the end of the month.

b Write a sentences using *speak, talk, say* and *tell*.

c The verb *tell* is used in several different contexts. Look at these examples and complete the phrases in the sentences.

to tell:
the truth a lie someone off tales
the difference between ... and ...
whether ... or not ...

1 She said she hadn't met him before, but I'm afraid she was telling _____ because I know she has known him for several years.
2 I can't tell _____ she is interested in the plan or not.
3 The secretary at work is always telling _____ to the boss about who comes in late, who leaves work early, and so on.
4 They told the police they had been at a party that night and I think they are telling _____ because other people at the party say the same thing.
5 I'm afraid I can't tell _____ French and Italian wine.
6 His teacher really told _____ for not taking the exam.

© SANTILLANA

4 Dictionary work

a Make the opposites of these words using prefixes. Use your dictionary to help you.

employed	________	responsible	________
profitable	________	dispensable	________
efficient	________	patient	________
expected	________	reputable	________

b Complete the sentences with an appropriate word from part A.

1 Mary is so _____. She never knows where anything is.
2 Nobody is _____ in this company, even the boss could lose his job.
3 He has such an _____ attitude to her work. I'm not surprised he makes so many mistakes.
4 The news was completely _____. Nobody thought they would ever get married.
5 That company is so _____. They have lost £100,000 in the last six months.

c Make the opposites of these compound adjectives by changing the first part of the word.

EXAMPLE:
well-made
badly-made

1 over-qualified
2 bad-mannered
3 narrow-minded
4 badly-behaved
5 slow-paced

5 Transformation

Rewrite these sentences without changing the meaning. Use the word or phrase in brackets.

1 She said to the police, 'I have never seen him before in my life.' (told)
2 'I'll see you tomorrow,' he said. (next day)
3 She has been working for the same office since 1989. (for)
4 He went to live in Paris in 1992 and he still lives there. (for)
5 There are 65 people who work in this company. (employees)
6 I can be interviewed at any time in July or August. (available)
7 If you give the plant too much water, it will die. (don't)
8 Germany uses double the amount of oil that Sweden does. (twice)
9 Don't wear those shoes. Your feet might get sore. (in case)
10 My boss always seems to have so little tolerance. (intolerant)

6 Project

a What qualities do companies ask for when they advertise a job vacancy? Look through the job section of a local newspaper and decide the five most frequent things that advertisements ask for.

EXAMPLE:
Two years experience ...
Enthusiasm and adaptability ...

b Choose a job that you would like to apply for. Write a checklist of skills, qualifications, experience and personal qualities you think the interviewer will look for in all the candidates. Give your checklist to another student. Ask your partner for advice and suggestions.

c Write a letter of application giving full details about yourself. Include information about your education, qualifications, skills, experience and personal qualities. Explain why you think you would be suitable for the job. Begin the letter by saying where you saw the advertisement and end the letter by saying when you are available for interview.

© SANTILLANA

Communicating in Code

1 Body language

A

C

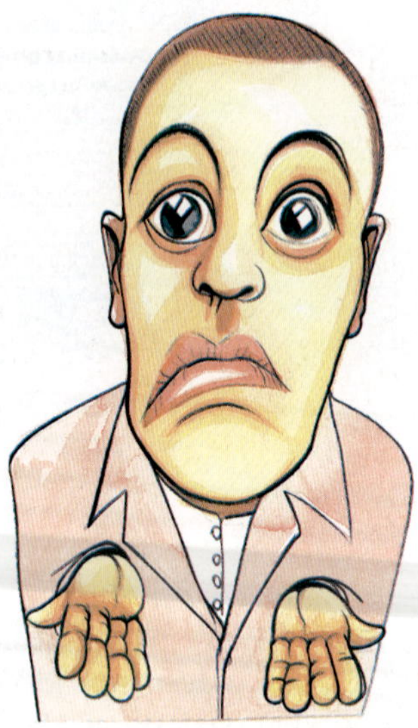

B

D

E

a What do you think the people in the pictures are saying?

b Which gestures do you use when you say these phrases?

Come here!	I'm full.	Hello. How are you?
Excuse me.	He's crazy!	So-so. Not so good.
Absolutely not!	I'm not interested.	That's enough!

Can you think of any other gestures you often use?

© SANTILLANA

A

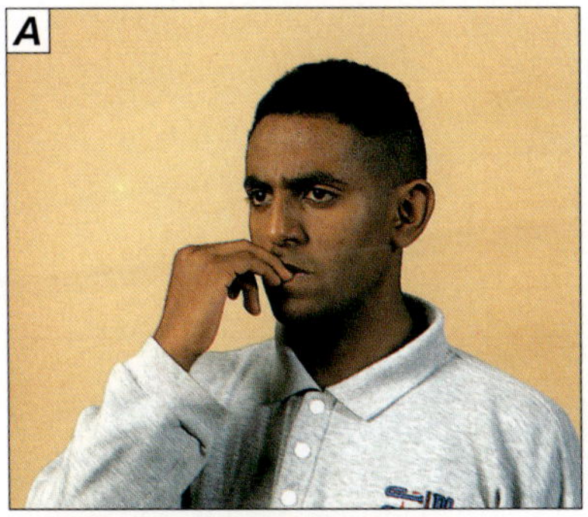

B

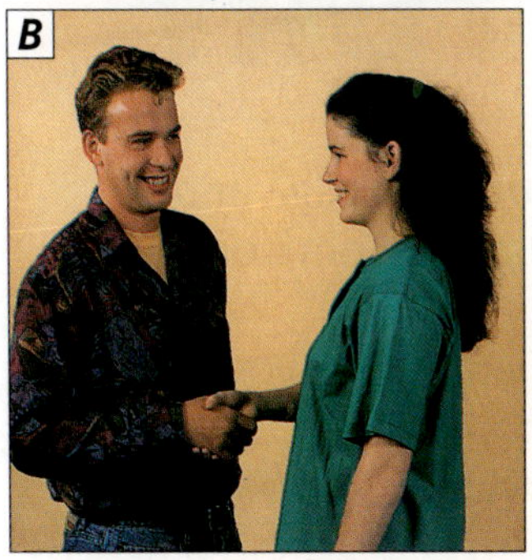

C

D

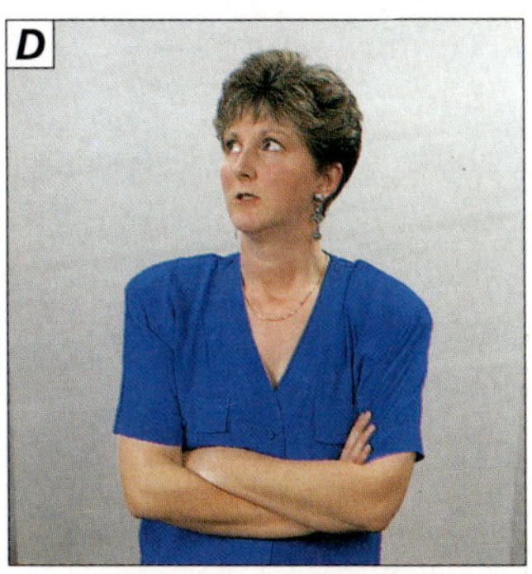

E

2 Meaningful gestures

a Read the descriptions of body gestures in column A and match them with the correct meaning in column B. The first one has been done for you. Try to guess the meaning of verbs you do not know.

EXAMPLE:

Shrugging your shoulders. What do you do with your shoulders when you say, 'I don't know'.

A	B
shrugging your shoulders	'Good luck!'
putting your thumb up	You are embarrassed.
crossing your fingers	'How do you do?/Goodbye.'
biting your nails	'I don't know.'
folding your arms and tapping your foot	'Hi!'
blushing	'Yes.'
nodding your head	'Everything's OK.'
shaking your head	'You are worried.'
waving your hand	'No.'
shaking hands with someone	You are losing your temper.

Match five of the body gestures and phrases with these five pictures. Say what the person in the picture is doing and what s/he is saying or feeling.

b Work in groups.

Write down five or six phrases we often say with special body gestures. Write each phrase on a different piece of paper. Exchange pieces of paper with another group. Members of the group make gestures for each of the phrases, other members of the class guess what the phrase is.

Pronunciation File

/ʌ/ and /æ/

a How do you say these words? cup cap

How do you say this word? understand

Notice the difference between the pronunciation the *u* and the *a* in these words.

Listen and repeat the words.

lunch love us nothing shrug worried blush young ugly

b Say these pairs of words.

cut	cat	sung	sang	tonne	tan
hut	hat	drunk	drank	some	Sam
cup	cap	fun	fan	crush	crash
but	bat	much	match	uncle	ankle

Listen and you will hear one word spoken from each pair. Tick (✓) the word you hear.

c Listen and repeat this sentence.

The cat cut my uncle's ankle.

© SANTILLANA

3 Meaning without words *Writing a summary*

a How important do you think body language is? Do you think you can 'tell a lie' with your body language? Read the article by an expert on body language and see if you agree with the experts.

Leaning to one side. This expresses understanding and support.

Leaning back and tilting the chair back. This shows disinterest and distance from the speaker.

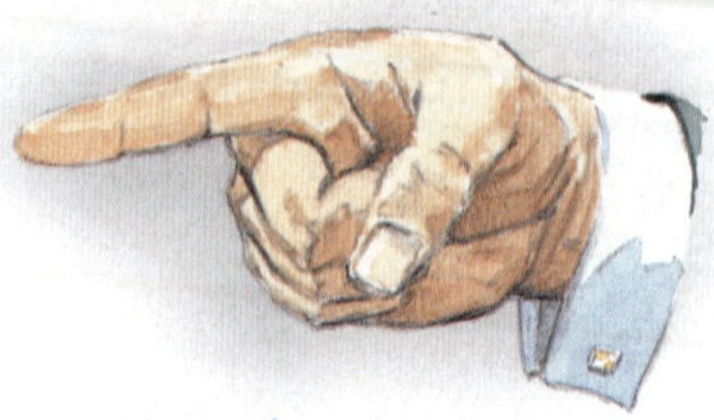

Extending the forefinger. Used when speaking threateningly.

Cupping hands. Used when speaking precisely.

EVERY GESTURE TELLS A STORY

WHEN WE THINK about language and communication we usually think of speaking. But our gestures and movements, in other words our body language, says much more about us than our words. Body language tells us what others are really thinking or feeling, too.

Psychologist, Susan Quilliam, says that words make up only seven per cent of the communicating we do, while 93 per cent comes from silent signals. Children understand it naturally, but as we grow up the emphasis shifts towards words and we lose the knack of picking up these silent signals. Adults become very good at saying things they don't necessarily mean. Body language works together with verbal language, but sometimes the two can be contradictory. For example, people may say they agree with you, at the same time tilting their chair back and leaning away from you. By physically distancing themselves from you, they are actually expressing disagreement.

'Some people are extremely good body language liars,' says Susan Quilliam. For example, politicians learn to use certain gestures to create the right impression. But maybe they are not as successful as they hope. Before believing what you see in a person's face you should move further back to see their whole body. The further you get from their face the more truthful people become. Feet are a really good indicator. Tapping feet show restlessness and a desire to escape.

Some facial gestures, however, we do instinctively. For instance, the pupils in our eyes dilate when we are attracted to someone. So much body language happens unconsciously. If we want to use and understand gestures successfully we need to be aware of them and their different meanings. Watching out for body language in ourselves and others helps us communicate better. If you learn to decipher and use body language well, you will become as fluent with it as you are with verbal language.

© SANTILLANA

b Find words or phrases in the text with a similar meaning to the words and phrases below.

1 also (line 7)
2 moves (line 11)
3 the ability to (line 12)
4 leaning (line 17)
5 people who tell lies (line 20)
6 a feeling of not wanting to stay still (line 27)
7 of the face (line 29)
8 for example (line 30)
9 become larger (line 30)
10 without us knowing it (line 32)
11 be conscious of (line 33)

c Which points in the text do you agree/disagree with?

d Read the text again and answer these questions in your own words. Do not read directly from the text when you give your answers.

1 Why is body language so important?
2 How are adults different to children in their understanding and use of body language?
3 How can our body language contradict our words?
4 Why should we not look at the face alone if we are trying to understand body language?
5 Why is it not possible to control all our gestures?

e Prepare a summary of the text. The questions and answers above will help you. Do not look back at the text until you have written your summary.

A

4 People's habits

a Do you, or does anyone you know, have distinctive habits? For example, pulling your hair or chewing your pen when thinking or pushing your glasses up your nose before speaking.

b Listen to these people talking about their particular habits and match the pictures to the speakers.

c Listen again and write sentences for each picture. Choose from the list of habits below and listen for the verbs and adjectives to complete the sentences.

biting my nails   coughing   twisting my hair

tapping my feet

biting my bottom lip

EXAMPLE:

Speaker 1 *Biting my bottom lip. I do it when I am thinking or concentrating.*

B

E

C

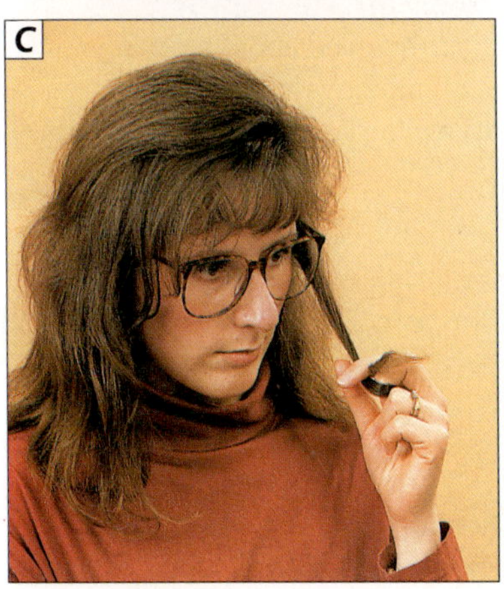

D

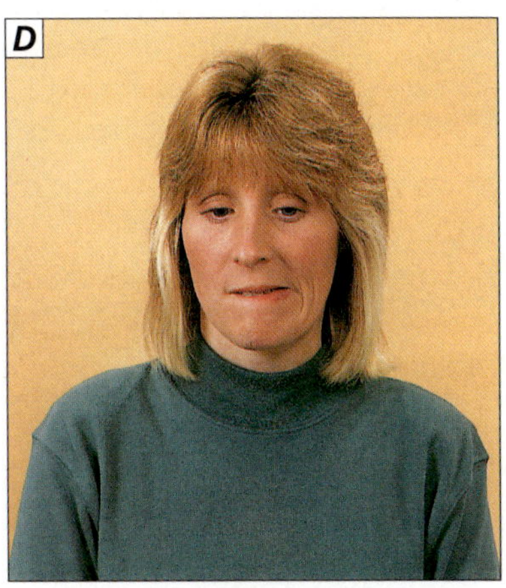

© SANTILLANA

Grammar File

1 *-ing* words

Look at these three examples from the text in exercise 3.

1 Words make up only seven per cent of the communicating we do.
2 Adults become very good at saying things they don't necessarily mean.
3 People may say they agree with you, at the same time tilting their chair back and leaning away from you.

The *-ing* words in sentences 1 and 2 are gerunds (nouns made from verbs).
The *-ing* word in sentence 3 is a participle (a form of a verb).
It is not so important to know the difference, but knowing when we use them is important.

2 Participles

Participles are often used with these adverbs of time: *before*, *after* and *while*.

Look at this example.
Before I leave home in the morning, I usually have a good breakfast. =
Before leaving home in the morning, I usually have a good breakfast.

Change these sentences using the participle instead of the complete verb.

1 After I finish work I like a cup of tea.
2 While I was looking through the dictionary, I found a word I'd never understood before.
3 He saw an unusual bird while he was walking through the forest.
4 While she was getting into the car, she dropped her ring on the floor.
5 She writes her reports out in pencil before she types them up properly.

Can you find any more examples of gerunds and participles in the reading text in exercise 3?

3 Gerunds

a We use gerunds to talk about an activity in general. Change these verbs into gerunds and put them into the correct place in the sentences.

do drink eat play swim smoke

1 ______ is very good exercise.
2 ______ too much chocolate makes you fat.
3 ______ a lot of water is good for you.
4 ______ is bad for you.
5 ______ housework is boring.
6 ______ the clarinet is my favourite pastime.

b We often use gerunds for an activity which follows a preposition. Use these phrases to make your own sentences. Use a gerund after each preposition.

interested in bored with good at bad at keen on tired of fascinated by worried about

EXAMPLE:
I am interested in learning about psychology.

c We use gerunds after certain verbs. Here is a list of common verbs followed by gerunds.

like dislike hate love enjoy mind stop finish suggest imagine avoid look forward to miss regret consider can't stand practise

EXAMPLE:
I love / *I can't stand* | *camping / skiing / acting / dancing*

Put these verbs into the gerund form and put them in the correct places in the sentences.

drive make up get up see type go waste leave

1 I dislike ______ early in the morning.
2 Would you consider ______ abroad for a few months?
3 I think he regrets ______ home, now he has to do all his own cooking and cleaning.
4 When you've finished ______ that letter, post it.
5 I really can't stand ______ my time.
6 He tries to avoid ______ his mind about anything.
7 I never enjoy ______ on motorways.
8 I've missed ______ all my family and friends since I've lived in New York.

© SANTILLANA

5 International signs

a Match the signs with the phrases.

No smoking
Beware of children crossing
Dangerous chemicals
Petrol
Hotel
Beware of falling stones
No entry
One way street
Wheelchair access
No right turn

b Decide whether the phrases are warnings, prohibitions or give information.

6 Signals and codes *Stress patterns*

a Look at the three code systems: the Braille alphabet, sign language and Morse Code. Which is used by ships, people who are deaf and dumb, people who are blind?

b Listen to this talk about communicating through codes and signals. Make a note about any other methods of using codes and signals which are not in the illustration on the right.

c Morse Code dots and dashes are similar to the stress patterns in words and phrases. Listen to these words and phrases and look at the dots and dashes.

• • •	—	• —	• — •
isn't it	now	today	Good evening

Look at the Morse Code chart and change the four Morse code symbols above the words, into letters of the alphabet. Which word does it make?

A •—	G ——•	M ——	S •••	Y —•——
B —•••	H ••••	N —•	T —	Z ——••
C —•—•	I ••	O ———	U ••—	
D —••	J •———	P •——•	V •••—	
E •	K —•—	Q ——•—	W •——	
F ••—•	L •—••	R •—•	X —••—	

d Listen to the stress in these words and phrases. Write the dots and dashes above each word or phrase. Change the dots and dashes into letters of the alphabet. Which word does it make? The first one has been done for you.

B
— • • •
Tall, isn't he? a blue one the Hello! Time for tea!

red tomatoes at eight isn't it Yes

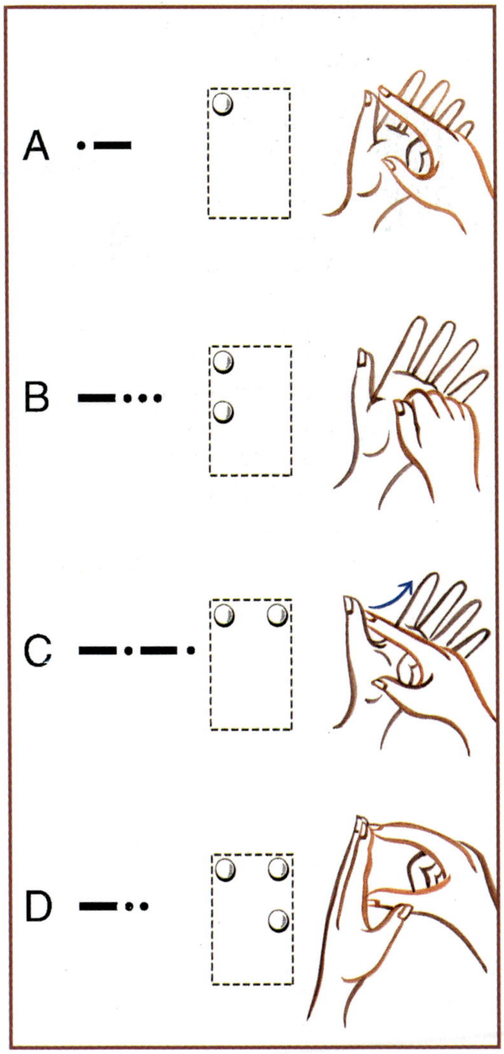

© SANTILLANA

7 Do you give off the right signals?

1 My mother has the knack of making me feel guilty, even though I do a lot for her. I call to see her six days a week, I clean her house, rush round after work to cook her an evening meal and take her presents. But nothing I do is good enough for her. She's such a martyr, always trying to make me feel guilty. Should I just put up with it – after all, she is my mother?

2 My new boss is such a bully and he's so aggressive. I'm finding the situation increasingly difficult. He's always shouting at me and sometimes makes threats so that, in the end, I give in and do whatever he asks. He seems to find all my weaknesses and I feel I have to pussyfoot around in order not to upset him. He thumps the desk, slams doors and he's extremely aggressive in other ways, too. For example, he always interrupts me or ignores my questions. I dread upsetting him. The situation is getting really impossible. What can I do?

3 Remember you are not responsible for the feelings and actions of other people. Stay calm, but make your point. Stay on the same level. For example, if you are seated then stand up and keep eye contact. If you are interrupted, say, 'You interrupted me,' and then continue with your point. If you feel angry, then say clearly, 'I am angry. I don't want you to ...' Don't shout, but make sure your facial expression and tone of voice show how you feel inside.

4 Ask yourself if you really need to do so much for her. Is she really so incapable? She may respect you more if you take time out for your own needs. Anyway, your own needs are important, whether she respects them or not. When she complains, don't apologise or make excuses, give her examples of what you do for her and how much you show your affection for her. Tell her you love her – and ask her if she loves you, too.

a The texts 1–4 are letters and responses on a magazine problem page. Match the responses to the letters.

b Find these words and phrases in the texts and match them with definitions on the left.

1 guilty	a serious warnings
2 put up with it	b say sorry
3 make your point	c does not pay any attention to
4 tone of voice	d a feeling of having done something wrong
5 a bully	e alone
6 threats	f suffer a situation in silence
7 pussyfoot around	g be afraid of
8 ignores	h unable to do things
9 dread	i way of speaking
10 incapable	j a very aggressive person
11 apologise	k say what you are thinking or feeling
12 on her own	l speak and move very quietly so that nobody is disturbed

c Which points in the responses to the letters do you agree or disagree with?

I'm one of two secretaries in an office, but my colleague is making my life a misery. Our boss encourages us to suggest ideas to improve efficiency in the office. Somehow, she always gives him my ideas as if they were her own. For example, I told her about a new computer program that I'd seen and the next minute she is telling the boss about 'her' idea. I thought it was ridiculous to contradict her so I said nothing. Or she waits until the boss is around and says things like, 'Oh, haven't you finished that report yet?' when I only got the report ten minutes ago. She always fixes the holiday timetable so that I am the one who is working between Christmas and New Year. It's really getting me down.

d Read the letter on the right and work out some possible responses to give to the writer of the letter. Then write up the response you would give.

© SANTILLANA

Vocabulary File

1 Adverbs ending in *-ly*

a Adverbs ending with *-ly* can be used:

1 with adjectives to make the adjective stronger.
Some people are extremely good liars.

2 with verbs to give more information about the verb.
Children understand it naturally

In both examples the adverb form is made by adding *-ly* to the end of the word.
Make a list of the *-ly* adverbs used in the text in exercise 3. Write down if they are type 1 or 2.

b Change the adjectives into adverbs and put them into the sentences.

good slow bad unconscious careful aggressive

1 Many of our gestures we make ______, without even thinking about them.
2 I can speak a little French, but I'm afraid I don't speak it very ______.
3 I hate driving with my dad. He drives so ______ we take hours to go anywhere.
4 When speaking ______ we often point our forefinger.
5 Do this exercise very ______, so that you don't make too many mistakes.
6 They played so ______, they lost 5 – 0.

2 Extremes

a Look at these examples from the text in exercise 7.

He's extremely aggressive in other ways, too.
The situation is getting really impossible.

When we use an adjective which has an absolute or extreme meaning, we cannot use the words *very* or *extremely* in front of the adjective.

We can say *very/extremely difficult*, but NOT *very/extremely impossible*. Because *impossible* is an absolute.

We can put the adverbs into two groups.

used with non-extreme adjectives (e.g. surprised)	used with extreme adjectives (e.g. amazed)
very very … indeed really extremely	really absolutely

The progression of meaning is like this.
surprised → very surprised → very surprised indeed → amazed → absolutely amazed

b Match the non-extreme adjective in column A with its extreme or absolute form in column B.

A	B
good	boiling
bad	tiny
hot	starving
cold	horrified
small	overjoyed
big	freezing
hungry	huge
shocked	dreadful
happy	excellent

c Write five sentences using one of the extreme adjectives with an adverb.

EXAMPLE:
When we went on holiday last year the temperature was 40°C every day. It was absolutely boiling!

Read out the sentences to the class but do not say the adjective. Other members of the class try to guess what the missing adjective is.

3 *-ing* or *-ed*

Look at the list of adjectives in exercise 8. Some end in *-ed* and some in *-ing*. Several adjectives can have two different endings.
EXAMPLE: *boring* or *bored.*

Adjectives ending in *-ed* describe someone's reactions or feelings.

Adjectives ending in *-ing* describe the quality of the thing (or person) itself.

EXAMPLE: *I was really bored by the film.*
The film was really boring.
He is a very boring person.

Put the correct adjectives into these sentences. Choose from the adjectives below.

interested/interesting disgusted/disgusting
worried/worrying frightened/frightening

1 There was a ______ smell in the room.
2 Walking through the backstreets of New York at night was quite a ______ experience.
3 The bank manager was not very ______ in their business plan.
4 When her daughter did not come home at eleven she was extremely ______.
5 I was ______ of my boss when I first worked there, but now I get on with him OK.
6 Rising unemployment is a very ______ problem at the moment.
7 I thought his last book was not as ______ as his first one.
8 I was ______ when I heard he hadn't visited his mother once while she was in hospital.

© SANTILLANA

8 Absolutely delighted! *Talking about extremes*

a Match four of the adjectives in column A with the faces in the photographs.

A	B
surprised	fascinating
interesting	exhausted
annoyed	delighted
pleased	amazed
frightening	furious
tired	terrifying

b Listen to this conversation and find the words which follow *very* and *absolutely*.

c Listen to five more conversations and match the words in column A with words of a similar meaning in column B. The first one has been done for you.

d Work in pairs. Make up dialogues using an adjective in column A and its extreme form in column B.

EXAMPLE:

A: Were you very ...?

B: Oh, yes. Very ... indeed. I mean, I was absolutely ...

A

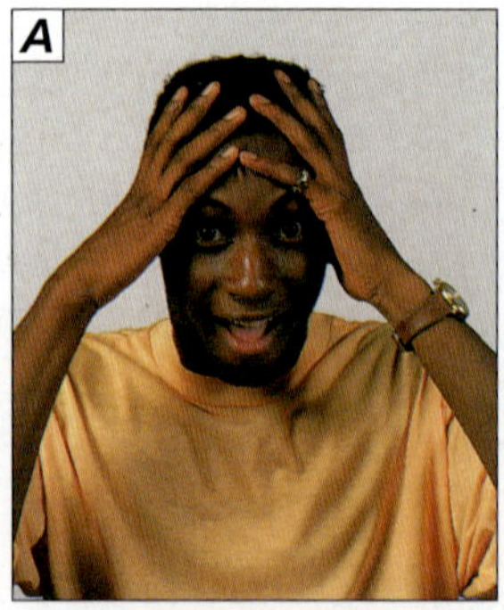

B

C

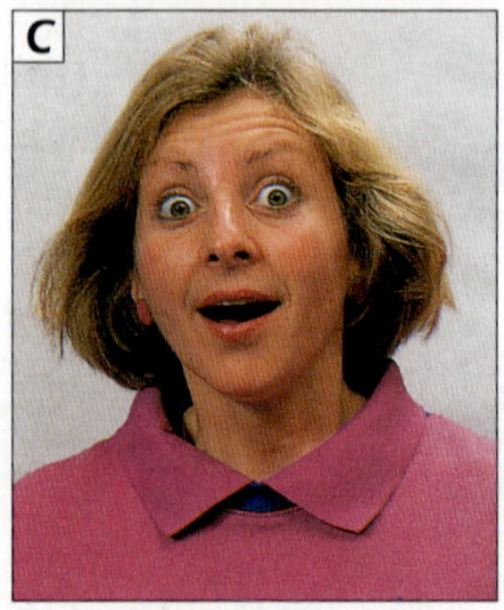

D

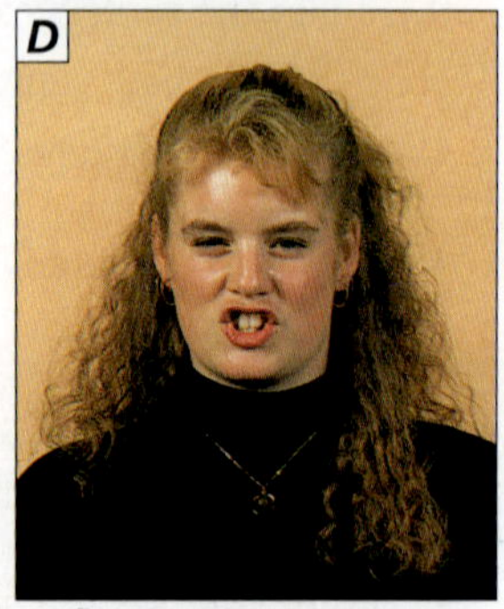

Learning Tips

Using phonetics

1

When you look up a new word in the dictionary, look at the phonetic transcript for the correct pronunciation. Say the word aloud several times. This will help you to learn its pronunciation.

> **vital** /vaɪtəl/. 1 Something or someone that is **vital** is extremely important and necessary in order that something else can take place, succeed, etc. EG *It is vital to keep an accurate record of every transaction... He is of vital importance if you want to get something urgently.* ◊ **vitally.** EG *The way we choose to bring up children is vitally important.*
> ADJ QUALIT = crucial
> ◊ ADV + ADJ ↑ crucially

Find three new words you have learned in this unit. Write out the phonetic transcript for each word. (Use the list of phonetic symbols on page 148 to help you.) Then check in a dictionary to see if you wrote the correct transcript.

2

Try to make up nonsense sentences with adjectives and adverbs, where every word begins with the same letter.

EXAMPLE: *Angry Adam ate apples aggressively.*
Perfect Peter paints pictures peacefully.

Pronunciation File

Intonation

a Intonation is very important to the meaning of what we say. When we make requests in English, it is important not to sound impolite or aggressive. Listen to these requests and notice if the voice starts the sentence high or low.

Can I have two coffees, please?
Could I borrow your pen for a moment?
Do you mind if I open the window?

It is not absolutely necessary to use the word 'please' in every request. But if you do not use 'please' you must be sure to use the correct intonation, if you don't want to sound very impolite.

b Practise saying these polite requests with the correct intonation.

Can you tell me where Dean Street is?
Have you got the time, please?
Where can I find the shoe department?
Is it OK if I use the telephone?

Now listen and repeat the sentences. Try to copy the intonation accurately.

© SANTILLANA

9 Coded writing *Using the phonetic alphabet*

a This article is from the *New Internationalist* magazine. Look quickly at the article and say what you think it is about.

b Read the first two paragraphs again and find words or phrases with a similar meaning to these words:
1 without hesitating
2 control
3 quick look
4 enjoyment
5 participating
6 influence
7 very important indeed

c Now read the second part of the article. Follow the instructions and discuss the questions.

Simply … the right to read

FOR THOSE of us who learned to read in primary school it is hard to understand what it would be like to speak and understand a language fluently, but not be able to read or write it. Imagine you were not able to decipher the signs and the documents that govern our lives in the modern world. This activity is designed to give you a glimpse of what it is like to learn to read. Try it – in a group, with a class, or just for fun …

Here are two statements about the importance of education. Imagine you are taking part in a referendum which is going to shape the future of your country's education system. Your vote may be vital, but first you have to understand the manifestos, which are written in International Phonetic Alphabet.

MANIF	*ESTOS*
edju:keɪʃən ʃʊd	edju:keɪʃən ʃʊd
ti:tʃ pi:pl tə ◀	▶ ti:tʃ pi:pl
kwestʃən ðə	tə rɪspekt
wɜ:ld əraʊnd ðəm	ɔ:θɒrɪtɪ

1 The class divides into groups of three.
2 One person in each group makes a copy of card A, one person card B and one person card C.
3 Everyone spends a few minutes learning the symbols on his/her card. People can draw pictures to help them learn the symbols but no-one must write anything in the normal alphabet.
4 Now teach the other two group members the symbols on your card.
5 Everyone should now know all the symbols on the three cards. In groups, look at the two manifestos and translate them into the normal alphabet.
6 As a group you can now discuss the two manifestos and vote on them.
7 Tell the result of your vote to the rest of the class.

- How do you think it feels to try to make a decision about something you do not completely understand?
- If people cannot read, they will probably only receive information through the radio or the television which are much easier for governments to control.
- How difficult was it to learn the new symbols?
- If people cannot decipher the symbols to interpret the message, they will probably feel very confused and powerless.

A

Vowels	Consonants	
e	j t	/jet/(yet)
aʊ	k	/kaʊtʃ/(couch)
ɪ	tʃ p	/tʃɪp/(chip)
ɒ	s l	/lɒst/(lost)

B

Vowels	Consonants	
u:	θ r	/θru:/(through)
ɔ:	w n	/wɔ:n/(worn)
ɜ:	l	/lɜ:n/(learn)

C

Vowels	Consonants	
ʊ	d	/ʃʊd/(should)
i:	ʃ r	/ʃi:/(she)/ri:d/(read)
eɪ	m	/meɪd/(made)
ə	ð	/ðə/(the)

10 In the manner of the word *Language round-up*

Work in groups.
Write down a list of adverbs that end in *-ly*. Other groups ask you to do a particular action such as comb your hair, speak to your boyfriend, etc. You must do the action in the manner of the adverb you have circled. The other members of the class must guess what the adverb is. If they do not guess correctly they then ask you to do other actions until someone guesses your adverb.

© SANTILLANA

What's it like?

1 Personal portraits

A

a Look at the photograph of this man and say what you think about him. Use the phrases below.

He is probably	in his thirties/forties/fifties …
He looks	kind/unhappy/tired …
He looks like a	fisherman/sailor/farmer …
He looks as if	he is …
He looks as though	he comes from …/lives in …

B

C

b Work in pairs. Say what you think about the other two people in the same way. Then tell the class what you think about all three people in the photographs. Agree or disagree with other members of the class like this:

Yes, I think	she he	is probably … looks … looks like … looks as if …	too.

No, I don't think so. I think	she he	is probably … looks … looks like … looks as if …

c Write a short paragraph about one of the people. Include what you think about his/her job, age, feelings, where he/she lives.

© SANTILLANA

2 *The Old Man and the Sea*

a Read this text from Ernest Hemingway's book *The Old Man and the Sea* and say which paragraph tells us:

1 the old man's attitude to the sea
2 what the old man looks like
3 that the old man is not as successful in his job as he used to be

b Read the text again and put the words at the end of the line into the correct place in each line. The first one has been done for you.

He was an old man ⁁(who) fished alone in a skiff[1] in the Gulf Stream[2] and he	who
had gone eighty-four days now without taking a fish. In first forty	the
days without a fish the boy's parents had told him that the old man	was
now definitely and finally *salao*[3], is the worst form of unlucky, and the	which
boy had gone at their orders in another boat caught three good fish in	which
the first week. It made the boy sad see the old man come in each day	to
with his skiff empty and he went down to help him carry the sail.	always
The old man was thin and gaunt[4] deep wrinkles in the back of his neck.	with
The brown blotches[5] of the benevolent skin cancer which sun brings from	the
its reflection on the tropic sea were on his cheeks. The blotches ran	down
the sides of his face and hands had the deep-creased scars from handling	his
heavy fish on the cords[6]. But none of scars were fresh. Everything	these
about him was old his eyes and they were the same colour as the sea	except
and were cheerful undefeated.	and
He always thought of the sea as *la mar* which is people call her in Spanish	what
when they love her. Sometimes those love her say bad things of her but	who
they are always said as she were a woman. Some of the younger	though
fishermen, those who had motor-boats, spoke of her as *el mar* is masculine.	which
They spoke of her as a contestant or a place or even enemy. But the old man	an
always thought of her as feminine and as something gave or withheld great	that
favours, and if she did wild or wicked things was because she could not help	it
them. The moon affects as it does a woman, he thought.	her

1 a small boat with a sail
2 a warm current in the North Atlantic ocean in the Gulf of Mexico, and moving north.
3 (Spanish) literally it means 'salted'. It means 'unlucky' in this context.
4 thin and showing the signs of suffering
5 dark spots
6 fishing lines

c Which words and phrases tell you where this story took place? What impression do you get of the old man? Which words and phrases give you this impression?

d This extract is from the beginning of the book. If you know this story, tell the class what happens next. Do you know any other books by this author?

3 Pet hates *Expressing annoyance*

a Different people are going to talk about their pet hates (things they don't like). Look at the pictures and guess some of their pet hates.

b Listen and match the pictures with each short conversation you hear.

B

C

A

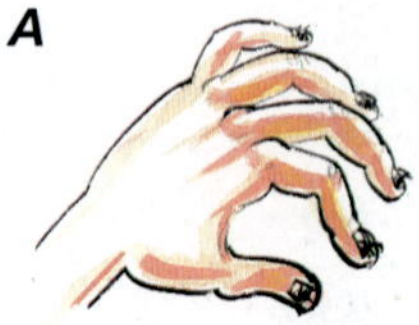

I

who

D

when

where

H

which

that

E

whose

G

F

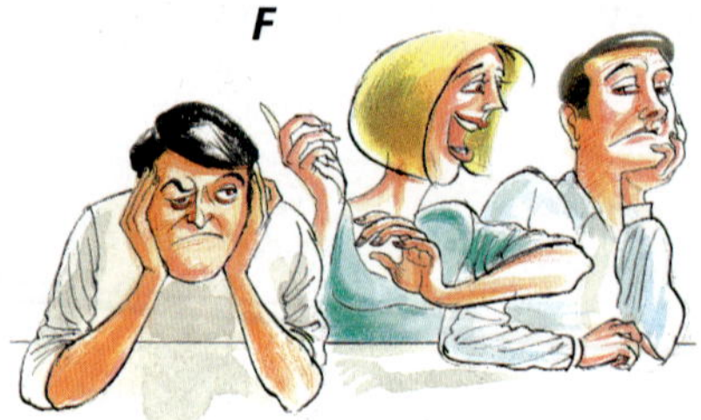

© SANTILLANA

c Listen again and give examples of their pet hates. Use the pictures in part A and the phrases below.

			who …
	can't stand	people/men/teachers/children	whose …
He	doesn't like	places/restaurants/towns	that …
She	really dislikes	things/films/machines	where …
	hates	times/the moment/the day	which …
			when …

EXAMPLE:
Speaker 1 can't stand people who never stop talking.

d Tell your partner your pet hates about people, places, things and times. Do you share any of your partner's pet hates?

e Write these words on a piece of paper in four columns like this.

people	places	things	times

Talk about your pet hates and listen to other members of the class talking about their pet hates. Make notes of as many as you can under the correct column. Look at your notes and say which are the most common pet hates.

Pronunciation File

/dʒ/ and /j/

a Can you pronounce these two words? job yob

Listen to see if you were correct.

Draw two columns on a piece of paper. Write the word *job* at the top of one column and the word *yob* at the top of the second column. Read these words aloud and put them into the correct column, according to the sound at the beginning of the word.

young	you	due	jump	yawn	John
duty	gin	useful	university	gentle	joke
yolk	yes	gesture	yet	jet	juice

Listen to see if you were correct.

b Listen to the words and tick (✓) the ones you hear.

c Listen to this sentence and say it aloud several times.

Just for a joke John used jam, gin and egg yolk in a yellow juice.

© SANTILLANA

Grammar File

1 Relative pronouns

a Look at this example from the text in exercise 2. Choose one of the relative pronouns *who*, *which* or *when* to complete the sentences.

He always thought of the sea as *la mar* [1]______ is what people call her in Spanish [2]______ they love her. Sometimes those [3]______ love her say bad things of her. Some of the younger fishermen, those [4]______ had motor-boats, spoke of her as *el mar* [5]______ is masculine. But the old man always thought of her as feminine.

b Choose one of the relative pronouns *who, whose, which, where* or *when* to complete each of these sentences.

1 I don't like machines ______ don't work properly.
2 That's the man ______ is staying in our hotel.
3 I hate the moment ______ we all pick up our pens at the start of an exam.
4 She's the woman ______ brother is on TV every Saturday.
5 Benidorm, ______ is one of the busiest holiday resorts in Spain, is extremely crowded in August.

2 Defining and non-defining relative clauses

a Look at these two examples of relative clauses.

1 There's the old man | who / that | fishes every day.

2 The boat | which / that | he uses is very old.

In sentence 1 it is possible to use *who* or *that*.
In sentence 2 it is possible to use *which* or *that*.
In these examples the clauses underlined are defining clauses. They tell us the exact person or thing we are talking about.

Now look at these examples.

3 My brother John, who is very tall, is a national basketball player.
4 His BMW, which is twelve years old, is always breaking down.

In these examples the clauses underlined are non-defining clauses. They do not tell us which person or thing we are talking about, we already know we are talking about John and his car.
In non-defining clauses it is not possible to use *that* instead of *who* or *which*.

b Look at the sentences in exercise 1b above. Which sentence has a non-defining relative clause? What do you notice about the punctuation in non-defining relative clauses?

c Look at these sentences. Put a tick (✓) if you can change the relative pronouns *who* and *which* to *that*. Put a cross (✗) if you cannot. Then punctuate the sentences which are non-defining relative clauses.

1 I can't stand films which are too violent.
2 This is the key which opens the front door.
3 Which restaurant did you go to? The one which is opposite the station?
4 Our English teacher who comes from Ireland is getting married in August.
5 I don't like people who look snobbish.
6 London which is the biggest city in Europe has a population of about seven millon.
7 My parents who have never been abroad before are going to New York next month.
8 The teacher who you spoke to this morning is the new French teacher.

3 Verb position in relative clauses

a Look at the position of the verbs in these clauses with *where* and *when*.

I can't stand restaurants where only well-dressed people go.
I hate the moment when the exam results arrive.

Translate these sentences into your language. Is the position of the verb in the relative clause different in English?

b Use the phrases below to write four sentences about your pet hates.

people who …/whose …
things which …
places which …/where …
moments when …

4 *What … like?*

Look at these questions and answers.

What's he like?
– He's quite old, with lots of wrinkles and dark skin.
What was the exam like?
– It was terrible. I could only answer half the questions.

Write questions using *What … like?* for these answers.

1 It's quiet and quite cheap and it serves a lot of Mexican food.
2 It was great. The hotel was excellent and the beaches were fantastic.
3 It's noisy and a bit dirty, but it has lots of interesting museums, theatres and so on.
4 It was really boring. I fell asleep in the middle.
5 Horrible! It tastes disgusting.

© SANTILLANA

4 What does it sound like? *Identifying sounds*

Listen to these sounds. What do they sound like?
If you do not know the name of the machine in English say what the machine does.

EXAMPLE:
It sounds like a thing/machine which …

5 Guess the object *Identifying objects*

a Look at the five objects and listen to descriptions of four of the objects. Match the description to each object and say which object is not described.

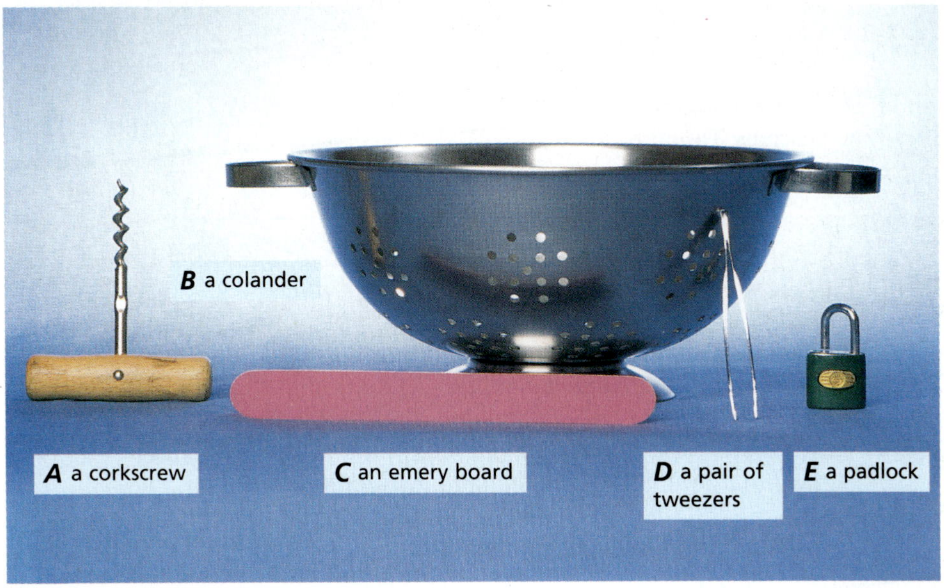

Give a description for the object which was not described. Use the phrases below.

It's something	which that which that	you find in … people have in … we use for …

b Work in groups and follow these instructions.

1. Think of an object that you do not know the name of in English.
2. Look up the name of the object in a dictionary. (Remember to check the correct pronunciation with the phonetic script.)
3. Prepare an accurate description of the object, as in part A.
4. Prepare two false descriptions of the object.
5. Write the name of the object on the board.
6. Each person in the group gives a description of the object, but only one is the true description.
7. Other members of the class try to guess which is the true description.

EXAMPLE:
I don't think it's something that …
I think it's something which …

© SANTILLANA

6 Identikit pictures *Describing physical appearance*

a Listen to someone giving a description of one of the people below to the police. Match the description to the identikit picture.

A
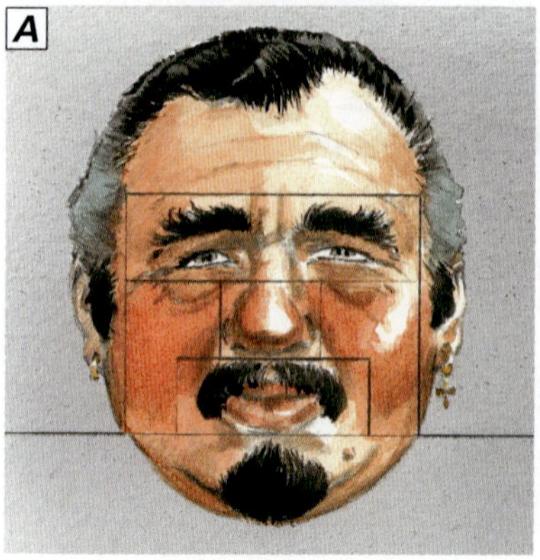

B
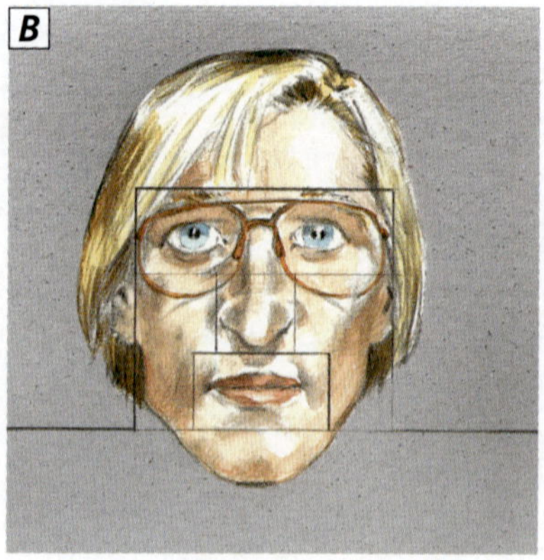

C
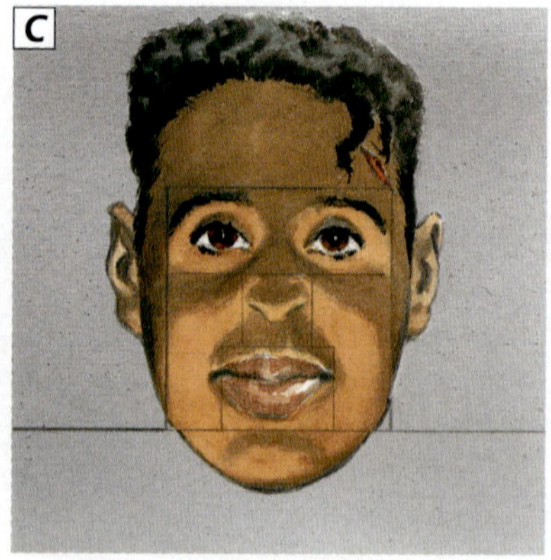

b Read the descriptions and look up any words which you do not know in a dictionary. Then read the Learning Tip on page 89 and check you have found the correct meaning.

Age:	mid-fifties	early thirties	late teens – early twenties
Build:	medium height well-built	small and thin slight	tallish, slim muscular
Skin:	white red-faced	white pale	black
Eyes:	narrow, grey bushy eyebrows	large, pale blue glasses	dark brown
Hair:	wavy greyish black	long, straight greasy, blond ponytail	short, curly black
Features:	round, plump face large nose wart on chin beard and moustache	thin face long, pointed nose mole on cheek	oval face small nose scar on forehead
General Appearance:	lots of jewellery flashy clothes	scruffy	smart, well-dressed

c In pairs, ask and answer questions about the identikit pictures. Use the phrases.

What does he look like?

What is / are his face / eyes like?

Has he got any special features?

What kind of clothes does he usually wear?

He's in his …
…-built
… with …

He's got …

He usually has/wears …

d Write a description of one of the people who was not described to the police.

© SANTILLANA

Vocabulary File

1 Order of adjectives

Look at the order of the adjectives in these sentences.

She has got short, curly, brown hair and large, watery, grey eyes.
He has got long, dirty nails and a big, pointed, red nose.
He is tall and slim.

When there is more than one adjective, which adjectives come first, second and third. Size, type or colour?

2 Words and phrases to describe people

Put as many describing words as you can, under these three columns. Look at exercise 6 for examples. Look in your dictionary if you want more examples.

build	facial features	hair
medium-height	*wart*	*wavy*

3 Saying things approximately

a Look at the ways of describing things approximately.

He's in his early / late teens/twenties/thirties/forties …
He's got greyish hair.
He's tallish.

How can you describe someone who:

1 is approximately twenty two or twenty three and is quite small, but not very small?
2 is approximately thirty five or thirty six and has hair which is a little blond?
3 is quite young but not very young and has eyes which are a little blue?
4 is approximately nineteen or twenty and has hair which is a little long, but not very long?

b Write a short description of someone you know. Describe his/her build, hair, eyes, facial features and general appearance. Use adjectives from the list in exercise 2. Remember the correct order of the adjectives.

Learning Tips

When you look up a word in a dictionary, there may be several meanings. Look at these examples.

mole[1] *n.* small dark raised spot on the skin.
mole[2] *n.* **1.** small burrowing mammal. **2.** *Informal* spy who has infiltrated and become a trusted member of an organization. **molehill** *n.* small mound of earth thrown up by a burrowing mole. **make a mountain out of a molehill** exaggerate an unimportant matter out of all proportion.
mole[3] *n.* **1.** breakwater. **2.** harbour protected by this.
mole[4] *n.* unit of amount of substance.

English – English

mole [məul] *n* (*animal, spy*) (*spot*) lunar *m*.

English – Spanish

mole [məul] *n* (*animal, fig*) talpa; (*spot*) neo.

English – Italian

mole [məul] *n* (*animal*) toupeira; (*spot*) sinal *m*, lunar *m*; (*spy*) espião/piã *m/f*.

English – Portugese

Match the definitions from the monolingual dictionary with those from one of the bilingual dictionaries.

Look at the possible translations of the word *mole*. You can check which meaning is correct for the context by:

1 the logical meaning of the word in the sentence
2 bilingual checking – look up the English word in your own language then check the translations back again with the original English. In this way you can double-check you have the correct meaning. If you don't check properly you could find:

A man with a large mole on his cheek.

© SANTILLANA

7 Turn a blind eye? *Using expressions*

a There are many expressions which include words for parts of the human body and face. Here are some with the words *eye* and *nose*.

Match the expressions in italics with the correct meaning. Which expressions match the cartoons?

1 He was wearing a very *eye-catching* shirt.
2 I've never *set eyes on* him before.
3 My boss *turned a blind eye* when I had two days off.
4 Will you *keep an eye on* my luggage?
5 That building is such *an eyesore*.
6 We have an *eyewitness* who saw you there.
7 He is really *nosy*, he wants to know everything about you.
8 She goes around *with her nose in the air*.
9 She really *gets up my nose* when she talks about how important she is.
10 Kindly *keep your nose out of* my business.

a annoys me
b ugly-looking thing
c bright, colourful and noticeable
d someone who was there at the time and saw everything
e anxious to know all personal information
f look after
g seen
h feeling superior to (someone else)
i don't interfere in other people's affairs
j pretended not to notice another person doing something wrong because it is not so important

b Do you know any other expressions using different parts of the head (face, cheek, mouth, teeth, hair, etc)? Use a dictionary to help you.

© SANTILLANA

Pronunciation File

Elision

a In spoken English many of the words run together without a break. Look at the linking marks between the words in the sentences below.

He's got‿a‿wart‿on his nose.

She's got‿a‿scar‿on her forehead.

She wears lots‿of‿fashionable jewellery.

He's‿scruffy‿and‿dirty.

She's‿tall‿and‿slim with curly blond hair.

Listen to each sentence then repeat it. Try to run the words together where you see the linking marks.

b Listen again and mark the stressed syllables. Then underline the schwa sounds. Now try to say each sentence with the correct stress and schwa sounds, joining the words together where possible.

8 Spot the difference *Language round-up*

A

B

Look at photographs A and B. In pairs, talk about the differences between the photographs.

EXAMPLE:

In picture A	*she looks as if she is …, whereas in picture B*	*she looks …*
	she is …	*she is …*
	she has got …	*she has got …*
	she is holding …	*she is holding …*

© SANTILLANA

1 Using gestures

a Think of five body or facial gestures then describe the gesture and its meaning.

EXAMPLE:

Leaning back in the chair with your hands behind your head often means you are not really interested.

Putting one thumb up usually means 'Good luck!'

b Work in groups. Describe the meaning of the gesture to other people in the group, but do not say what the gesture is. Others in the group guess the gesture.

EXAMPLE:

This usually means 'Be quiet!'

– Putting your finger to your lips.

c Change these verbs into their *-ing* form and complete the sentences.

scratch talk bite suck pull twitch

1 Scientists have proved that _____ your nails is bad for you.
2 People often say that _____ to yourself is the first sign of madness.
3 Most children like _____ funny faces when they have their photograph taken.
4 She has this nervous habit of _____ her chin.
5 It always happens. I sit down to eat and my leg starts _____.
6 Why do babies spend hours _____ their thumbs?

2 What people look like

Write a description of one of the people in the photographs. Describe the person's face, body and distinguishing features. Also describe their clothes and general appearance, and make guesses about their personal characteristics.

EXAMPLE:

S/he looks as if ...

3 Powerful words – *look*

a Look at this dictionary definition of the word *look*. How do you translate this word into your own language?

look /lʊk/, **looks, looking, looked. 1** If you **look** in a particular direction, you direct your eyes in that direction, especially so that you can see what is there or see what something is like. EG *She turned to look out of the back window... They looked across the room at each other...* — V: USU+A

2 If you **look** at something that is moving or happening, or at the television, you watch it. EG *People like to look at animals and birds... You spend far too much of your time looking at the television.* — V+A (at)

11 You say **look** when you want someone to pay attention to you because you are going to say something important. EG *Bill? Look, I want to go to Europe for six months... Look, Paul, this is ridiculous... Now look, Mrs Kintner, you've got it wrong.* — CONVENTION

15 You say that someone or something **looks** nice, ill, sad, etc when describing or commenting on their appearance or expression. EG *You look very pale... Doesn't she look lovely?...* — V+C, OR V+A (as/like) ⇑ appear, seem

Now look at these definitions of phrases using the word *look*.

look into. If you **look into** a particular problem, subject, situation, etc, you find out and examine the facts relating to it. EG *In 1959 a working party was set up to look into the problem... They wanted an independent financial controller to look into the city's accounts.* — PHRASAL VB: V+PREP, HAS PASS = investigate

look out. 1 You say or shout **'look out'** to warn someone that they are in danger. EG *'Look out,' I said. 'There's something coming.'* — CONVENTION = watch out

look over. If you **look** something **over**, you examine it quite quickly in order to get a general idea of what it is like. EG *Sometimes he used to look over the article I had written, shrug, and tear it up...* — PHRASAL VB: V+O+ADV

b Check the meaning of these words and phrases using the word *look* in your dictionary.

look down on	look forward to
look up to	look after
look for	overlook
look into	look up

c Complete these sentences with a word or phrase from part B. Put the verb into the correct form where necessary.

1 I'm really _____ going to Canada next summer.
2 She thinks she is so superior, she _____ everyone else.
3 Hold on. I'm _____ my keys. I can't find them.
4 When I was an au pair in France I had to _____ three children for five hours a day.
5 When I was a child I used to _____ my uncle. He seemed so clever and he was always very kind to everyone.
6 The police are _____ the crime right now, but so far they don't know who did it.
7 You were breaking the speed limit by 20mph. I'll _____ it this time, but if I catch you again I'm afraid I'll have to fine you.
8 If you can't find her number in your address book, _____(it) in the telephone directory.

© SANTILLANA

4 Dictionary work

a You can use dictionaries to find the meanings of new words, but also to learn how to pronounce words correctly. All of these words have silent letters. Use a dictionary to check the pronunciation of these words and cross out the silent letter. Practise saying the words aloud.

EXAMPLE:
bom~~b~~

1 comb	5 handkerchief
2 listen	6 muscle
3 should	7 knowledge
4 knee	8 answer

b Match the words in column A with their phonetic transcription in column B. Use your dictionary to help.

A	B
colleague	/kərɪzmə/
knowledge	/li:shəʊld/
leisure	/fənetik/
leasehold	/kɒlə/
Christmas	/kɒli:g/
charisma	/leʒə/
furniture	/nɒlɪdʒ/
phonetic	/kʌlə/
collar	/krɪsməs/
colour	/fɜ:nɪtʃə/

c Look at these four words. Each word has two different meanings.

face wave sack nails

Use each word twice in this exercise. Each word is used with its two meanings.

1 A stereotypical burglar wears a striped shirt, a black mask and carries a large _____ on his back.
2 I always bite my _____ when I feel nervous.
3 I didn't do enough revision and I couldn't _____ doing the exam because I knew I would fail.
4 His boss gave him the _____ yesterday for coming to work late all the time.
5 The puncture was caused by rusty _____ lying in the road.
6 He smiled and gave me a cheerful _____ when I saw him across the street.
7 She still has a scar on her _____ from when she fell over when she was a child.
8 As the enormous _____ rolled in, all the surfers jumped on their surfboards.

5 Error correction

There is one mistake in each of these sentences. Find the mistake and rewrite the sentence correctly.

1 *If the baby doesn't stop crying soon, I had to take him home.*
2 *Come on! Decide up your mind. Do you want to go to the cinema or the pub?*
3 *Hey, that man looks as if Bill Clinton.*
4 *My sister doesn't stand her English class, she says it is boring.*
5 *When I go to Scotland, I will to buy you some whisky.*
6 *I'm really looking up to seeing John at the weekend.*
7 *A vacuum cleaner is something who you clean the carpets with.*
8 *Whose that man over there? I'm sure I recognise him.*
9 *What is Susan look like?*
10 *I am tired of get up so early in the morning.*

6 Project

a In groups, talk about who you go to for advice when you have a problem. Is it better to get advice from people who are very close to you (family, boyfriends, girlfriends, etc) or from people who are not so intimate (friends, colleagues, teachers, etc)?

b Conduct a class survey. Ask these questions and record the answers.

Have you ever read a problem page in a magazine? When?/How often?
Do you enjoy reading the problem page in magazines? Why?/Why not?
Why do you think people write to magazines with their problems?
Do you think they receive good advice? Why?/Why not?
Have you ever written to the problem page of a magazine?

Write a short report about your survey.

EXAMPLE:
Everybody in the class has read a problem page at some time, but only ... people read problem pages regularly.

c Find an English magazine that has a problem page and choose two 'problem' letters. (If you can't find an English magazine, use a magazine in your language and translate the letters into English.) Give the 'problem' letters to a partner. Your partner imagines that s/he is editor of the problem page and writes responses to the letters. Do you agree with your partner's advice?

© SANTILLANA

Living Outside the Law

1 Survey

a Read the survey and work out the meaning of the words underlined.

1 hard drugs
2 a classmate's purse
3 your friend was the thief
4 a hit-and-run accident
5 try to persuade your friend to
6 stolen goods

b In groups, ask and answer the questions. Write down the answers of each person in the group.

c Now look back at your answers. Check if you have given the answer for what you would actually do or what you think you should do.

Check the answers of each person in the group.

EXAMPLE:

For question 1, you said you would …
Would you really do this or do you think this is what you should do?
– I would really do this.
– I would actually … , but I think I should …

What would you do if …	Would you …
1 you found out one of your friends was taking hard drugs?	*a* tell the police ☐ *b* discuss your friend's problem with everyone who knows him/her ☐ *c* try to talk to your friend about it ☐ *d* say and do nothing ☐
2 you saw a friend stealing a classmate's purse?	*a* tell everybody that your friend is a thief ☐ *b* tell the person whose purse was stolen that your friend was the thief ☐ *c* talk to your friend and try to persuade him/her to give the money back ☐ *d* tell no-one and do nothing ☐
3 you knew your friend was the driver in a hit-and-run accident? S/he had seriously injured another person who was now in hospital. The police wanted to find the driver of the car.	*a* tell the police ☐ *b* tell the family of the injured person that your friend was the driver ☐ *c* try to persuade your friend to go to the police ☐ *d* not say anything to anyone ☐
4 you knew your friend often stole things? On your birthday this friend gave you a very expensive CD player which you knew was stolen.	*a* tell the police that somebody offered you stolen goods ☐ *b* get angry and say you do not want anything which is stolen ☐ *c* thank the friend, but politely refuse the present ☐ *d* thank the friend, accept the present and say nothing more about it ☐

© SANTILLANA

2 Chris's Story *Taking notes*

a This is a true story of a teenager's experiences with drugs. Read his story and look at the possible endings.

I was into alcohol and cigarettes from about the age of 12. Before long, I started sniffing glue and smoking cannabis. When I was about 15, I used go to clubs and parties where most of my friends were taking 'E' (Ecstasy). So I tried it. It gave me this feeling of 'Everything's wonderful.' That's what it was like. At the time it was great, but the worst thing was the next day. I often used to stay in bed all day feeling terrible. Sometimes I went to school on Monday morning still feeling bad. But most of my friends were taking drugs; parties wouldn't seem any good if you didn't take anything.

I wasn't taking drugs because I had any problems. I just wanted to have a good time and drugs made me feel good. Soon I started to take all sorts of different things. One time I took 'E's, acid (LSD), speed (amphetamines) and cocaine, all in one night. After a night like that, I remember thinking, 'I'm lucky to be alive!' And I probably was.

I started getting bored of going to clubs and parties, but I really had a need for 'charlie' (cocaine) by then. I wanted it more and more, but it was becoming harder and harder to get. People who used to sell me cocaine said, 'Why don't you try crack?' (a stronger type of cocaine). The first time I took it, it was fantastic. Crack is the most psychologically addictive drug because you like it instantly. It destroys you, but you don't think about that because you like it so much. I would spend all my money on crack. The crack takes your money, but it also takes your morals – I ended up stealing money from people I loved and I used to get violent and aggressive. That's what it does to you. I knew I had a problem. It had all got out of control.

Possible endings:

1 His parents found out about his drug problem. They took him to a local drug centre where he is now on a detoxification programme.

2 He went to a drug centre by himself. He no longer takes drugs and now works as a volunteer on a youth project. He visits schools, talking to the pupils about drugs.

3 He met a girlfriend who was not interested in drugs. She has helped him a lot. He now has a new set of friends and hasn't taken any drugs for several months.

4 He has been in and out of hospital several times. Each time he has always gone back to drug taking. He is a now registered drug addict.

b In groups, discuss the four possible endings and say which one you think was the real ending to Chris's story. Now decide what you think is best ending to his story.

c Complete the notes on Chris's story.

history of drug taking	his reasons	his feelings/ behaviour
alcohol and cigarettes	most of his friends …	at the time …

d Write up the notes on Chris's story. Add what you think is the real ending.

© SANTILLANA

3 Attacked in the street

a Look at the picture. What do you think happened? Listen to the story to see if you were correct.

b The sentences below give a summary of the story. Put them into the correct order, then listen again to check.

1 Someone put a light on in the house opposite.
2 When I turned round, I came face-to-face with a man I had never seen before.
3 Someone called the police and they came a few minutes later.
4 He let go for a second and I screamed and screamed.
5 As I was putting my key in the door, someone tapped me on the shoulder.
6 They drove me round to see if we could find him, but he had disappeared.
7 He grabbed my throat as if he was trying to strangle me.
8 The attacker ran off.
9 I took a taxi home after a party.
10 I twisted round and elbowed him in the stomach.

c Underline any words in the sentences you do not know and try to guess their meaning. Look up the words you cannot guess.

d What advice did the police give?

If I were you, | *I'd ...*
I wouldn't ...

Do you agree with this advice?

© SANTILLANA

4 Streetwise *Giving advice*

a Read this advice to teenagers on how to fight street crime. Put in the words *don't* or *never* where necessary.

If you are by yourself after dark, ...

- walk home with other people if possible
- listen to personal stereos when you're out in the street
- try to walk in the centre of the pavement and away from bushes or dark buildings
- wait at a bus stop by yourself
- carry an attack alarm
- accept a lift in a car from a stranger
- carry a lot of money
- wear expensive jewellery
- take short-cuts through parks or dark and lonely places

For more information on street safety, send a stamped addressed envelope to: Kidscape, 152 Buckingham Palace Road, London SW1W 9TR.

b Read each piece of advice and say what you would/wouldn't do and why.

EXAMPLE:
I wouldn't carry an attack alarm because if someone attacked me, it would be too late to get the alarm.

Pronunciation File

/ʊ/ and /uː/

a Listen to the pronunciation of these two words. Repeat the words and the sounds.

foot food

Now listen and repeat these words and phrases.

pull	pool	would you
full	fool	could you
book	boot	should you do

b Listen and write down the words in the order you hear them.

c Look at these different ways of spelling the /uː/ sound. These words all have the same sound.

you do shoe blue flew through fool rude

d Listen and repeat these phrases.

Would you ...?	What would you do?
Could you ...?	What should you do?
Should you ...?	Would you do what you should do?

© SANTILLANA

Grammar File

1 Conditional clauses with *would*

a Look at these examples.

1 What would you do if you saw a friend stealing a classmate's purse?
2 If I saw a friend stealing a classmate's purse, I wouldn't tell the police. I would (I'd) talk to my friend about it.
3 I wouldn't wear expensive jewellery if I were out at night in the city centre.

Which verb form is used in the clauses with *if?* Which word is always used in the clause without *if?*

b Imagine you are in these situations. Write sentences to explain what you would do in each case.

EXAMPLE:
You find a wallet in the street which contains bank cards and £100 in cash.

If I found a wallet in the street, I'd look for the owner's name and address.

1 You find a £50 note in the classroom.
2 Someone steals your handbag in the street.
3 You hit someone while driving your car.
4 Your friend has drunk too much alcohol and offers you a lift home in his/her car.
5 You don't have enough money to buy your mother a birthday present next week.
6 You don't have any chance of getting a job in your hometown.

2 *If I were you, ...*

a Look at this example.

If I were you, | *I'd fix a light over your front door.* / *I wouldn't let the taxi go before you're inside the house.*

These sentences follow the same rule as the examples in part A. What do you notice about the form of the verb *to be* in the *if* clause?

b Give advice to these people. Write sentences beginning: *If I were you*...

1 A friend is going to live and work in Paris for one year, but she does not speak any French and does not know anything about Paris.
2 A foreign visitor is going to spend a two-week holiday in your country, but he does not know where to stay.
3 A friend thinks her brother is taking hard drugs and she doesn't know what to do about it.
4 A colleague needs to learn English quickly and wants to know the best and quickest way to learn.

3 *some-, any-, no-, every-*

a Look at exercise 1 on page 94. How many words can you find beginning with *any-*, *no-* and *every-*?

EXAMPLE: *everything, nobody*

Is there any difference in meaning between *everyone* and *everybody* and *no-one* and *nobody*?

b Look at these examples.

Say nothing and tell no-one.
Do not say anything or tell anyone.

The words beginning with *no-* and *any-* both have negative meanings. But which do we use with negative verbs and which do we use with positive verbs?

Look at these examples.

It's really easy. Anybody could do it.
(a specialist does not need to do it)
You can find these new computer games anywhere.
(not in a special place/shop)

Complete these sentences with *anybody, no-one, everything, somewhere*, etc.

1 I don't want ______ thank you, I'm not hungry.
2 ______ came to the meeting so we went home early.
3 I didn't buy her ______ for her birthday and she bought me ______ for mine.
4 It's not a difficult question, ______ could answer it.
5 She promised she wouldn't tell ______, but she didn't keep her promise because ______ knew about it the following week.
6 When they moved from Italy they brought ______ with them, so they didn't need to buy ______ when they arrived here.
7 ______ has moved the books. Who was it?
8 It's a fantastic shop. You can buy ______ you want there.
9 ______ must speak now, the exam has started. You can't have ______ on your desk except the exam paper and a pencil.
10 I've looked ______ for my purse, but I just can't find it. I think ______ has stolen it.

© SANTILLANA

5 A Mafia widow

a Read this article from *The Guardian* newspaper and try to work out the meaning of the title of the article.

Widowed by the Mob

There was something different about Piera Aiello. She was not the typical Mafia widow,' says Judge Alessandra Camassa. 'My colleague first saw her at her husband's autopsy; there was a stark contrast between his family, who were all weeping, all dressed in black, keeping their distance from the police – and this girl who stood on her own, silent, dry-eyed. She looked more dignified, better-dressed … more intelligent.'

Piera Aiello was 25 when her husband was shot dead in front of her; their daughter was three. Her husband was a heroin dealer and killer for the Sicilian Mafia. She had tried for years to change him – she would destroy packets of drugs if she found them in the house, and she would hide his gun. If she knew he was going out to do a contract killing, she would throw herself between him and the door; he would punch and kick her out of his way. Piera's parents bought them a pizzeria to help him go straight. It was only open a week before he was murdered.

At the time of his death in August 1991, a team of young magistrates, including Judge Camassa, were investigating the western Sicilian Mafia. They were making good progress by using Mafia informers. They were offering a government salary, police protection and a safe place to live, in return for information about the Mafia. A number of women whose husbands had been murdered came forward.

After her husband's autopsy, the police contacted Piera Aiello. 'With my background I didn't have a very positive idea of lawyers and magistrates,' said Signora Aiello, speaking on the telephone from a secret location. 'The first time I went to the magistrate's court was pretty frightening.' Judge Camassa adds, 'If you become an informer, you lose everything – your job, your home, your family. We have to guarantee people their safety. Signora Aiello wasn't interested in vendetta. She wasn't the type, and I don't think she had that much respect for her husband. She talked because she was frightened for her child, and because she wanted to escape from her future as a Mafia widow, shut indoors day after day in a small town. This collaboration gave her the chance of a new life.'

Camassa says Piera Aiello always felt she had to prove she wasn't doing it for the money. 'She used to turn up in a fur coat, looking very elegant – as if to say "I don't need anything from you." ' It was true, her family was well-off. Signora Aiello's testimony uncovered a series of Mafia murders, going back 20 years. Thirty three members of the western Sicilian Mafia have now been convicted and sentenced to prison, with a number of others in hiding. Piera Aiello also lives in hiding with her young daughter. She sometimes moves house as often as three times a month. 'There have been some very dark times,' she says. 'But I'm getting on with my life. I've just got a university degree. I speak to my family on the phone. Maybe what I have done will help to change things in Sicily and make people wake up. You know, I can't even remember what my life was like before.'

b Read the article again and answer these questions.

1 How was Piera Aiello different from the typical Mafia widow?
2 How did Piera and her family try to stop her husband committing crimes?
3 Why did the magistrates and the police want to contact Piera after her husband's death?
4 Why did she agree to talk to the police?
5 What is her life like now?

Do you think you would have the courage to do what Piera did if you were in her situation?

c Find words or phrases with a similar meaning to the following:

1 crying (line 5)
2 not crying (line 7)
3 in smarter clothes (line 8)
4 a person who sells drugs (line 11)
5 a person who murders (line 11)
6 hit with your fists (line 16)
7 start to lead an honest life without breaking the law (line 18)
8 people who give information to the police, usually for money (line 23)
9 volunteered to give information (line 27)
10 quite scary (line 33)
11 arrive (line 44)
12 had a lot of money (line 47)

© SANTILLANA

6 The crimes people commit *The vocabulary of crime*

a Look at these two public notices. What are they warning us about?

b Read these extracts from newspaper articles and public notices. Work out the meanings of these words.

kidnap ram-raider robber
kidnappers forgery ransom
shoplifting forger
burglary pickpocketing

Banknote Forgery

Shopkeepers are checking $10, $20 and $50 notes very carefully before accepting them. It is believed that a group of Sydney-based forgers have produced $200,000 worth of forged banknotes in the last month.

Ram-raiders Attack Jeweller's Shop

£1,000,000 worth of diamonds were stolen in the latest ram-raid attack on a jeweller's shop in Glasgow last night. Robbers drove their car straight through the shop window and ran off with the diamonds. This robbery is the second this month.

ʘʘ Watch Out! ʘʘ *There's a Burglar About!*

Is your home safe? Insurance companies are refusing to pay for losses through burglary where homes do not have secure locks fitted on all windows and doors. If your home is burgled, you might find

Miami Stores Lose 23% Profit from Shoplifting

Shoplifters are causing serious damage to profit in Miami shopping malls. Food, electrical goods, alcohol and tobacco are the most popular items to steal.

Kidnappers Demand $500,000 Ransom

Yesterday afternoon, 10 year-old Maria Chevez was kidnapped 50 metres from her home.Later that evening, kidnappers contacted her father, millionaire businessman Cesar Chavez, demanding $500,000 ransom for her release. Police say

Beware of Pickpockets!

If you carry a handbag, keep your bag close to you. Do not put your wallet in your back pocket. Pickpocketing has increased dramatically

c Does anyone in the class know of similar examples of crimes committed in your town?

© SANTILLANA

7 If you ask me … *Expressing opinions*

a **Listen to these people talking about crime. They use these phrases to give their opinions.**

As far as I'm concerned …
Well, in my view …
If you ask me, …
If you want to know what I think, I think …
In my opinion, … *1*

Number each phrase in the order you hear it. The first one has been done for you.

b **Listen again and match each phrase with the correct opinion.**

1 parents are to blame. Parents don't teach their children the difference between right and wrong properly.
2 the police are at fault. They are not interested in small crimes like burglary and pickpocketing.
3 it's terrible. Most crimes are committed by young people, teenagers who should be in school. I can't understand it, we didn't do things like that.
4 I blame unemployment. People today don't see any future. A lot of people have no job, no money and so they turn to crime.
5 people watch too much television. They see all this violence and crime and they copy what they see on television.

c **Do you agree or disagree with any of these opinions?**

8 Things we say *Using expressions*

a **Complete the sentences in column A with the correct expressions in column B.**

A	B
I'm working 16 hours a day at the moment,	I'm just killing time.
I've got nothing to do now,	I could kill him.
My brother has taken my socks again,	my feet are killing me.
I'm really hungry,	my new job is murder, believe me.
Ooh! These new shoes,	I could murder a plate of steak and chips.

b **Match the cartoons with two of the expressions.**

A

B

Pronunciation File

Intonation

a Listen to this sentence and look at the arrows on the syllables where the voice rises.

She looked more dignified, better-dressed and more intelligent than the others.

When we give lists of things, the voice usually rises at each item on the list until we get to the end. Listen again to the sentence and repeat it.

b Say the sentences aloud. Mark the intonation as in part A.

There are so many crimes today: murder, robbery, kidnapping, all sorts of things.

Would you tell the police, speak to your friend, tell everyone else, or what?

I'm afraid my brother is better-off, better-educated, better-dressed and more intelligent than I am.

c Now read the sentences and mark the syllables where you think there is a schwa sound. Listen and repeat the sentences with the correct stress and intonation.

© SANTILLANA

Vocabulary File

1 Vocabulary of police and crime

a Look at the article in exercise 5 and write more words and phrases in the columns.

crime and criminals	the police and the law
shot dead	autopsy
heroin dealer	judge

b Look at the newspaper extracts in exercise 6 and find vocabulary about crime and criminals. Write the vocabulary in these columns. Use your dictionary if necessary.

crime	criminal	action
kidnap	kidnapper	kidnap
burglary	burglar	burgle

c Complete the sentences. Use the words below.

kidnappers	investigating	murders
shoplifting	prison	shot
dealer	forgery	pickpockets

1 The man convicted of murder was sentenced to 20 years in ______.
2 The ______ demanded £250,000 ransom for her release.
3 He was a drug ______ who sold cocaine, crack and heroine.
4 The Mafia are responsible for hundreds of ______ in Sicily.
5 When you walk through the town centre, keep an eye on your handbag – there are a lot of ______ about these days.
6 I'm sorry I can't accept this £10 note. I'm afraid it's a ______.
7 Police are ______ the death of a 35 year-old man who was ______ by gunmen last night.
8 Some large department stores lose thousands of pounds every year because of ______.

2 Compound adjectives with *well-* and *better-*

a Look at these two examples from the text in exercise 5.

She looked more dignified, better-dressed … more intelligent.

It was true, her family were well-off.

Well- can combine with many words to make a compound adjective. These are some common examples.

well-	off	well-	made
	dressed		designed
	paid		mannered
	informed		educated

b When we make comparisons with these adjectives, *well-* changes to *better-*.

EXAMPLE:

She looked dignified, well-dressed and intelligent.

She looked more dignified, better-dressed and more intelligent than the typical Mafia widow.

Rewrite these sentences with *better-* so that they have a similar meaning.

EXAMPLE:

My brother has quite a lot of money, but I don't have so much.

My brother is better-off than I am.

1 My sister passed a lot of exams at school and then went to university, but I did not have such a good education.
2 He is very polite and always remembers to say please and thank you, but his brother is quite rude.
3 My boss receives a good salary, but my salary is much less than his.
4 I think Japanese watches are good quality, but I don't think these new watches from Korea are so good.
5 The secretary knows a lot about the company, but the sales manager knows very little.
6 My colleague has some very smart and fashionable clothes, but I never look very smart or fashionable.

© SANTILLANA

9 You judge *Language round-up*

a Read the biographies of these two people and the crimes each one has committed. In groups, discuss the crimes and decide on the sentence you would give if you were the judge.

Case 1

Biography: Karen Mitchell is a 19 year-old woman. She is not very well-educated and has a boyfriend who seems to have a lot of money and travels abroad a lot. She is very impressed with her boyfriend, but she knows he has been to prison twice before. Karen's boyfriend asks her to go to Turkey to bring back a suitcase he left there on his last visit. He tells her it contains important papers for his business and she can earn £5,000 for collecting the suitcase. Karen thinks it is a little strange that her boyfriend asks her to go, but she goes without asking questions. She does not want to ask too many questions because she wants the money.

Crime: Drug smuggling – she smuggled £½million worth of heroine from Turkey in a suitcase. She was caught at Heathrow Airport, London, as she returned, but she said she did not know what was in the suitcase.

Case 2

Biography: Mrs Theresa Arlott has five children. She is unemployed and her husband left her three years ago. He is much better-off than she is, but he does not give much money to her for the upbringing of her children. Mrs Arlott would like to go on holiday with her children but she has no money. She spends all her money on food and clothes for the family. Last week she committed a crime.

Crime: Shoplifting – she stole £100 worth of food and clothes from a supermarket.

Sentences:

no sentence, but a warning not to do it again

a fine of £_____

_____ years community service

_____ years in prison

b Write down the advice would you give to both these people so that they can stay away from the police and the courts in future.
If I were … , I would/wouldn't …

c Work in groups.
Make a list of ten crimes and give each crime a number from 1–10 (number 1 is the most serious crime and number 10 is the least serious). Say why you think a particular crime is more serious than another. Remember to use some of the phrases in exercise 7 when you give your opinion.

EXAMPLE:
In my view, …
As far as I'm concerned, …

Learning Tips

Lexical sets

1 Word spiders

a Add as many words or phrases as you can to these word spiders, without looking back at the unit.

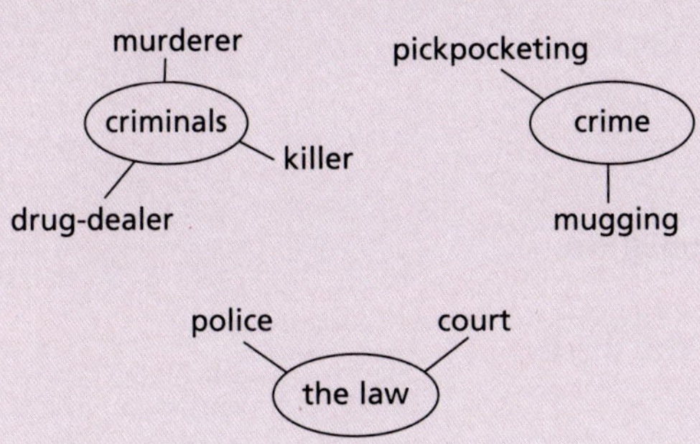

b Now look back through the unit and add any more vocabulary you can find.

c Whenever you learn a new vocabulary set, make a word spider to test how much vocabulary you can remember. Then check to see if you can add any more words.

2 Example sentences

Say or write your own sentences to help you remember new words and phrases.

EXAMPLE:
The judge investigated a lot of Mafia crimes.
The kidnappers demanded £200,000 ransom for the release of his daughter.

© SANTILLANA

Living with Animals

1 The story of the 'Gingerbread Boy'

a **The sentences below are missing from the story of the 'Gingerbread Boy'. Listen and number the sentences in the order that they should appear in the story.**

'I have run away from a little old woman, a little old man, a cow, a horse and a flock of birds. And I can run away from you, I can.'

'Run, run, as fast as you can! You can't catch me, I'm the Gingerbread Man!'

Oh dear! I'm afraid the water is getting deeper. Jump on my nose and I can hold you out of the water.'

After that the Gingerbread Boy never said anything more at all.

And he had a cap made of orange sugar.

'Please stop, little Gingerbread Boy,' said the horse, 'You look very good to eat.'

And the cow couldn't catch him.

Out jumped the Gingerbread Boy and away he ran, out of the door and into the street.

b **Listen to these sentences from the story and notice the pronunciation of the words *can* and *can't*.**

'And I can run away from you, I can. You can't catch me I'm the Gingerbread Man.'

Notice how *can* is pronounced in the middle of sentences and at the end of a sentence.

Repeat the two sentences with the correct pronunciation of the words *can* and *can't*.

c **Re-tell the story in groups.**

© SANTILLANA

2 Fighting for life in the Antarctic

a Read the text about emperor penguins in the Antarctic. Put the phrases 1-6 into the correct place in the text.

1 that humans would be totally unable to survive, no matter what clothes they were wearing.
2 It is necessary to complete this exchange in about 10 seconds,
3 has to recognise its mate by its particular song.
4 by which time the chick should be too large for the pouch.
5 could never survive the freezing winter temperatures in the southern Antarctic.
6 it is possible for penguins to increase their body temperature by 50 per cent.

Life in the freezer

Bringing up young emperor penguins is one of the greatest acts of survival in the natural world. In early April, when the sea ice is starting to form again and most of the Antarctic's life is escaping north, the emperor penguins head south. Emperor penguins have a truly remarkable lifestyle. Most other animals [A] ...

Mating is a noisy business as male and female penguins sing loudly to each other. This is a very important process because each bird [B] ... . Emperor penguins do not have individual territories.

The female lays a single egg in early May and immediately passes it to her mate. The male emperor penguin does not make a nest, but keeps the egg in a pouch (a small pocket) just above his feet. The temperature inside the pouch may be 80 degrees centigrade higher than the temperature outside. The egg must not freeze solid in the depths of winter. As soon as the male has the egg, the female has to leave to spend the next 65 days at sea in search of food. The male must incubate the egg alone, spending much of his time in total darkness and in winds of up to 300 kilometres an hour. Temperatures may drop to minus 60 degrees centigrade, so cold [C]... . In addition, the male has to spend 115 days without food and may lose as much as 200 grams a day in body weight.

Male emperor penguins can only survive through the winter if they huddle together for warmth. Thousands of penguins squeeze together in a large group and any bird who does not join in the group is sure to die. In such groups, [D]... . All the birds cooperate together by taking it in turns to stand in the coldest position. The group is constantly shifting as each bird stands on the cold, and then the warm side of the group. Huddled like this in silence, penguins have to spend days in total darkness with temperatures cold enough to crack the teeth.

In mid-July, just as the eggs are hatching, the females return. They have to walk up to 100 kilometres over the ice in permanent darkness. On arrival at the colony, each female sings at the top of her voice to find her mate in the gloom. Once the pair are reunited, the female feeds the chick while it is still in the male's pouch. The male then passes the chick to the female. [E]... or the chick will die. Now the males make their long journey north to the open sea. Many of them are dangerously thin by now. If the males keep going, round the clock, for two days they will be able to reach their destination and find food. Meanwhile, the mother keeps the chick in her pouch and feeds it for about three weeks. Her mate returns and takes over again. This process continues for about two months [F]... . At this stage the chick looks like a perfect, soft, cuddly toy. Unfortunately, usually only about 19 per cent of emperor penguin chicks survive to adulthood.

b Mark the statements True or False.

1 Emperor penguins are very unusual animals.
2 They are always silent.
3 Emperor penguins build their nests in May.
4 The male penguins are not involved in hatching the egg.
5 Humans could not live in the southern Antarctic in winter.
6 Penguins are very cooperative birds.
7 A female penguin can find her mate by the colour of his feathers.
8 It is very difficult to raise a penguin chick.

c Find words and phrases in the text to match the meaning of these phrases.

1 very unusual (line 5)
2 looking for (line 15)
3 as well as this (line 18)
4 stay very close to each other (line 21)
5 press against each other (line 21)
6 will certainly (line 22)
7 moving all the time (line 24)
8 very loudly (line 30)
9 every hour of the day and night (line 35)
10 takes back the responsibility (line 38)

© SANTILLANA

3 Humans and animals

a How are humans superior to animals? Make a list of three examples. Compare your list with your partner's.

b Listen to the first part of this interview about human and animal behaviour. Note down any examples you hear of:

1 animals having superior abilities to humans
2 animals behaving in a better way than humans

c In the sentences below, the second part of each sentence is missing. Write down what you think the second part should be. Listen to the second part of the interview and check if you guessed correctly. You do not need to write down the exact words you hear on the tape.

In the past	we were able to catch or grow our own food, we could travel for days on foot, we had to build our own houses, we had the ability to entertain ourselves, we had to respect nature, we didn't have to use and understand so much information,	whereas now … however, now … Now, on the other hand …

Pronunciation File

Final consonants

a Listen to these two sentences.

I can type. She can't type.

What is the pronunciation of the words *can* and *can't* in these sentences?

We do not hear the final *t* on the word *can't* because the next word begins with *t*. We can hear the difference between *can* and *can't* by the short and long vowel sound.

Listen to these sentences and put a tick (✓) if you hear the word *can* and a cross (✗) if you hear the word *can't*.

1 He … dance very well.
2 I … swim quite fast.
3 She … hear us.
4 I … do it.
5 He … type very fast.
6 They … help us.
7 We … tell you.
8 You … take it upstairs.

Practise saying the sentences with a schwa sound /ə/ for *can* and a long a sound /ɑ:/ for *can't*.

b The letters *d* and *t* at the end of a word are often not pronounced when the next word begins with a consonant. Listen to these sentences and cross out the *d* and *t* letters which are not pronounced. The first one has been done for you.

1 The ol~~d~~ lady wen~~t~~ home.
2 Desmond Mooney doesn't live here, he must live next door.
3 I learned to read when I was five.
4 He told me to go there, but I couldn't find my way back.
5 That old shirt must belong to Simon.
6 She said David might bring some sandwiches.

© SANTILLANA

4 It's a fact *Talking about ability and necessity*

A

B

C

D

a Read the descriptions and name the animals in the pictures.

The giant anteater has no teeth. It is able to destroy ant hills with its long claws, then poke its tongue, 60cm long, into the nest. With one lick the anteater can pick up 500 ants.

Bright colours on an animal often indicates that the animal tastes foul or is poisonous. The fugu fish, an extremely brightly coloured and poisonous fish, is a delicacy in Japan. This means that an expert chef has to remove the poisonous part before cooking. Even so, about 80 people die each year from fugu poisoning.

Oysters have the unusual ability to change sex. An oyster starts life as a male and gradually becomes female. After laying her eggs the female becomes male again. Oysters can change sex several times in one year.

Reptiles are cold-blooded which means they have to keep their body temperatures at about 30°C. It is necessary for warm-blooded animals, like ourselves, to eat frequently, whereas some snakes don't have to eat at all for several months. The tuatara, a New Zealand reptile, has a body temperature of only 12°C. This means that it must move very slowly. When moving it breathes about once every seven seconds. However, when it is still it only has to breathe about once an hour.

b Read the texts again and find examples of ability and necessity.

EXAMPLE:

It is able to destroy ant hills with its long claws.

An expert chef has to remove the poisonous part before cooking.

© SANTILLANA

Grammar File

1 Ability

a There are several ways to express ability. The most common ways are *can/could* and *be able to*. (See the Grammar Reference on page 145 for the different meanings of *can*.)

b There are only two forms of the verb *can*: *can* and *could*.
For ability, *can* = *am/is/are able to*
could = *was/were able to*

EXAMPLE:

Cheetahs	*can* *are able to*	*run at a speed of* *100 kilometres an hour.*
We	*couldn't* *weren't able to*	*translate the poem.*

For other verb tenses we change the tense of the verb *to be*.

EXAMPLE:

If you practise every day, you'll soon be able to play the guitar.
If he spoke with a strong American accent, we wouldn't be able to understand him.
I've been able to ski since I was a child.
I used to be able to read without glasses, but now I can't.

c Use *can* or *could* where possible in these sentences. Where it is not possible, use *be able to* with the correct tense of the verb *to be*.

1 I'm afraid I ______ (not) speak Italian.
2 I ______ (not) walk since I broke my leg skiing.
3 When I was younger, I ______ swim much faster than I can now.
4 You're doing very well. I think you ______ type 40 words a minute by next month.
5 He ______ run much further if he got some good running shoes.
6 I ______ do this exercise, but I ______ (not) do the one we had last week.
7 How long ______ you ______ read and write Chinese?
8 I'm afraid you ______ (not) hear properly for a few days. You have a very bad ear infection.
9 I ______ stand on my hands, but I can't do it now.
10 ______ you play any musical instrument?
11 I ______ (never) understand why people like opera.

2 Necessity

a The two most common ways to express necessity are *must* and *have to*. (See Grammar Reference on page 145 for the difference in use between *must* and *have to*.)

EXAMPLE:

Emperor penguins	*must* *have to*	*keep the egg warm* *throughout winter.*

b The verb *must* only has one form. When talking about necessity in other tenses we use the verb *have to*.

EXAMPLE:

Centuries ago we had to build our own houses and catch our own food.
We'll have to learn to live with nature if we want to preserve our environment.
I've had to learn a lot of new vocabulary since I joined the English class.
If there were a later train, we wouldn't have to leave so early.

c Look back at the reading texts in exercise 2 and exercise 4. Find examples of sentences, or parts of sentences, which express necessity. Write them down and underline the verbs expressing necessity.

3 Negatives of *must* and *have to*

a Look at these examples.

1 The egg must not freeze solid in the depths of winter.
2 Some snakes don't have to eat at all for several months.

Must not and *do/does/did not have to* have different meanings. In sentences 1 and 2 above, which one means:
it is not necessary or important?
it is very important that this does not happen?

b Write *must not* or *do/does/did not have to* in these sentences.

1 Students ______ smoke in the classroom.
2 Reptiles ______ get too hot or they will die.
3 You can give me your homework next week. You ______ finish it today.
4 In the past, we ______ learn so much information as we do today.
5 You ______ eat the poisonous part of a fugu fish.
6 Many insects ______ eat for several weeks because they can store food for a long time in their bodies.

© SANTILLANA

5 Are we like animals? *Expressions with animals*

a Complete these sayings with the correct animal. Check your answers with a partner.

As	quiet	as a/an	bat
	strong		mouse
	blind		mule
	stubborn		ox

b Look at the pictures and complete the sentences below using the correct animal.

monkey bee sheep bull fly

1 She is a real busy-______, always doing something, never relaxing.
2 He is not at all diplomatic. He's like a ______ in a china shop.
3 I wish I could be a ______ on the wall for that conversation. I'd love to know what they are saying.
4 They followed the leader like a lot of ______.
5 My daughter is a little ______ sometimes – she can be so naughty.

Are any of these expressions the same in your language?

c Look at these examples. It is possible to make the words ***spider*** and ***fish*** into adjectives by adding the letter *y*.

'Look at this horrible spidery writing.'

'I'm not sure. The whole thing sounds very fishy to me!'

© SANTILLANA

6 Sweet dreams *Contrasting ideas*

a Before reading the text about dreams, look at the illustration of animals in dreams. Say what you think some of the animals could indicate in our dreams.

The 'Dream Dictionary'

Dreaming is one of our most intimate experiences. We all dream – every night – and every dream is unique. Some people say they never dream, but this is because they don't remember their dreams. When we fall asleep each night, deepest sleep comes upon us almost immediately. This is followed by a shorter period of lighter sleep in which our eyeballs move around under our closed eyelids. This period of Rapid Eye Movement – or REM – is when we dream. It happens about five times in an eight hour period. We usually wake up after the last one and so this is the dream we remember best. On average we sleep for a third of each day; by the time we are 75 we have slept for about 25 years – and dreamt for ten of them. That's a lot of dreaming! Every human emotion and experience can be reflected in our dreams: they mirror our deepest desires, hopes, fears and fantasies. That is why our dreams are so important.

By using this 'Dream Dictionary' you will be able to interpret your dreams – and understand your inner self – more completely. Sweet dreams!

6

Animals

An **alligator** is a sign you're surrounded by enemies. If you see several of them, you should take care if you are thinking of starting up a new business – it's probably risky.

Bats flying around in daylight are a symbol of peace and quiet, whereas if you see one at night it means a problem is just around the corner – and it's either a family or a financial one.

Cats are generally not a good omen. They spell deceit and are often a sign that your partner is being unfaithful. A black cat is a sign of illness to come. However, if you chase one away, you may get a surprise stroke of good luck.

Dogs symbolise friendship. A friendly dog means happy times ahead in good company. A snarling dog means don't trust one of your friends. If the dog actually bites, then a so-called friend is up to some trickery which could harm you.

Elephants show you are in good health. You are also about to meet someone who will influence your career.

A long-necked **giraffe** is a sign to stop meddling in other people's affairs.

A **horse** is a good sign as long as it isn't black. A black horse predicts sadness. On the other hand, riding a horse indicates happiness through independence.

Pigs are good news for the family, but bad for business. The fatter the pig, the better at home and the worse at work.

7

© SANTILLANA

b **Find phrases in the text which have a similar meaning to the phrases below.**

EXAMPLE:

1 in general (line 16)
2 show our secret wishes (line 23)
3 it will be possible for you to understand (line 26)
4 it may not be very secure (line 33)
5 is waiting for you in the very near future (line 36)
6 a sign of good luck (line 38)
7 signify dishonesty (line 39)
8 a person who says s/he is a friend, but is not really a true friend (line 46)
9 change your job prospects in some way (line 50)
10 putting your nose into things which are not your business (line 51)
11 that is, if it is not (line 53)
12 but the other side of this is (line 54)

c **Work in groups.**

Write down one or two dreams which members of the group have had. You can make up a dream if you prefer. Write each dream on a separate piece of paper and give the paper to another group. See if the second group can interpret your group's dreams.

Say which is the most interesting dream you hear about.

Vocabulary File

1 Words for contrast

a Look at these examples.

1 Bats in daylight are a symbol of peace and quiet, whereas if you see one at night, …
2 A black horse predicts sadness. On the other hand, riding a horse indicates …
3 A black cat is a sign of illness to come. However, if you chase one away, you may get …

Whereas, however and *on the other hand* all indicate that the second part of the sentence is going to contrast with the first. Choose the correct ending for sentences 1, 2 and 3. Write out the complete sentences.

a a surprise stroke of good luck.
b it means a problem is just around the corner.
c happiness through independence.

Underline the phrases in each part of the sentence which contrast with each other. Now check with the text in exercise 6 to see if you were correct.

b Use the words/phrases *whereas, however* and *on the other hand* to write sentences which contrast:

1 human and animal behaviour
2 human behaviour now and a few hundred years ago
3 two different animals

2 Time phrases

Look through the reading text in exercise 7. Find the time phrases used in this text and put them into three columns.

point in time	duration	frequency
almost immediately	for a third of each day	every night

Look through the reading text in exercise 2 and add more phrases to the first two columns.

3 Contrasting nouns and adjectives

a Look at the text in exercise 6. Find the words which describe good things and bad things in life. Draw four columns and copy these headings.

good		bad	
noun	adjective	noun	adjective

Write the words in the correct column. Write both forms of each word where possible. Use a dictionary if necessary.

b Look back at other units to find more words.

© SANTILLANA

Pronunciation File

Rhythm

a Some phrases in the sentence are said very quickly in English, especially common phrases. Listen to the rhythm in these sentences.

Humans would be totally unable to survive, no matter what clothes they were wearing.

A horse is a good sign, as long as it isn't black.

As far as I'm concerned, it's a load of rubbish.

Let's say I believe in it to some extent. I think it's all very interesting, but I don't take it too seriously.

You will only be able to say the phrases quickly if you use the correct weak and strong stress. Mark 1 the stressed syllables and 2 the syllables pronounced with a schwa sound.

b Now listen again and notice any linking sounds between the syllables. Mark the words which sound joined together. Say the sentences with the correct rhythm, stress and linking sounds.

Learning Tips

Keeping records

1 Linking phrases

You will see many phrases which link two parts of the sentence together. Make a note of these phrases because they are very useful.

EXAMPLE:

Humans would be totally unable to survive, no matter what clothes they were wearing.

A horse is a good sign as long as it isn't black.

Write your own sentences using these useful linking phrases.

EXAMPLE:

She told me a lie and now I never believe her, no matter what she says.

I love ice-cream as long as it isn't banana flavoured.

Look through this unit and pick out useful linking phrases. Write your own sentences using the phrases. Look back at other units to find more phrases.

2 Grammar references

Look at these examples from the *Cobuild English Grammar*.

When you revise grammar, try to put the grammar into categories.

EXAMPLE:

talking about the past, the present, the future
talking about ability and possibility
talking about necessity and importance
making comparisons

Indicating ability

4.119 'Can' is used to say that someone has a particular skill or ability.

You can all read and write.
Some people can ski better than others.
He cannot dance.
...the girl who can't act.

'Could' is used to say that someone had a skill or ability in the past.

...the good old days when everyone could read, write and do arithmetic.
I could barely walk.
He could kick penalty goals from anywhere.

Indicating importance

4.215 Modals can be used in declarative sentences to say that it is important that something is done. Different modals indicate different degrees of importance.

4.216 'Must' is used in three common ways to talk about the importance of doing something.

You use 'must' with 'you' or 'we' to urge someone to do something, because you feel it is important. 'Must not' is used to urge someone not to do something.

You must come at once.
We must accept the truth about ourselves.
You must not worry.
You mustn't let her suffer for it.

You use 'must' to say that something is required by a rule or law.

People who qualify must apply within six months.
European Community standards must be met.

You use 'must' to say that it is necessary that something happens or is done, in order that something else can happen.

Meadows must have rain.
To identify a poison you must be able either to carry out a chemical analysis or observe the poison at work on the victim.

'Have to', 'have got to', and 'need to' can be used instead of 'must' to talk about the importance of doing something. This is explained in paragraphs 4.248 and 4.249.

© SANTILLANA

7 One mouse – two mice!

a Read the text and work out the two meanings of the word *mouse*.

b Write down any vocabulary you do not know. Guess the meaning of the unknown words. Do not look up any words in a dictionary before guessing the meaning.

Random access mouse

Computer technician, Errol Ingleton, is used to fixing 'mouse' problems on company computers. But last week he found a very unusual computer mouse.

He first noticed small drops of brown liquid on his desk beside the computer. He cleaned them up, but each day he would find more. Then he began to notice a few white hairs and tiny shreds of paper as well. Errol was baffled, so he decided to open up the computer and investigate inside. He discovered a collection of carpet fibres and shredded paper – a perfect nest for a real mouse! The mouse had got inside through a hole in the back of the computer and built its nest right in the centre. The warmth inside made it an ideal place for a mouse nest. 'Remarkably, the machine still worked perfectly,' says Ingleton.

8 Talking about beliefs *Expressing opinions*

a Listen to these people talking about interpreting dreams. Number the phrases in the order you hear them.

Let's say I believe in it to some extent …
As far as I'm concerned, it's a load of rubbish …
Well, yes and no. I mean I do and I don't …
Yes. I definitely believe in it …
I haven't got time for all that nonsense …

b Now listen again and complete the phrases above. Summarise what people say.

c Which opinion is closest to yours?

d Use the expressions in part A to say what you think about:

superstitions
(e.g. opening an umbrella in the house)

telling the future
(e.g. with tarot cards or horoscopes)

alternative medicine
(e.g. aromatherapy, homeopathy)

personal therapy
(e.g. managing stress, assertiveness training)

9 Test yourself *Language round-up*

Now test yourself. See how many different ways you know of talking about the past, the future, the present, necessity, etc. Working in groups, choose one topic each and write example sentences for your topic.

EXAMPLE:
Talking about the past:
Where did you go for your holidays last year?
One day I was watching TV when I heard a strange noise.
I used to live in Rome, but now I live in Milan.

© SANTILLANA

1 Rules and regulations

a Draw up a list of rules and regulations for either:

1 employees in a company
2 students at a school or university.

Then imagine you were living 50 years ago. Write up a set of rules and regulations for the company, school or university as they might have existed 50 years ago.

EXAMPLE:

50 years ago	now
All pupils must wear school uniform.	Pupils don't have to wear a uniform.

b Write five comparisons between 50 years ago and now.

EXAMPLE:

Fifty years ago all pupils had to wear a uniform, whereas now they can wear casual clothes.

2 Giving advice

Write down the advice you would give in these situations. Begin each sentence like this:

If I were you I'd .../I wouldn't ...

1 Your friend tells you that he is sure his girlfriend has been seeing someone else quite regularly, but he hasn't told his girlfriend what he suspects.
2 Your sister, aged 18, wants to leave home and go and live in a flat with her boyfriend. She hasn't told your parents what she plans to do yet.
3 A friend has applied for 30 jobs so far. He hasn't had a single interview yet. He wonders if he is writing his letter of application properly.
4 Your nephew, aged 10, seems very anxious about going to school. Sometimes he pretends to be sick so that he doesn't have to go to school. His mother asks you for some advice.

3 Powerful words – *have*

a Look at these examples.

I have breakfast at eight o'clock every morning.

She was having breakfast when she heard the news.

In these examples, it is possible to use the verb *have* in both the present simple and continuous tense. Read the Grammar Reference on page 145 for when it is not possible to use the verb *have* in the continuous tense.

b Look up the meaning of any expressions with *have* in the list below which you do not know. Write 12 sentences using each of the phrases.

to have	a bath/a shower/a wash
	a shave
	a meal
	dinner/lunch/breakfast*
	a good time
	a party
	an exam
	a conversation
	a holiday/a rest/a break
	an affair with someone
	a heart attack
	a nervous breakdown

*(N.B. no article)

© SANTILLANA

4 Dictionary work

a Antonyms are words which have the opposite meaning of other words.

EXAMPLE:
strong/weak

These words have more than one meaning. Use your dictionary to find the different meanings and then find the antonyms.

EXAMPLE:

1 hard *soft/difficult*
2 light ——/——
3 fresh ——/——
4 single ——/——
5 dull ——/——
6 rich ——/——
7 cold ——/——
8 tight ——/——

b **Complete these sentences with five antonyms from part A.**

1 Who left the bread out? It's gone _____.
2 A _____ ticket is usually much cheaper than two single tickets.
3 She seemed pleased to see me and gave me a very _____ smile.
4 I don't like this wine. I tastes too _____ for me.
5 This suitcase is _____. What have you got in it?

c **Write three sentences with the antonyms from part A that you did not use in the sentences in part B.**

5 Transformation

Rewrite these sentences without changing the meaning. Use the word or phrase in brackets.

1 My advice is not to get involved with people who deal in drugs. (if I were)
2 The reason he fails all his exams is because he doesn't work hard. (if)
3 Don't tell him anything. He can never keep a secret. (nothing)
4 Not a single person saw the pickpocket. (no)
5 In my opinion, murderers should be put in prison for life. (concerned)
6 He behaves very well, but his younger sister is quite badly-behaved. (better)
7 I couldn't swim until I was 16. (able)
8 It is not necessary for students to wear a uniform. (have)
9 It is important that you do not touch this switch. (must)
10 A black cat can be a sign of good luck. However, if it crosses your path, it means danger. (other hand)

6 Project

a **Interview other students, friends and members of your families to find out what they think are the most frequent crimes in your town/city. In groups, discuss your answers and write a list of the five most frequent crimes in your town/city.**

b **In groups, discuss how these crimes could be prevented. Write a report on your decisions.**

EXAMPLE:
Car theft is the most frequent crime in ... . I think that if all cars had car alarms and better locks there would be less car theft.

c **Work in groups.**
Collect four or five crime stories from newspapers or magazines. Prepare a summary of the crime stories and tell other people in your group about the crimes and the criminals. Do not tell them the judge's sentence. Other members of the group listen to the summary and decide the sentence. How similar is it to the actual sentence?

© SANTILLANA

Strange Stories

1 Bad timing

a This is an American short story called *Nightmare in Yellow* by Fredric Brown. Read the story and decide what you think the ending is.

Nightmare in Yellow

He awoke when the alarm clock rang, but lay in bed awhile going over the plans he'd made. Every little detail had been worked out, but this was the final check. Tonight at forty-six minutes after eight he'd be free, in every way. He'd picked that moment because this was his fortieth birthday and that was the exact time of the evening when he had been born. It had struck his sense of humour to have his new life begin at forty, to the minute.

As a lawyer who specialized in handling wills, a lot of money passed through his hands – and some of it had passed into them. He had carefully sold a lot of property, and by this afternoon he'd have well over a hundred thousand dollars, enough to last him the rest of his life. And they'd never catch him. He'd planned every detail of his trip, his destination, his new identity, and it was foolproof. He'd planned it for months. His decision to kill his wife had been an afterthought. The motive was simple: he hated her.

He'd hardly been able to keep from laughing at the birthday present she'd given him; it had been a new suitcase. She'd also talked him into celebrating his birthday by having dinner at seven. Little did she guess how the celebration would go after that. He planned to get her home by eight forty-six and make himself a widower at that exact moment. There was a practical advantage, too, in leaving her dead. If he left her alive but asleep, she'd guess what had happened and call the police when she found him gone in the morning. If he left her dead, her body would not be found for two or three days, and he'd have a much better start.

Things went smoothly at the office; by the time he went to meet his wife everything was ready. But she dawdled over drinks and dinner and he began to worry whether he could get her home by eight forty-six. It was ridiculous, he knew, but it had become important that his moment of freedom should come then and not a minute earlier or a minute later. He watched his watch.

He would have missed it by half a minute if he'd waited till they were inside the house. The dark of the porch of their house was perfectly safe, as safe as inside. He swung the cosh viciously once, as she stood at the front door, waiting for him to open it. He caught her before she fell and managed to hold her upright with one arm while he got the door open and then got it closed from the inside.

Then he flicked the switch and yellow light filled the room. …

b What do you think the end of this story is? Look on page 159 to find the answer.

c These sentences summarise some of the events in the story. Put them into the order each event happened. Be careful, this may be different to the order they appear in the story.

1 He sold other people's property and kept some of the money.
2 He went out for a birthday celebration dinner with his wife.
3 His wife invited some of their friends round for a surprise party.
4 He planned to kill his wife.
5 He planned to run away with the money he made on selling property.
6 He awoke on the morning of his birthday and went over the plans in his mind.
7 He switched on the light, holding up his wife.
8 He and his wife returned home at approximately quarter to nine.
9 He hit his wife on the head with a cosh.

d Look back at the reading text. There are 13 examples of *'d* in the text (eight of these = *had* and five = *would*). Find each example and write down if *'d* means *had* or *would*.

© SANTILLANA

2 Unsuccessful robber

a Put these pictures in the correct order. Say what you think happened.

b Listen to this true story of a robber who failed. Check you have the correct order for the pictures.

c Answer these questions and then listen again to check your answers.

1 How was the robber's face covered?
2 What was he holding when he came into the bank?
3 Why couldn't the cashier give him a lot of money?
4 Why couldn't he get out of the bank?
5 What happened to him in the end?

d Do you know any similar stories of unsuccessful crimes?

© SANTILLANA

3 Thanks to the video *Talking about past events*

a Look at this photograph. Identify the bride and groom.

b Read the short story about their wedding. Put the verbs into the past participle form and put them into the correct place in the story.

drink pay do have leave disappear arrive
play save steal invite turn

The camera never lies

A young couple were planning their wedding on very little money. Neither the bride's family nor the groom's family were well-off, but the bride's father had a little nest-egg he'd [1]_____ over the years. He very generously offered to pay for his daughter's wedding.

The big day came and everything went according to plan. By the end of the evening, everyone had [2]_____ a wonderful time. The moment had [3]_____ for the father to pay for the band, the disc jockey and all the catering services.

He had [4]_____ quite a lot of wine by this time and he took a few minutes to find his jacket. It turned out he had [5]_____ it on the back of his chair. When he finally found it, he was horrified to discover that his wallet, with all his savings, had been [6]_____. Everyone searched high and low, but it became obvious that the cash had [7]_____.

Feeling totally humiliated, he had to ask the guests to contribute some money to pay the hotel. At least he was glad that he had already [8]_____ for the video and the honeymoon.

When the married couple returned from their honeymoon, the first thing they did was to plan a showing of the video of their special day. All the in-laws were [9]_____ to see it. Everyone sat down, the lights were [10]_____ down and the video was [11]_____ for the whole family. At first there was lots of laughing and joking about the various guests, who had [12]_____ what, who had said what, how so-and-so had dressed, etc. Then came the speeches. The viewers suddenly fell silent at the bride's father's speech. There he was – caught by the camera lens – the pickpocket! The groom's father!

© SANTILLANA

c If your in-laws are your wife/husband's family, who is your brother-in-law, mother-in-law and son-in-law?

d Look at these phrases from the text.

Neither … nor (line 2)

everything went according to plan (line 10)

It turned out (line 18)

searched high and low (line 23)

so-and-so (line 40)

Rewrite the sentences using one of the phrases above.

EXAMPLE:

I thought someone had stolen my purse, but finally I realised I had left it in the library.

I thought someone had stolen my purse, but it turned out I had left it in the library.

1 The party was a big success and things happened just as I had planned them.
2 He wanted to know all the details – what this person said to that person, etc.
3 My daughter never eats meat and my son doesn't eat it either.
4 I looked everywhere for my jacket, but I couldn't find it anywhere.

4 It serves you right … *Everyday expressions*

a Match the sentences 1–7 with a suitable expression a–g.

1 I'm getting married next summer.
2 And when I looked, all my money had been stolen.
3 So he was caught and arrested by the police.
4 And we're going on our honeymoon in the morning.
5 The wedding was cancelled because his mother was so ill.
6 I'm really nervous about getting married.
7 I'm so sorry. I've spilled some wine on your jacket.

a Oh dear! I'm really sorry to hear that.
b Congratulations!
c Well, it serves him right.
d Don't worry. I'm sure everything will be fine on the day.
e Never mind. It's not worth bothering about.
f Oh no! I bet you were furious, weren't you?
g I hope you have a fantastic time. I'm sure you will.

b Now write your own sentences to match the expressions. Read your sentences to a partner who responds with a suitable expression.

Pronunciation File

/θ/, /ð/, /s/ and /z/

a There are two pronunciations of the letters *th*. They are written /θ/ and /ð/ in the phonetic alphabet. How is the *th* pronounced in these words?

thin this

Copy the two phonetic symbols and write the words *thin* and *this* under the appropriate symbol. Listen to how they are different.

Listen to the *th* sound in these words and write the words under the correct phonetic symbol.

this thing that those with fourth think both then

b Listen to the sounds /s/ and /z/ in these two words.

this those

Copy the two phonetic symbols and write the words under each symbol. Listen to these words and write them under the correct phonetic symbol.

puts teaches finds comes advice (noun) advise (verb)
lose choose boss costs

© SANTILLANA

Grammar File

1 Passive voice

a Look at this example from the story about the unsuccessful robber in exercise 2.

The manager explained that every Friday morning the cash is taken out of the bank. They only had a small amount of cash because it was Friday afternoon and most of the money had been taken away that morning.

We use the passive form when we do not know, or it is not important who does/did the action of the verb. Look at this example.

The money is taken out of the bank.

It is important that the money is taken out. It is not important who takes the money out, or we do not know who takes the money out.

b The passive is formed by using different tenses of the verb *to be* + the past participle. Look at these examples.

The money is taken out of the bank every Friday morning.	(present simple tense)
The money was taken out this morning.	(past simple tense)
My money has been stolen.	(present perfect tense)
He found that his money had been stolen.	(past perfect tense)
He is going to be caught and he should be punished.	(infinitive)

c Change these sentences from the active to the passive form.

EXAMPLE:

Someone has stolen my money.

My money has been stolen.

1 Someone has taken my purse.
2 Every weekend someone cleans our classroom.
3 When he came back, he found that someone had eaten his dinner.
4 Someone built this theatre in 1921.
5 Somebody can repair this watch for you.
6 Someone robbed the bank last night.
7 Somebody has kidnapped his daughter.
8 Somebody should tell her how rude she is.
9 Next week someone is going to give out the exam results to the students.
10 Some people made these toys in China.

d Look back at the story in exercise 3. Find four examples of the passive form.

2 Past perfect

a Look at these two examples from the story in exercise 3.

1 The bride's father had a little nest-egg he'd saved over the years.
2 By the end of the evening, everyone had had a wonderful time.

Both these sentences use the past perfect tense to show that one event had happened before another.

In sentence 1, the father had saved money before the wedding day.

In sentence 2, people had enjoyed themselves before the end of the party.

b Notice the preposition *by* in sentence 2. *By* is often used with the past perfect tense. Find another example of the past perfect tense used after *by* in the story in exercise 3.

c Read through the story in exercise 3 and find more examples of the past perfect tense. Write down five examples and underline the past perfect tense of the verb in each sentence.

d Look at the reading text in exercise 1. Write a summary of the events which had happened before his fortieth birthday.

EXAMPLE:

He had carefully sold a lot of property and had saved over one hundred thousand dollars.

Write a summary of the events which had happened on the day of his birthday, before he walked through the door and switched on the light.

EXAMPLE:

He had gone over his plans to kill his wife when he woke up.

© SANTILLANA

5 Myths from the past

a A myth is a story which has been told for hundreds of years. It may be true or untrue. Each of the paragraphs tells the story of an old myth. Each of the stories has words missing. The missing words are written at the end of each line. Put the missing words in the correct place in each line.

b Look at these words and tick (✓) the words you already know. Circle the words if you can guess the meaning and underline the words you have to look up in a dictionary. Try to guess as many words as you can before you look them up in the dictionary.

cocoon	storms	fog
silkworm	centuries	icebergs
thread	explorers	sightings
dust	edge	exaggerated
dragons	tortoise	vivid

c Do you know any famous myths from your country or another country?

Silk comes the cocoon of the silkworm. One cocoon contains about a	from
kilometre of thread. It originally came China, where it had been kept	from
a secret for hundreds of years. It is said that 140BC, a Chinese princess	in
hid some silkworm eggs her hair and took them to Turkestan. Silk was	in
brought Europe from Turkestan a few years later.	to

Off the coast of Ireland there are several huge pillars rock in the sea.	of
These volcanic rocks look large stepping stones. According to the	like
legend, the rocks were steps made a famous giant called Finn	by
McCool. They were supposed be for the Irish giants to cross the	to
water to fight the giants over Scotland.	in

The ancient Chinese believed that dragons formed rain clouds their	with
breath. It thought that the rain fell when the dragons walked over the	was
clouds and that storms came they fought each other.	when

Many centuries ago, world was believed to be flat. It was thought	the
that any explorers who travelled too far could fall the edge. Some	off
people also believed that the world was supported a giant tortoise.	by

Early sailors faced many dangers, such storms, fog and icebergs.	as
Sailors were also afraid the many stories of sea monsters. These stories	of
probably came from sightings of whales other sea creatures. Such	and
stories then exaggerated by sailors returning home and telling of their	were
great adventures. More vivid details were then added the stories by	to
writers and artists – and so the stories grew myths.	into

© SANTILLANA

6 Ghosts and spirits *Re-telling a story*

a 🖭 **You are going to hear two stories about strange experiences. Listen to the first story and answer the questions.**

1 When did the story take place?
2 What was Mrs Jackson doing at the time?
3 What did she suddenly do?
4 Why?
5 What was the driving instructor's response?
6 By the time Mrs Jackson stopped the car, what had happened to the strange woman?
7 How had she been dressed?
8 What was the explanation thought to be?

b 🖭 **Listen to the second story and complete the notes.**

In 1_____, Mr P.J. Chase was 2_____. He was 3_____ when he noticed 4_____. One of the cottages had 5_____.

When he mentioned this to 6_____, he was certain that 7_____.

When Mr Chase went back to check, 8_____. The space was occupied by 9_____, not the 10_____ he thought 11_____.

When some of the local people who 12_____ around there a long time 13_____ asked about the site, they said 14_____, but 15_____ demolished several years ago.

c 🖭 **Listen to the two stories again. Re-tell one of the stories in your own words. Use the questions or the notes to help you remember the details.**

d **Do you know any similar stories about strange experiences? Write a short summary of your story.**

Pronunciation File

Linking sounds /w/ and /j/

a 🖭 This paragraph from exercise 7 has been marked to show how the words are pronounced together when read aloud. Notice the /w/ and /j/ sounds which help join the words together. Listen to the paragraph being read aloud and notice how the words are linked together.

The Great Pyramid at Giza, just outside Cairo, /w/ Egypt, has been discussed and investigated more than any /j/ other monument on earth. It was one of the seven wonders of the /j/ ancient world and is the /j/ only one to survive to this day. It was the largest monument that had ever been built before this century.

b How is the word *the* pronounced when it comes before a vowel sound?

c Practise reading the paragraph aloud, linking the words together. Practise linking words with other texts in the book.

© SANTILLANA

7 Wonders of the ancient world

a What do you know about the pyramids of Egypt? Do you know when, how and why they were built? Read the text to find out.

The Pyramid of Giza

The Great Pyramid at Giza, just outside Cairo, Egypt, has been discussed and investigated more than any other monument on earth. It was one of the seven wonders of the ancient world and is the only one to survive to this day. It was the largest monument that had ever been built before this century.

One fact is clear, the Great Pyramid is huge. It is equivalent to seven blocks in midtown Manhattan. It was originally made from more than two and a half million blocks of stone. The structure contains more stone than all the cathedrals and churches that have been built in the whole of England since the time of Christ.

It is believed that the Great Pyramid was built as a tomb for the Egyptian Pharaoh Khufu who ruled Egypt from about 2592 BC to 2569 BC. The Great Pyramid was not the first pyramid to be built and it is not the only one left in Egypt. There are two more pyramids beside the Great Pyramid and there are one or two more a few kilometres away. But it has become the most famous and most talked about pyramid in the world.

Building a pyramid, particularly with only the simple tools available to the Egyptians at that time, was an enormous task. The truth is, we are still not sure exactly how they managed to do it. We do not know how the heavy stone blocks were carried. One single block of stone is so heavy it could not possibly be carried by men. We do not know how the construction was planned. For example, to calculate the correct angles for constructing such a huge pyramid needs a detailed knowledge of geometry. Most historians think that this knowledge of geometry was not known to the world until much later.

Another astonishing fact is that one of the sides of the Great Pyramid runs exactly north to south. The measurement is so perfect that it could not have been an accident. But, as far as we know, the ancient Egyptians did not possess compasses and did not know the exact line of true north. Such information only became available several centuries later.

Many people believe that the Pyramid at Giza is still one of the world's greatest mysteries.

b Read the text again and write down all the time phrases used.

EXAMPLE:
until today, before this century

Then find as many phrases of place as you can.

EXAMPLE:
at Giza, just outside Cairo

Compare your list with another person. If s/he has any more, add them to your list.

c Prepare notes about another famous monument in your country or in another country. Write a short paragraph describing the monument, then read the description to the rest of the class but do not say the name of the monument. Use some phrases of time and place. Members of the class try to guess which monument it is.

© SANTILLANA

Vocabulary File

1 Prepositions with verbs and adjectives

a Match each verb or adjective with the correct preposition. You can use two different prepositions with some of the verbs/adjectives, depending on the meaning.

in at of to by for from with about

EXAMPLE:

What do you think <u>*of*</u> *the new shopping precinct? (What's your opinion?)*

What do you think <u>*about*</u> *while you are jogging? (What thoughts are in your mind?)*

verbs	adjectives
believe ______	bored ______
think ______	afraid ______
decide ______	nervous ______
arrive ______	dressed ______
(be) made ______	different ______
apologise ______	similar ______
listen ______	
look ______	
(dis)agree ______	

b Write ten sentences using some of these verbs/adjectives + prepositions.

EXAMPLE:

I decided to arrive late this morning.
I apologised for arriving late this morning.

c Can you add any more verbs and adjectives and their prepositions to the list?

2 General opinions, ideas and beliefs

a Look at these examples from exercise 5.

It is said that …
According to …
(people) believed that …
… were supposed to be …
It was thought that …
… was believed to be …

All these phrases express people's ideas, beliefs or opinions. The verb tenses change, depending on the time referred to.

EXAMPLE:

According to my friend Claudia, Rome is the most beautiful city in Europe.
For many years it has been thought that there can be no life on the planet Mercury.
In the time of the ancient Romans, there were believed to be hundreds of gods.

b Write six sentences using each of the phrases above. Describe ancient legends from your country and popular beliefs of the past or present.

3 Noun, verb and adjective word spiders

Look back at the texts in exercises 5, 6 and 7. Add as many words and phrases as you can to the word spider.

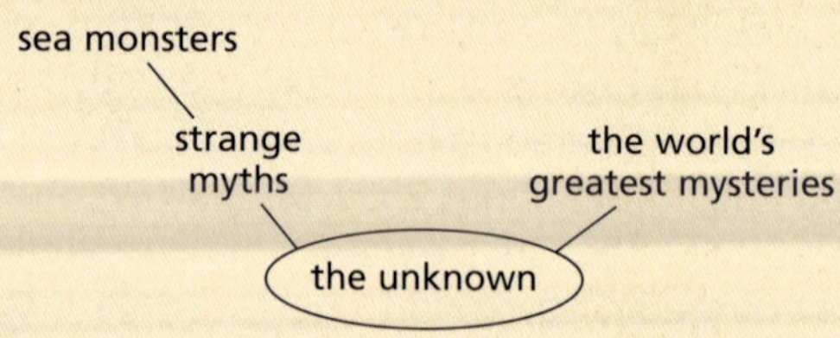

Learning Tips

Recycling

1 When you read or listen to English, try to make a note of the prepositions which are used with certain verbs and adjectives.

Write example sentences for each one to help you remember the correct preposition.

2 Look back through the written work you have done in this unit. Check you have used some of the new phrases you have learned.

EXAMPLE:

As far as I'm concerned …
We searched high and low, but …

© SANTILLANA

8 One dark night ... *Language round-up*

a In pairs, look at the picture and make up a story of what happened one dark night. Include these details in your story:

Who the person/people in the story was/were.
When the story happened.
What the person/the people was/were doing just beforehand.
What suddenly happened.
What the person/people did next.
Who was told what had happened.
What was thought to be the explanation for the story.

b First tell the story to a partner. Then write the story.

© SANTILLANA

Languages

1 Can you read Japanese?

1 人 2 大 3 川 4 山 5 木 6 森

a Maybe you can understand more Japanese than you think. Look at these Japanese symbols. Each symbol is a kind of word-picture. Try to match the symbols with these words. The first one has been done for you.

mountain	forest
river	person *1*
tree	big

b Now listen to these people guessing the meaning of each symbol. Did you guess the correct meanings?

c Listen again and complete the sentences in column A with the correct tag question in column B.

A	B
I think this is big,	doesn't it?
If that was tree, this would be forest,	isn't it?
This looks like a river,	mustn't it?
So this must be a mountain,	wouldn't it?

2 Can you guess the accent? *Listening to different accents*

a Listen and try to identify these different accents.

American	Australian
Irish	Scottish

b Now listen to people identifying each accent. Did you guess correctly? Complete the reasons each speaker gave when identifying the accents.

conversation 1	He can't be … , can he? He didn't … It must be …
conversation 2	That must be … because she said … instead of … , didn't she?
conversation 3	It can't be … because she said … . It must be … , mustn't it?
conversation 4	That must be … , mustn't it?

© SANTILLANA

3 A letter in time

a This is a story by Rudyard Kipling written in 1902. In the story Rudyard Kipling describes how Taffy, a young Neolithic girl, invented the beginnings of the alphabet. Read the story and put these three illustrations in the correct boxes in the story.

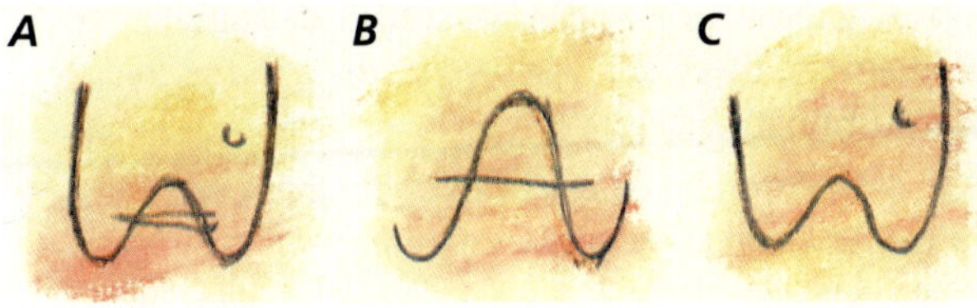

b Now match these words with the illustrations.

bone bark shark carp cave mud

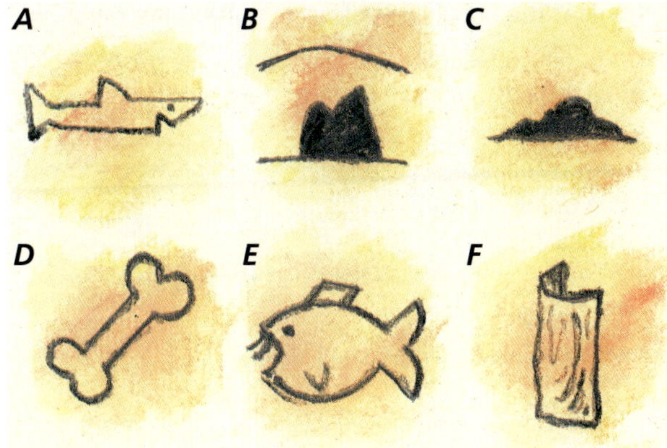

How the alphabet was made

Taffy took a bone and sat mousy-quiet for ten whole minutes, while her Daddy scratched on pieces of bark with a shark's tooth. Then she said "Daddy, I've thinked of a secret. You make a noise – any sort of noise."

"Ah!" said her Daddy, Tegumai. "Will that do?"

"Yes," said Taffy. "You look just like a carp-fish with its mouth open. Say it again, please. And keep your mouth open at the end."

"Ah! ah! ah!" said her Daddy.

"Now lend me that tooth. I'm going to draw a carp-fish's mouth wide-open."

"What for?" said her Daddy.

"Don't you see?" said Taffy, scratching on the bark. "When I draw a carp-fish with its mouth open, it will remind you of that ah-noise."

"Really?" said her Daddy, in the voice that grown-ups use when they are truly interested.

"Oh, bother!" she said. "I can't draw all of a carp-fish, but I can draw something that means a carp-fish's mouth. You know how they stand on their heads looking in the mud? Well, here's a carp fish and here's his mouth and that means *ah*."

And she drew this.

1

"That's not bad," said Tegumai, and scratched on his own piece of bark. "But you've forgotten the feeler that hangs across his mouth."

"But I can't draw, Daddy."

"You needn't draw anything except the opening of his mouth and the feeler across. Then we'll know he's a carp-fish because the other fish haven't got feelers. Look here, Taffy."

And he drew this.

2

"Now I'll copy it," said Taffy. "Will you understand this means *ah* when you see it?"

And she drew this.

3

"Perfectly," said her Daddy.

c Find words and phrases in the text with a similar meaning to the words and phrases below.

silent (line 1)
Is that OK? (line 6)
Why? (line 14)
help you remember (line 17)
adults (line 20)
really (line 20)
don't have to (line 34)

d Find one example of an incorrect verb in Taffy's speech. Is this a logical mistake? Can you think of examples of young children making similar mistakes in your language?

© SANTILLANA

Pronunciation File

Consonant clusters

a Sometimes when we join words we need to say two or three consonant sounds together. Several consonants together are called consonant clusters. Look at the consonant clusters underlined here.

Now, will you all take your things into the green room, please, and wait there for Mrs Morris. She'll be along very soon.
If anybody wants some lemonade and cookies, I've put some out in the yard.
-Thanks, Mum.
We're all fine, thanks. Is your dad keeping well?
-Yes thanks, Mrs Marsh.
Well, we'll probably all meet at the railway station at quarter to nine. If anyone misses the train, there's another in three quarters of an hour.

b Look at these consonant clusters.

ngs nr mpl

Now say the words where consonant clusters occur. (Remember, there are no vowel sounds in the middle of a consonant clusters.)

Now listen again to the extracts from the conversations and repeat the sentences.

4 Baby talk *Tag questions*

a Listen to the first part of this interview with a linguist explaining how babies learn to speak. She explains how babies often say their first word. What do you think the first word often is?

b Listen again and count the number of tag questions you hear. Can you remember which tag questions were used?

c Do you think small children learn to speak by imitating adults' speech? Listen to what the linguist says in the second part of the interview and see if you agree with her.

d Read the sentences below and listen again to what the mother says. Tick (✓) the sentences if the mother says them and put a cross (✗) if she doesn't.

1 Have you finished?
2 Put your spoon down.
3 Do you want an apple?
4 Do you want some milk?
5 What do you want?
6 What are you doing?
7 Don't do that.
8 Wipe your mouth.
9 Did you like that?
10 Don't put your apple in the water.

Write down what the mother said. Use these phrases:

She asked him if/whether ...

© SANTILLANA

5 Howlers *Making logical mistakes*

a Howlers are mistakes in language which make other people laugh or sometimes make people angry. Look at these examples. What mistakes did these speakers make?

'I would like to become* a sausage.'

*(The German verb *bekommen* = to get or to have in English.)

'I was really boring at the party.'

'Give me a coffee.'

b Work in groups.

Write down some examples of mistakes you sometimes make when speaking English. These do not have to be 'howlers', just normal mistakes. Show the group your typical mistakes and see if other people make the same mistakes. Why do you think people make these mistakes? Are they 'logical' mistakes?

© SANTILLANA

Grammar File

1 Tag questions

a Tag questions must change according to the form of the main verb. Look at these examples from exercises 1 and 2.

This looks like a river, doesn't it?
He can't be Scottish, can he?
It must be Australian, mustn't it?

When do we use 1 a negative form or 2 a positive form in a tag question?

What punctuation do we use before and after a tag question?

b Write the correct tag question at the end of each sentence. Put in the correct punctuation.

1 You've seen that film before ______
2 I think she would help if she could ______
3 Look? He must be her brother ______
4 You don't smoke ______
5 She worked here last year ______
6 You'll send us a post card ______
7 He's going to live in Turkey ______
8 She shouldn't work so hard ______

2 *Must* and *can't* for deduction

Look at this example from exercise 2.

It can't be American. It must be Australian.

Must/*can't* + infinitive are used for making deductions. *Can't* is usually used for negative deductions and *must* for positive deductions.

Use *must* or *can't* to make deductions about these situations. For some examples you can use both *must* and *can't*.

EXAMPLE:

Look at that man. He looks exactly like Ann's brother. But he told me he would be on holiday in Canada this month.

Well, it can't be her brother. It must be somebody else.

1 That group of tourists over there can only speak French. Susan is speaking to them and they're all smiling.
2 He spent £2,000 on a holiday last month and £25,000 on a new car four months ago. But he is always saying how poor he is.
3 The man who lives in the house opposite is always on his own and nobody every visits him.
4 That student always looks tired and he rushes away after every lesson.
5 I'm sure my answer is right, but everyone else has a different answer. The book has a different answer too.

3 Reported instructions

Look at these examples.

'Don't do that.'
'Wipe your mouth.'

She told him	*not to*	*do that.*
	to	*wipe his mouth.*

Write down things parents often tell young children to do or not to do. Use direct speech.

EXAMPLE:

'Sit down here.'
'Don't drop your food on the floor.'

Exchange your sentences with another pair. Change the instruction from direct to indirect speech.

EXAMPLE:

She told him to sit down there.
He told her not to drop her food on the floor.

4 Reported questions

a Look at these examples.

1 'What are you doing?'
2 'How old is her child?'
3 'Do you want an apple?'

If we report these questions we change the verb tense in the same way as reported statements. (see unit 5, page 54) When the question has no question word we use *if* or *whether*.

EXAMPLE:

1 *She asked him what he was doing.*
2 *He asked me how old her child was.*
3 *She asked him if/whether he wanted an apple.*

What do you notice about the position of the verb in reported questions? Does it come before or after the subject (e.g. *he, her child, he*) of the verb?

Look at the punctuation. How is it different to direct questions?

b Change these direct questions into reported questions.

1 'Do you want a cup of tea?'
She asked him ______.
2 'What time is it?' I asked him ______.
3 'Where have you been?' They asked me ______.
4 'Are you leaving before or after six?'
She asked him ______.
5 'What time did you finish work?'
We asked them ______.
6 'Can I help you?'
He asked her ______.
7 'Will you need the computer next week?'
John asked me ______.
8 'Have you got any brothers or sisters?'
She asked him ______.

© SANTILLANA

6 Logical spelling? *Spelling vs pronunciation*

a Look at these pairs of words. The spelling is similar but the pronunciation is different in each pair. Can you pronounce these pairs of words? Check the pronunciation in a dictionary.

woman	women
give	five
read (present tense)	read (past tense)
pour	flour
break	speak
road	broad
enough	through
patio	station
boot	door
moustache	headache

Now listen to the correct pronunciation.

b Read this short text and answer the questions below.

FOR THE PAST hundred years, American and British linguists have attempted to simplify English spellings. The Americans have been a little more successful in their attempts. These are some examples of the differences between British and American spelling where the American spelling is simpler.

British English	American English
colour	color
grey	gray
practise (verb)	practise (both verb and noun)
practice (noun)	

Unfortunately, the great majority of spellings have never been simplified, even in American English.

About fifty years ago, a famous British writer, George Bernard Shaw, also tried to simplify English spelling. He thought it was illogical and too difficult for children to learn. However, he did not succeed in his ambition – in the last century, British English spellings have not been simplified. George Bernard Shaw gave an example of how illogical English spelling is. He said that a non-existant word 'ghoti' could be pronounced 'fish' in English.

gh - o - ti = f - i - sh

George Bernard Shaw

1 Can you work out the 'logical' spelling of the word ghoti? Look at the list of words in part A to help you. Find the words in the lists where *gh* is pronounced *f*, *o* is pronounced *i*, and *ti* is pronounced *sh*.

2 Do you know any more differences between British and American English spelling or vocabulary?

7 Why English?

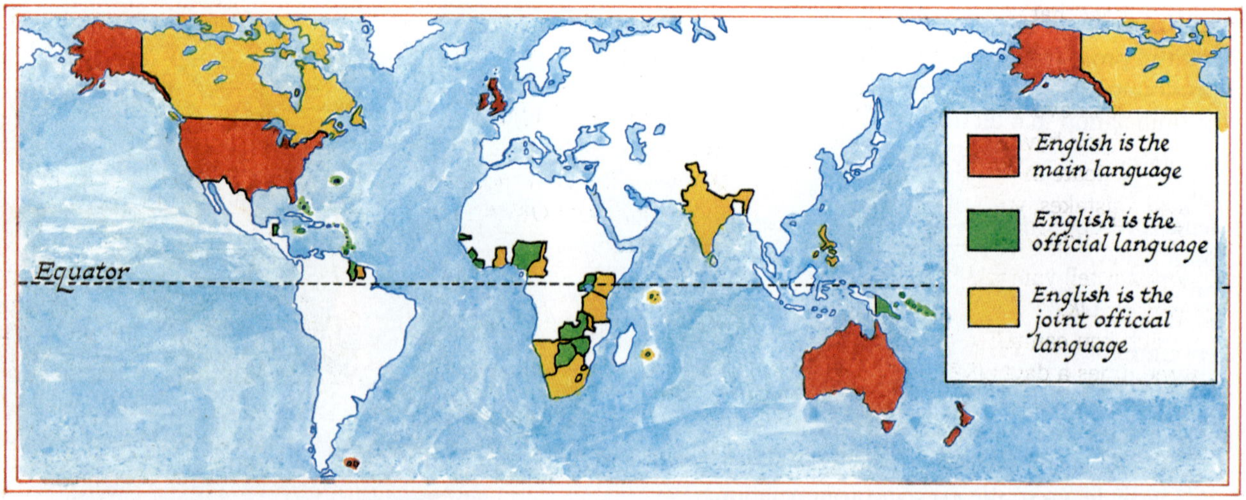

a You are going to listen to a talk about the development of the English language. You will hear the answers to these questions in the talk. Before you listen, suggest answers to these questions.

1 Why has English become such an important language in the world?
2 Why are artificial languages, like Esperanto, not used for international communication?
3 What is the origin of the word OK?

Now listen to the talk and then answer the three questions above.

b Here are some notes on the talk.

Listen again and arrange these notes in the order you hear them in the talk.

French, Spanish ... Arabic–Islamic Empire
200 years from now — English?
100 yrs ago Esperanto — artificial – natural?
Early U.S.A. — Dutch? English?
2,000 yrs ago — English
OK — President Jackson → OK = Oll Korrect
2,000 yrs ago — colonies
USA – technology, communications → English

c Look at the notes above and re-tell what the speaker said.

Pronunciation File

Homophones

a In exercise 6, you looked at words where the same vowel letters are pronounced differently. There are also words which are pronounced the same way, but spelt differently. They are called homophones. Here are some examples.

see	sea
be	bee
there	their
here	hear
flower	flour
aloud	allowed
weather	whether

Can you think of any more examples of homophones in English?

b When you learn a new word in English, make sure you look at the phonetic transcription of the word in the dictionary. The connection between pronunciation and spelling is not always logical in English.

Look at the possible ways of spelling the /eə/ sound as in the word hair:

hair pear there their stare

How many ways can you think of spelling the /i:/ sound as in the word *meet*, and the /əʊ/ sound as in the word *so*? Write down as many examples as you can.

© SANTILLANA

Learning Tips

Be confident

Remember that using a language is about communicating. It is not possible to be one hundred per cent accurate in everything we say or write. If you have the confidence to communicate in English, even if you make mistakes, you will probably learn much more effectively.

Why not tell yourself: '*My English is definitely OK.*'
In fact, you can tell yourself that three times a day! OK?

8 Everything's OK *The meaning of OK*

Listen to these four short conversations. You will hear the word OK in each conversation. Look at the four words and phrases below, and match them with the meaning of OK in each conversation.

Fantastic!

give your approval to

Stop! That's enough!

Fine

Vocabulary File

1 Homophones

Be careful to write the correct spelling of a word, especially if it has a homophone. The words in the list below all have homophones. Write them in the sentences below.

<u>scene</u> blue so pear sight there find rain

EXAMPLE:
It's the best film I've ever <u>*seen*</u>.

1 My grandmother used to ______ for a living. She made all kinds of clothes for people.
2 No, those children haven't got a father. I think that man is ______ grandfather.
3 The ______ of Queen Elizabeth II has lasted over 40 years.
4 The wind ______ so hard all the tents fell down in the night.
5 He was ______ £200 for leaving his car in a no parking zone.
6 They originally planned to have the building on this ______, but they decided it was too far from the airport.
7 Your black jeans are dirty? You'll have to wear another ______.

Keep a list of any other homophones you find.

2 Similarities and differences

a Look at the text in exercise 9 on page 134 and find these phrases.

from … to
ranging from … to …
various forms of …
(be) compared to …
similar to …
a long way from …
is closely connected to …

b Use the phrases in part A and make up sentences to describe some of these things.

different European languages
varieties of a language (not English)
the scenery in a particular area
two different types of music/art/films
a town that has changed over the years
the facilities available in a city you know
different fashion styles

3 American and British English

There is very little difference in grammar between British and American English. Most of the differences are in slang words and expressions. However, some common vocabulary is different. Here are some typical examples.

British English	American English
biscuit	cookie
toilet	bathroom
insect	bug

Match the words in British English on the right with the correct American English word on the left.

flat	sidewalk
rubbish	movie
chips	VCR
film	crosswalk
aubergine	garbage
garden	eggplant
pavement	fries
pedestrian crossing	apartment
video recorder	yard

© SANTILLANA

9 The story of English

In his lifetime, Bob Marley was the most famous Jamaican in the world. His success gave Jamaican English an international audience.

Bob Marley

Michael Smith

a This is an extract from a book called *The Story of English*. This extract describes what is happening, and what might happen in the future to the different forms of English throughout the world. The text decribes the 'Latinization' of English. Can you guess what this process could mean? Read the text to find out.

The Latinization of English

English is an official language in some thirty-four countries, from islands as far apart as Jamaica and Singapore, to states ranging from Sierra Leone to the vast sub-continent of India. English is scattered far and wide and has produced Caribbean English, Indian English, various forms of African English and Singapore English, sometimes known as 'Singlish'.

The emergence of these new Englishes has been compared to the spread (and subsequent break-up) of Latin throughout the Roman world. In the late 1970s, the Chief Editor of the Oxford English Dictionary, Doctor Robert Burchfield, predicted that English would disintegrate into separate languages. He said it would be similar to Latin which broke up into separate European languages such as French, Spanish and Italian, with the decline of the Roman Empire.

Jamaica probably offers the best example of the beginning of this process of 'Latinization' – the separate development of English. A British or American visitor to Jamaica would probably notice two basic levels of language. The newspapers use Standard English and many middle-class Jamaicans will use a spoken form of Standard English very similar to British or American English. On another level, however, Jamaican English will be almost unintelligible to an outsider and the meaning and pronunciation is a long way from the English of London or New York. Until recently, Jamaican English was an oral form only. But now, with the rise of reggae and a style of poetry, called 'dub poetry', Jamaican English appears in both written and spoken form. One Jamaican dub poet with an international reputation was Michael Smith. Unfortunately his career was short and tragic. At the age of twenty-nine he was stoned to death, a victim of Jamaica's political violence. His fellow poet and friend, Mervyn Morris, says the language of dub poets is closely connected to the language of pop stars like Bob Marley and Peter Tosh:

> The concerns are very much the concerns you find in Jamaican pop music. They're usually talking about oppression. The need to return to some kind of sense of identity which often connects with Africa.

Many of the dub poets have had a university education. They are turning their backs on Standard English out of choice. They have chosen to write in the language of their own culture and to spread it throughout the English-speaking world in poetry readings, music and books. They know that the language of their poetry might become the future standard language of the Caribbean and give their society a distinct Caribbean identity that is not overshadowed by British or American English.

© SANTILLANA

b Look back at the text and find the words in the text which are the same, or very similar to, words in your own language.

Now find words and phrases which are new to you, but you can guess the meaning from the context.

EXAMPLE:

as far apart as … and …
ranging from … to …
scattered far and wide

Make a list of these words and phrases.

c Here is Michael 'Micky' Smith's most famous poem, 'Mi cyaan believe it'. (I can't believe it)

Mi cyaan believe it

Mi seh mi cyaan believe it
Mi seh mi cyaan believe it
room dem a rent
mi apply widin
but as me go in
cockroach rat an scorpion also come in
waan good
nose haffi run
but me naw go sideung pan igh wall
like Humpty Dumpty
mi a face me reality

Michael Smith's poem talks about Humpty Dumpty. Look at the illustration of Humpty Dumpty.

He is a famous character in a children's rhyme. He was a man made from an egg.

Listen to the original rhyme.

Humpty Dumpty sat on a wall.
Humpty Dumpty had a great fall.
All the King's horses and all the King's men,
Couldn't put Humpty together again.

d Listen to the reading of Michael Smith's poem. After the first reading of the poem there is a translation into standard English.

Look back at Michael Smith's poem.

Remember he was a Jamaican writer who believed in the value of Jamaican English. His history was connected to Africa, Europe and the Caribbean. He was an idealist who wanted a definite identity for the people of the Caribbean which was not exactly African, not British and not American. In your own language, can you explain why this Jamaican poet thinks he is like Humpty Dumpty sitting on a high wall, looking at his own reality?

10 Learning strategies *Language round-up*

You have practised many strategies for understanding and learning new words and phrases in this book. Here is a list of what you know.

- guessing the meaning from the context
- looking for cognates (words which are the same or similar to words in your language)
- using prefixes (*un-*, *in-*, etc to make the opposite meaning)
- using suffixes (*-ful*, *-less* to make the opposite meaning)
- changing part of a word to make nouns, adjectives, verbs or adverbs (education, educated, educate)
- using synonyms (words with the same or similar meaning such as allowed – permitted)
- homophones

Now look through this unit and find examples of all the above. Then, in pairs, look through earlier units to find more examples.

© SANTILLANA

REVIEW UNITS 11-12

1 The most famous statue in the world

a Work in pairs. Partner A reads this text and partner B reads the text on page 159. Ask questions to complete your text.

THE STATUE OF LIBERTY situated on ____ in New York Harbour, is one of the world's most famous monuments. The statue was originally designed by ____ in the ____. She was made from thin copper panels and Bartholdi was given advice on the construction of the metal by Gustav Eiffel – the creator of the famous Eiffel Tower in Paris. The statue is ____ high, it weighs ____ and each eye is ____ wide. The statue itself was paid for by the French public and it was only the pedestal that was funded by the Americans. In fact, the statue had been planned for ____ before the Americans came up with the money for the pedestal. Everything was finally completed in 1885.

The Statue of Liberty can be reached by ____, every 30 minutes from 10.00am to 4.00pm. The tickets are sold in the Castle Clinton National Monument. The ____ is housed inside the statue and the story of the immigrants to America, who helped to create a nation, is told by ____. The Statue of Liberty was restored in 1986 for her centennial celebration.

b Read the complete text then cover it. Write six facts from memory about the Statue of Liberty.

2 Powerful words – *make* and *do*

The words *make* and *do* are used in certain phrases. Look at these examples.

make		do	
	plans		the housework
	breakfast/lunch/dinner/etc		your homework
	the bed		the washing/cooking/ironing/cleaning
	a mess		English/maths/geography/etc
	a noise		a job
	a fuss		someone a favour
	a mistake		someone a good turn
	a decision		something stupid/clever
	money		an exam
	friends (with someone)		what you want/like

Take care to use the correct word after *make* or *do*.

EXAMPLE:

I made the beds, then I made breakfast.
In the morning I did all the housework then I did my homework.

Choose five expressions with *make* and five with *do*. Write sentences using the expressions then exchange sentences with someone else. Check that your partner's sentences use the expression correctly and that the verbs are in the correct tense.

© SANTILLANA

3 Dictionary work

a Synonyms are words which have the same or similar meanings to other words.

EXAMPLE:

an intelligent person = a clever person

Match a word in column A with its synonym in column B. Use a dictionary to help you.

A	B
short	holiday makers
famous	select
whole	try
tourists	wealthy
rush	brief
attempt	entire
pick	happen
hardly	well-known
well-off	hurry
take place	barely

b Use your dictionary to find synonyms for the following words. Then complete the sentences with a suitable synonym.

amusing ________
beautiful ________
frightened ________
anxious ________
dear ________

1 I was really _____ about the history exams.
2 This shirt was _____, but I think it was worth it because it's so nice.
3 She was very _____ when she was a little girl.
4 If you think that joke is _____, wait till you hear this one.
5 Are you _____ of snakes?

4 Error correction

There is one mistake in each of the following sentences. Find the mistake and rewrite the sentences correctly.

1 *This car was manufacture in South Korea.*
2 *I got bitten three years ago and I'm still very nervous by dogs.*
3 *That mustn't be your book. It's got my name on it.*
4 *She wouldn't do that, wouldn't she?*
5 *Are you afraid from ghosts?*
6 *ICI make products ranging as fertilisers to jeans.*
7 *The policeman told the reporter that he turn off the camera.*
8 *This ring is done from pure gold. It's worth over £3,000.*
9 *37 cars been stolen in Bristol last night.*
10 *Oh no. I've done another mistake.*

5 Project

a How much do you know about famous monuments around the world? In groups, prepare ten quiz questions for the rest of the class.

EXAMPLE:

Where is the Statue of Liberty?

Ask other groups in the class your questions. Keep a score of the answers.

b Choose an historic building or monument in your town or city. Find out as much information as you can about the building or monument. Find information on:

where it is
why it is important
who built it
when it was built
why it was built
what it is made of
any special features it has
any myths/stories that are associated with it
how you can get to it
when it is open/closed

c Write a fact sheet for the building/monument for tourists visiting your town or city. Use photographs or pictures to illustrate your fact sheet. Try to 'sell' it as much as possible - you want people to visit the building/monument. Look at the work of other students. Which building/monument would you most like to visit?

© SANTILLANA

Grammar Reference

Unit 1

1 Present simple

Examples

I live in Granada.
Peter plays football every Saturday.
Karen comes from Germany.
The Earth goes around the Sun.
The bus leaves at 8.35.
Do you speak Arabic?
We often visit our sister in Paris.
The boys don't like chocolate.

Form

We put **-s** on the end of the present simple for the third person singular (**he/she/it**).
Sometimes we put **-es** or **-ies** on the end for (**he/see/it**).
Look at these examples:
He watches/he finishes/he dresses/she fixes/it buzzes
She goes/he does
He tries/she worries
We use **-es** after the letters **ch**, **sh**, **s**, **x**, **z** and with the verbs **go** and **do**.
We use **-ies** when verbs end with the letter **y**.
Negatives and questions are formed like this:
I don't smoke.
Tom doesn't smoke.
Do you come from Brazil?
Does she come from Brazil?

Use

We use the present simple in the following ways:

1 To talk about permanent or long term states. (when giving personal information, etc)
2 To talk about scientific facts.
3 To talk about actions we often do. (daily routines, habits, etc)
4 To talk about fixed future events. (timetables, itineraries, etc)

Pronunciation

The third person singular **-s** or **-es** may be pronounced in three different ways.
/z/ as in opens, goes, stays, lives, worries
/s/ as in waits, stops, asks, laughs
/ɪz/ as in catches, washes, dresses, fixes, loses, closes

2 Present continuous

Examples

I'm leaving for Venice tomorrow.
Are you going on holiday this summer?
I'm learning to windsurf.
It's raining.
We're waiting for Joe.
The boys are playing football later.

Form

The present continuous is formed like this:
present of **to be** + **-ing** form of the main verb

Use

1 To talk about actions happening now.
What are you doing?
– I'm looking for my keys.
2 To talk about continuous actions or states.
I'm living with my brother while my flat is being redecorated.
I'm learning to drive.
3 To talk about future plans.
What are you doing next Saturday?
– I'm going to a party.

Pronunciation

These contracted forms are often used in speech and writing.

I'm / *you're* / *s/he/it's* / *we're* / *they're* } reading

3 Imperatives

Examples

Pass the salt.
Go away.
Don't forget to call Pilar.
Take one of these tablets every day.
Don't put your dirty hands on that clean shirt.
Don't worry about it.

Form

Imperatives are made from the infinitive without **to**.
Negative imperatives are made from **don't** + infinitive without **to**.
Note: It is also possible to use the word **never** in negative imperatives.
Never accept lifts from strangers.

© SANTILLANA

Use
Imperatives are used to tell someone to do something. Imperatives can be requests, orders, invitations, advice or prohibitions.

Pronunciation
Intonation is very important in imperatives. Notice how the intonation of the example changes according to the function.
'Sit down.' polite request
'Sit down.' order
'Sit down.' invitation

Unit 2

1 *Going to*

Examples
It's going to rain.
We're going to have a party on Saturday.

Form
Going to is formed like this:
present tense of the verb **to be** + **going to** + main verb in the infinitive

Use
Going to is used to talk about the future. It has three main uses.

1 Planned events in the future
We're going to stay with my sister for a few days.
(it is all arranged)
I'm going to see the dentist at 10.30.
(I have an appointment)

2 Events which are expected to happen soon, or predictions supported by a lot of present evidence.
He's going to fall.
(he's already in a dangerous position)
It's going to be hot today.
(it's already getting warm)

3 Personal resolutions
I'm going to stop smoking and get fit.

Pronunciation
In informal spoken English, **going to** is often pronounced 'gunna' /gənə/. However, it is never written this way. This form is unstressed, the main stress falls on the verb that follows.

/gənə/ ●
We're going to visit the National Museum.

/gənə/ ●
I'm going to see her tomorrow.

2 *Should*

Examples
I should go.
He should explain.
We shouldn't do that.
Should I phone Alex?
She should have told me earlier.
Free medical care should be available to everyone.

Form
Should is a modal verb like **can**, **must**, **may** and **might**. There is no **-s** in the third person in the present tense and there are no past or continuous forms of **should**. There is a perfect form, **should have**, which refers to past events.
You should have said something.

Should is formed like this:
should + main verb in infinitive form without **to**
Questions are made with an inversion, negatives with **not**.
Note: **Ought to** means the same as **should**.

Use
Like all modal verbs, **should** has several meanings. Three are given here.

1 Probability
The bus should arrive in a few minutes.

2 Advice or criticism
You look awful. You should see a doctor.

3 Moral obligation
Everyone should have access to clean water.

Pronunciation
In speech **should not** is usually contracted to **shouldn't**.
They shouldn't worry so much.
Shouldn't you be in class?

3 *Make* and *let*

Form
Make and **let** are verbs with present, past and continuous forms. They are formed like this:
make/let + object + infinitive without **to**

The head teacher made me clean all the desks.
object / \ infinitive

Why don't you let Maria go to the dance?
object / \ infinitive

Use
Make means to force to do something. **Let** means allow to do something.
My parents were very strict. They made me get home by 8 pm. They never let me stay out late.

© SANTILLANA

Unit 3

1 Present perfect

Examples

I have telephoned the doctor.
The doctor has arrived.
We haven't told Peter.
Have you seen the manager?

Form

The present perfect simple is formed like this: present tense of the verb **to have** + past participle of the main verb.
For a full list of irregular past participles see page 160 in your student's book.

Use

The present perfect has several meanings. Each of them relates past to the present in some way.

1 Indefinite past (at any time up to now)
Have you ever visited Avignon?
This is often used with **ever** and **never**.
Have you ever read Hamlet?
I've never eaten snails.

2 Recent past (with relevance to the present)
News is often given using the present perfect.
The President has announced that elections will be held next April.
I've seen Jack (and this is what he told me ...)
This is often used with **just**, **already** or **yet**.
She's just had a baby.
I've already finished the report.
The nurse hasn't arrived yet.

3 Starting in the past and still continuing now
He's written five novels. (and he could write more)
This is often used with **for** and **since**.
She's lived in Austria for five years.
My brother hasn't written to me since 1988.
Note: The present perfect continuous (**have been doing**) is often used in this meaning.

Contrast with the past simple

The past simple is used to talk about events which happened at a specific time in the past. The contrast can be seen in this short dialogue.

A: Have you ever been to the USA?
(indefinite – at any time?)
B: Yes, I have. Only once though.
A: Oh? When did you go?
(definite – at what time?)
B: I went to Los Angeles in 1992.

Contrast with the present continuous

The present continuous talks about what is happening now.
Where are you living now?
– I'm living in a small flat in the town centre.
The present perfect talks about time up to now
How long have you lived there?
– I've lived there for about six months.

2 *Been* and *gone*

She's been to Majorca.
She's gone to Majorca.
Been means travelled away and come back.
Gone means travelled away.
Look at this example.
Horacio lives in Madrid. In May he goes to Athens for three months. In July he returns to Madrid. His wife Elena stays in Madrid.
In May Elena phones her mother and says: 'Horacio's gone to Athens.'
In August she phones her mother again and says: 'Horacio's been to Athens.'

3 *For* and *since*

Since tells you when something started. **For** tells you the length of time it has been happening.
Alan has studied computer science since 1992.
Alan has studied computer science for three years.
Both are used with the present perfect simple and present perfect continuous.

Unit 4

1 Past continuous

Form

The past continuous tense is formed like this: past simple of the verb **to be** + **-ing** form of the main verb.
The sun was shining.
Some boys were playing football.

Use

The past continuous refers to a single activity in the past which was in progress, usually as something else happened.

1 An action in progress may be interrupted by another action and therefore not completed, or possibly not completed.
I was getting into the bath when the phone rang.
She was crossing a busy road when a car knocked her down.

© SANTILLANA

2 To describe an action happening at the same time as another action.
It may describe the surroundings to that action, but be unaffected by it.
I was living in London when I first met my girlfriend.
He looked out of the window. It was raining.
Often the past continuous is used with the past simple. Look at these examples.
While we were staying in Morocco, we saw Samira.
I lost my keys as I was getting out of the car.

2 *Used to*

Examples

I used to live in London.
Begona used to work in a furniture shop.
She didn't use to spend so much money on clothes.
Did you use to play football at school?

Form

Used to + infinitive
Questions and negatives are formed with **did** and **didn't**, like ordinary verbs in the past tense.

Use

Used to talks about repeated actions in the past that no longer happen. It also refers to things that continued for a long time in the past, that no longer happen.
We used to live in Madrid.
(but we don't live there now)
I used to play the piano.
(but I don't play it now)
He didn't use to be so rude.
(but now he's often rude)

Pronunciation

1 **Used to** is pronounced /ju:stə/. The **-s** sound is not voiced.
2 **Used to** and **didn't use to** are pronounced the same. The two words are linked in one sound.
used to /ju:stə/
(didn't) use to /ju:stə/

Note: The past tense of the verb **to use** is pronounced /ju:zd/.
The **-s** sound is voiced.
/ju:zd/
I used a dictionary to help me understand the newspaper article.

3 Comparisons with adjectives

Revision

There are two main patterns for comparison of adjectives.
tall *taller than* *the tallest*
interesting *more interesting than* *the most interesting*
Can you remember the rule?

Using modifiers

You can use modifiers to give more information about the comparison. Look at the examples below.
Manchester is a bit bigger than Edinburgh.
Sheffield is slightly bigger than Liverpool.
London is much bigger than Bath.
Birmingham is a lot bigger than Oxford.
Glasgow is considerably bigger than Swindon.

Unit 5

1 Indirect speech

Examples

Alice says she never eats pizza.
Sarah said she wants to go to the cinema tonight.
He told me he would see me tomorrow.
Felipe said he was studying biology.
The old man told me he had been married for 40 years.

Form

1 Reporting verb **say** or **tell** is in the present.
'I don't like coffee.'
Alice says she doesn't like coffee.
Notice that the tense does not change, but **I** changes to **she**.
2 Reporting verb is in the present.
The speech is recent or relevant to the present, or still true at the time of reporting.
'I want to go swimming.'
He said he wants to go swimming.
Notice that the tense does not change, but **I** changes to **he**.
3 Reporting verb is in the past.
The speech happened a long time ago or refers to something that is no longer true or the reporter thinks it may not be true.
'I can type 60 words a minute.'
She said she could type 60 words a minute.
(but she can really only type 20 words a minute)
'I've just come back from Hungary.'
When I saw him last September, he told me he had just come back from Hungary.
(reporting several months later)
Notice that the tense changes in these two examples. See overleaf.

© SANTILLANA

Tense changes in past reporting

Look at the examples and notice the tense changes.

Direct speech	Reported speech	Tense change
'I'll ask Peter.'	He said he would ask Peter.	will → would
'I love Mozart.'	She told me she loved Mozart.	present simple → past simple
'We're leaving.'	They said they were leaving.	pres. continuous → past continuous
'We saw Tony.'	They said they had seen Tony.	past simple → past perfect

Say and *tell*

The two most common reporting verbs are **say** and **tell**. **Say** is followed only by the reporting words. **Tell** is followed by the person who is told and then the words. **That** can be used, but is usually omitted.

Luis said (that) he was good at football.
Luis told Eva (that) he was good at football.

Other reporting verbs are: **announce**, **explain**, **reply**, **add** and **answer**.

Time phrases in indirect speech

Remember that time phrases change from direct to indirect speech.

Direct speech	Indirect speech
today	that day
this morning/afternoon	that morning/afternoon
tomorrow	the next/following day
next week/month/year	the next/following week/month/year

2 Present perfect continuous

Examples

I have been learning English for three years.
She has been crying all morning.
I haven't been waiting long.
He hasn't been swimming.
Have you been working here long?

Form

The present perfect continuous is formed like this: present tense of the verb **to have** + **been** + **-ing** form of the main verb.

Use

1 Sometimes there is no difference in meaning between the present perfect simple and continuous.
I have worked in Birmingham for three years.
I have been working in Birmingham for three years.

2 Sometimes the present perfect simple means recent completion, but the present perfect continuous means that the action is still in progress.
He has just typed the report.
He has just been typing the report.

3 The present perfect continuous implies duration, or an unfinished period of time.
How long have you been waiting?
– Oh, about ten minutes.
Note: When we ask the question **How long ...?** we often use the continuous form. When we ask the question **How many ...?** we use the simple form.

Contrast with the past simple

Look at the examples.

How long have you been working in Madrid?
– Six months.
(I still work in Madrid)
How long did you work in Madrid?
– Six months.
(I don't work in Madrid now)

You can only use the present perfect tense if the activities continue up to the present. If not, you must use the past tense.

How long has Peter lived in Argentina?
How long did Peter work for the Swiss bank?

Unit 6

1 *Will*

Examples

I will call you tomorrow.
The doctor will arrive soon.
He won't arrive on time.
Will you give me a hand?

Form

Will is a modal verb like **should**, **can**, **may** or **must**. It is followed by a verb in infinitive form without **to**.

The negative of **will** is **will not** or **won't**.

In spoken English, and in informal written English, **will** is usually shortened to **'ll**.

She'll be late.
Peter'll show you everything.

Use

Will has several meanings.

1 One basic meaning relates to future time. **Will** is used for a general prediction about the future events.
There'll be a general election later this year.
He'll be pleased to see you.

© SANTILLANA

2 **Will** is also used as a promise or a spoken decision about the future.
I'll mend it for you tomorrow.
We won't be late.
I think I'll phone Andy.

3 **Will** is also used with **if** for conditional clauses. See part 2 below.
If you don't work hard, you won't pass the exam.
Sandra will call you if there's any news.

2 If sentences relating to future time: The first conditional

Examples

If I see Mike, I'll tell him to phone you.
She won't pass her driving test if she doesn't practise.

Form

This is often considered the basic form:
If + present simple + **will/won't**
or **will/won't** + **if** + present simple
However, there are other forms. Look at the examples below.
If Alan can't come, ask Mike instead.
If it's cold this evening, you shouldn't go out.
If you like swimming, why don't you come with us tomorrow?
She must send the letter today if she wants it to arrive by Thursday.
It is also possible to use other modal verbs, imperatives and verbs in the present simple.

Unit 7

1 *-ing* words

Examples

a *Most of all I enjoy playing tennis.*
b *She's really interested in working with computers.*
c *Leaving the library, I ran into Karen.*
d *Realising that there was hardly any time left, he rushed into the station and bought a ticket.*

Use

As well as being used for continuous tenses and adjectives, **-ing** forms of the verb can be used in the following ways:

1 Gerunds
In examples a and b, the **-ing** form takes the place of a noun.
Instead of saying: *I enjoy playing tennis*, we could easily say: *I enjoy tennis*. Similarly, instead of: *She's really interested in working with computers*, we could say: *She's really interested in computers*.
When an **-ing** form is used instead of a noun, it is often called a gerund. A gerund is an activity or an action. We often use gerunds to generalise about things.
Watching too much TV is bad for you.
We can also use gerunds after some verbs or adjectives with prepositions. These include:
enjoy like love stop interested in
good at keen on tired of

2 Participles
In examples c and d, the **-ing** form is used instead of a main verb.
Leaving the library, I ran into Karen, means the same as: *As I was leaving the library, I met Karen.*
In examples c and d, the **-ing** form is called a participle. Participles are used instead of a verb clause only when the subject of the main clause is the same as the (unspoken) subject of the participle.
Look at the examples below. Both contain two clauses. However, only in the second example can the verb in the first clause be changed to a participle.
As she was getting in the taxi, a man snatched her bag.
As she was getting in the taxi, she twisted her ankle.

2 Adverbs ending *-ly*

Revision

Adverbs ending **-ly** are made from adjectives. In most cases, just add **-ly** to the adjective. There are some spelling rules.

Adjective	**Adverb**	**Spelling rule**
quick	quickly	(+ly)
strange	strangely	(+ly)
happy	happily	(change y to i +ly)
careful	carefully	(double l+y)
historic	historically	(ally after ic)

Use

Adverbs can be used to give more information about verbs, adjectives and sometimes about other adverbs.

1 With verbs
The adverb tells us how the action of the verb is being performed.
He wrote the memo hurriedly.
She shouted angrily at the children.

2 With adjectives
The adverb often tells us how strong the adjective is.
He's terribly aggressive.
I felt slightly worried.

3 With other adverbs
Especially with adverbs of frequency.
I hardly ever go to the cinema.

© SANTILLANA

Unit 8

1 Defining relative clauses

Examples

The man <u>who we saw yesterday</u> was the fisherman.
She still lives in the village <u>where she was born</u>.
A squirrel is a small animal <u>which lives in trees</u>.
The man <u>whose window you broke</u> wants £60 for repairs.

1 In all the examples above, the relative clause introduced by **who**, **which**, **where** or **whose** gives information essential to the clear understanding of the sentence. The sentences would not be very clear without the relative clause. So, they are called defining relative clauses.

2 **Who** and **which** can be replaced by **that**.
The man that we saw yesterday was a fisherman.
A squirrel is a small animal that lives in trees.

3 When the pronoun **who**, **which** or **that** is the object of the verb in the relative clause, it can be omitted.
The man we saw yesterday was the fisherman.

2 Non-defining relative clauses

Examples

My brother John, <u>who is very tall</u>, is a national basketball player.
Her BMW, <u>which is twelve years old</u>, is always breaking down.
This is a photo of my cousin Anna, <u>whose husband you met at our party</u>.
Sudbury, <u>where Anna has her studio</u>, is a very quiet town.

1 In these examples the information in the relative clauses is not really needed for the sentence to be clear. The underlined clauses contain additional or 'extra' information. So, they are called non-defining relative clauses.

2 Non-defining relative clauses have a comma (,) at the beginning and end, or a full stop (.) at the end.

3 **That** cannot be used instead of **who** or **which**.

4 The relative pronoun cannot be omitted.

3 *Look/look like/look as if*

Examples

She looks annoyed.
He looks like a soldier.
You look as if you need a glass of water.

Form

look + adjective			*The children look tired.*
look like + noun			*The children look like their mother.*
look as	if / though	+ verb	*The children look as if they're waiting for you.*

Unit 9

1 Conditional clauses with *would:* The second conditional

Form

The second conditional is usually formed in the following way.
If + past simple + **would/wouldn't**
or **would/wouldn't** + **if** + past simple
If I lost my passport, I would go to the police.
I wouldn't be able to go if I didn't have a car.
The past continuous is also possible in the **if** clause. **Could**, **should** and **might** are sometimes used instead of **would** to talk about possibility or probability.
If he was taking drugs, you would know from his behaviour.
He could pass the exam if he didn't spend all of his time playing football.

Use

1 The second conditional is used to talk about imaginary or hypothetical situations. Unlike the first conditional, it does not refer directly to the future. Look at these examples.
*If I was President of the USA, I would do more to protect the environment.**
(there is no possibility of you becoming president)
If I moved to Paris, I could get a better job.
(general statement of possibility, not a real situation)
*Note: It is possible to use **were** instead of **was** in the first person singular.

2 The second conditional can also be used to give advice.
*If I were you, I'd go to the doctor.**
*Note: We say *If I were you …* not *If I was you …* .

Pronunciation

Notice that **I would** is often shortened to **I'd**, **you would** to **you'd**, **he would** to **he'd**, etc.

© SANTILLANA

2 *Have*

Examples

I have a shower every morning.
Where's Tony?
– He's having a shower.

In these examples it is possible to use the verb **have** in both the simple and continuous forms. When **have** means to possess, it cannot be used in the continuous form. However, when **have** + noun describes an activity (to have a bath, a shower, dinner, lunch, breakfast, etc) it can be used in the continuous form.

Unit 10

1 Ability: *can/could/be able to*

Form

In the Grammar File in this unit, **can**, **could** and **be able to** are used to talk about ability. Look at the table and note the present, past and future forms.

	can/could	**be able to**
Present	I can drive	I am able to drive
Future	—	I will be able to drive
Past	I could drive	I was able to drive

Note: There is no future form of **can** and **could**.

Use

In the present, **can**, **could** and **be able to** are similar in meaning. In the past, **could** usually means a general past ability, but **was able to** usually refers to one particular occasion in the past.

When I was younger, I could run 100 metres in 10 seconds.
(general ability)
The river was deep, but not very wide, so I was able to swim across it easily.
(on one occasion)

2 *Can/could*: other meanings

Note: **Be able to** is not used in these meanings.

Asking for permission	*Can/could I leave early today?*
Giving permission	*You can take tomorrow off if there's a problem.*
Requests	*Can I borrow £10?*
Polite requests	*Could I use your phone?*
Offering	*I can give you a lift home.*
Deducing (can't)	*That can't be Tom. He's got red hair.*
Prohibiting (can't)	*He can't stay here. He must go now.*

Note: In requests and asking for permission **could** is more polite than **can**.

3 *Must* and *have to (have got to)*

Form

In the Grammar File of this unit the negative forms of **must** and **have to** are contrasted. In the positive form they can both be used to talk about obligation or necessity.

Present	I must ring Simon.
	I have to ring Simon.
Future	She'll have to tell the nurse.
Past	They had to call the police.

Note: There is no past or future form of **must**.

Use

1 In the present, **must** is usually used when the obligation is felt personally – It is an 'internal' obligation or necessity.
I must leave now.
(this is my personal feeling)

2 **Have to** is usually used when the obligation is 'external' – perhaps someone has ordered you to do this.
I have to leave now.
(someone requires me to leave)
Note: **Must** is usually used on public notices.
All security passes must be shown at the entrance.
All passengers must wear seat-belts.

Unit 11

1 Past perfect

Examples

I had written to Alice earlier.
He was very nervous. He hadn't flown before.
Had they paid before they left the restaurant?
She had been working all day.
They had been looking for John for over an hour.

Form

The past perfect simple is always formed with **had/hadn't** + the past participle of the main verb.
He had spoken to James earlier that day.
The past perfect continuous is formed with **had/hadn't** + **been** + **-ing** form of the main verb.
He had been waiting for the bus for 20 minutes.
The past perfect continuous is used to show that an action lasted a long time and was possibly unfinished.

(continued overleaf)

© SANTILLANA

Use

1 Establishing the sequence of events. The past perfect expresses the earlier event. The past simple is often used to describe the later event.
When David finally rang, they had already left the hospital.
As soon as they had unpacked, they went to the bar for a drink.

2 Sometimes the past perfect is used to show the cause of a past event.
As he had missed the last bus home, he decided to take a taxi.
The road was closed because the bridge had collapsed.

3 In reported speech (see unit 5)
The past perfect is used in reported speech to replace both the present perfect and past simple.

Direct speech	Reported speech
'I've lost my keys.'	She said she had lost her keys.
'We went to Granada.'	They said they had been to Granada.

4 The past perfect is also used to report thoughts or ideas about the past.
She wondered why she hadn't phoned her yet.
I realised I had taken the wrong coat.
He thought he had met her somewhere before.

2 Passive voice

Form

Look at the table below. Notice that all passive verbs contain:
different tenses of the verb **to be** + past participle

Tense or modal	Example in passive
Present continuous	My car is being repaired.
Present simple	Cocoa is grown in Ghana.
Past simple	The hospital was built in 1986.
Past continuous	I realised I was being followed.
Future simple (will)	The boxes will be delivered tomorrow.
Present perfect (simple)	My car has been stolen.
Past perfect (simple)	The house had been badly damaged.
Future perfect (simple)	She will have been told by five o'clock.
Modals	She must be taken to hospital immediately.
Infinitive (after a verb)	He wanted to be introduced to the director.

Note: The passive voice exists in all tenses, in simple and continuous forms and with modal verbs. Passive forms are rarely used with: present perfect continuous, future perfect continuous, past perfect continuous.

Use

1 The passive is often used when the person doing the action is unknown.
My car has been stolen.
(I don't know who did it)
The plane was delayed.
(we don't know who or what delayed it)

2 The passive is often used when a process, result or consequence is the focus of attention.
The liquid is heated to 200°C.
The fish are caught in huge nets.
Our house has been completely redecorated.
The two men were killed in an avalanche.
Suddenly, I realised I was being followed.

3 To make general statements or to suggest something is generally accepted to be true.
He is said to be the best chef in town.
It is widely accepted that there is life on Mars.
The escaped prisoner is believed to be very dangerous.

Unit 12

1 Tag questions

Form

Positive statements have a negative tag. Negative statements have a positive tag.

1 Present and past continuous: tag with **to be**
She's working late, isn't she?
He was expected to see you, wasn't he?
They weren't coming tonight, were they?

2 Present and past simple: tag with **to do**
He plays for Manchester United, doesn't he?
She phoned last Friday, didn't she?

3 Present and past perfect (simple and continuous): tag with **to have**
She's started smoking again, hasn't she?
He's been watching TV all evening, hasn't he?
I hadn't been feeling well, had I?
We hadn't known Linda long, had we?

4 Modal verbs: tag uses same modal
You won't tell Andy, will you?
David can't swim very well, can he?
He must stay in bed and rest, mustn't he?

Intonation on tag questions

1 Rising intonation
This is a real question. You are asking the listener whether what you believe to be true, is true.
Alan speaks Italian, doesn't he?
(you are not sure, you are asking for confirmation)

© SANTILLANA

2 Falling intonation
This is a comment, not a question. You're asking the listener to agree with your comment.
Alan speaks Italian really well, doesn't he?
(this is your opinion, you expect the listener to agree)

2 Reported instructions

Form

Imperatives change to an infinitive in reported instructions. Negative imperatives change to a negative infinitive.

Direct speech	Reported speech
'Sit down.'	He told me to sit down.
'Don't make a noise.'	She told me not to make a noise.

Reporting verbs

There are other verbs in addition to **tell** which are used to report instructions. They all take an object before the infinitive.
She asked him to lend her £10.
He persuaded his sister not to get married.
She ordered the waiter to fetch the manager.
The doctor advised him to take more exercise.
She requested George not to wake her too early.

3 Reported/indirect questions

Form

In the Grammar File you noticed that the word order changes in reported questions.

Direct question	Reported question
'Where's the bank?'	He asked me where the bank was.

Use

1 Sometimes we use an indirect question because it is more polite than a direct question. Then we make the same word order changes. We also use **if** and **whether** when there is no question word.
Could you tell me if the banks stay open until 8 pm?
Do you know how long it takes to get to the airport?

2 We can use an indirect question form to express doubt (as if we are asking ourselves a question). Look at these examples.
I wonder whether Ann's left a message on the answering machine.
I'm not sure where the bus goes from.
I don't know what time they are expected to arrive.

© SANTILLANA

Phonemic chart

Vowels Monothongs

Symbol	Example	
/iː/	he	/hiː/
/ɪ/	sit	/sɪt/
/e/	red	/red/
/æ/	hat	/hæt/
/ɑː/	start	/stɑːt/
/ɒ/	not	/nɒt/
/ɔː/	sport	/spɔːt/
/ʊ/	foot	/fʊt/
/uː/	shoe	/ʃuː/
/ʌ/	cup	/kʌp/
/ɜː/	bird	/bɜːd/
/ə/	father	/fɑːðə/

Vowels Dipthongs

Symbol	Example	
/eɪ/	make	/meɪk/
/aɪ/	why	/waɪ/
/ɔɪ/	boy	/bɔɪ/
/aʊ/	how	/haʊ/
/əʊ/	no	/nəʊ/
/ɪə/	beer	/bɪə/
/eə/	where	/weə/
/ʊə/	tour	/tʊə/

Semi-vowels

Symbol	Example	
/j/	yes	/jes/
/w/	when	/wen/

Consonants

Symbol	Example	
/p/	pen	/pen/
/b/	bad	/bæd/
/t/	ten	/ten/
/d/	dad	/dæd/
/k/	cold	/kəʊld/
/g/	girl	/gɜːl/
/m/	me	/miː/
/n/	near	/nɪə/
/ŋ/	ring	/rɪŋ/
/f/	fast	/fɑːst/
/v/	very	/verɪ/
/θ/	three	/θriː/
/ð/	father	/fɑːðə/
/tʃ/	cheese	/tʃiːz/
/dʒ/	John	/dʒɒn/
/s/	see	/siː/
/z/	zoo	/zuː/
/ʃ/	she	/ʃiː/
/ʒ/	vision	/vɪʒən/
/h/	house	/haʊs/
/l/	lot	/lɒt/
/r/	run	/rʌn/

© SANTILLANA

Tapescripts

Unit 1

Exercise 2a

I = Interviewer S = Steve

I: So, Steve, you're leaving next month.
S: Yeah. I'm really looking forward to it.
I: Where are you going first?
S: First to Madrid. I'm visiting a friend there for a few days. Then I'm leaving Madrid on the 19th and I'm flying direct to Mexico.
I: Fantastic. How long are you staying in Mexico?
S: About ten days, then I'm leaving Mexico for Cuba. I'm flying to Havana.
I: Do you know anyone there?
S: No. I'm staying with friends in Mexico, but in Cuba I think I'm staying in a hotel.
I: Are you going on your own, by the way, or with your girlfriend?
S: No. I'm going on my own.
I: Uh-uh. And from Cuba?
S: Well, from Cuba I'm going to Buenos Aires, Argentina.
I: These are all Spanish speaking countries. Do you speak Spanish?
S: Yes. Fortunately, I can speak Spanish fluently. I did Spanish at university.
I: Oh, well, that's OK.
S: And my last stop in Latin America is Santiago, in Chile. I've got friends there, too. And I'm staying with them for two weeks.
I: So, a fortnight in Chile.
S: Uh-uh.
I: And then?
S: On to Australia. My cousin's getting married there on the 15th of November. So, I'm going to her wedding then I'm thinking of travelling round Australia for a while.
I: How long are you staying there?
S: I'm not sure yet. If I can work there for a few weeks I'll get a job and earn some money, but I don't know about that just yet.
I: And then you're coming back to London?
S: Not directly. I've got a ticket for Harare and Nairobi so I'm planning on staying a few days in each place. See a little bit of Africa.
I: Lucky man. Have you got friends in all these places where you're staying?
S: Well, I'm staying with friends mostly. I don't know anyone in Cuba or in Harare, but I've got an uncle in Nairobi so I can stay with him there. No, just in Havana and Harare I'm probably staying in hotels and everywhere else with friends.
I: And then, after Africa, back to London?
S: Yes. I'm coming back to London after Nairobi.
I: Sounds really great.

Exercise 8a

conversation 1

A: Excuse me.
B: Yes.
A: Can you tell me where the currency exchange desk is, please?
B: Yes. Go down here.
A: Yes.
B: Take the third turning on the right.
A: Mm-mm.
B: And it's next to the duty free shop.
A: Thanks a lot.

conversation 2

A: Excuse me. Do you know where the nursery is?
B: Let me see. Yes, it's -er. Go straight on.
A: Yes.
B: Go past the international telephones and it's there opposite the women's toilets.
A: Oh, right. Thanks very much.
B: OK.

conversation 3

A: Excuse me. Where can I find the flight information desk?
B: The flight information desk is -er. Yes, go down here. Take the third turning on the left.
A: Yes.
B: Go past the restaurant.
A: Right.
B: And it's just next to the car hire desk.
A: OK. Thank you.

Exercise 9

conversation 1

A: Can I see your boarding card, please?
B: Yes.
A: Sorry, madam. You can only take two litres of wine into Italy.
B: Oh, I see. Well. I'll just take these two bottles then.
A: Right. How are you paying?
B: With American Express.
A: Fine. Sign here, please.

conversation 2

A: Yes. Can I help you?
B: Yes. What time does the next flight to San Francisco leave?
A: Let me see. The next one is at 10.45. It leaves from gate 37.
B: Thanks.
A: Would you like to book a ticket?
B: Yes.
A: Go to the TWA desk over there. They'll book a seat for you.
B: Thanks a lot.

conversation 3

A: Can I change these Swiss francs into German marks, please?
B: Certainly, sir.
A: This is the rate of exchange today. OK?
B: Yes, fine.
A: Just sign here please.
B: Right. Oh, have you got a pen?
A: Yes. Here you are.

conversation 4

A: Could you give me two teas and three coffees, please.
B: The milk's over there.
B: Thanks.
A: Any sugar?
B: No, thanks.
A: Anything else?
B: No, that's all thanks
A: Right. That's £3.25, please.

conversation 5

A: Good morning ladies and gentlemen. Can I ask all passengers to fasten their seat-belts and to observe the no-smoking sign. We're taking off in two minutes. We hope you have a pleasant journey with us. Thank you.

conversation 6

A: Can I see your ticket, please?
B: Right.
A: You're going to Madrid.
B: That's right.
A: How much hand luggage have you got?
B: Just one bag.
A: OK. Would you like a seat in the smoking or non-smoking section?
B: Non-smoking, please.
A: Would you like a window seat or an aisle seat?
B: Window, please.
A: OK. Thank you. You can go through to passport control now.

Exercise 11c

I = Inteviewer A = Air stewardess

A: So, one day we were flying back from … from … -er, I'd better not say which country.
I: OK.
A: And, first of all I heard this banging noise. Like someone banging on the window.
I: Uh-uh?
A: We were 20,000 feet in the air by this time.
I: Mmm.
A: So, I turned round and I saw this man, standing up, banging on the window and then he smiled at me and said …
I: What?
A: He said, 'Excuse me, miss. It's a bit hot in here. Can you open the window, please? I don't know how to open it.'
I: Oh, no! He tried to open the window in the plane. Thank goodness he couldn't.
A: And then, later on, this was on the same flight, I heard this other funny noise coming from the back of the plane. And when I went down there there were these two men sitting in the aisle.
I: Sitting in the middle of the aisle?
A: Yes, on the floor, in the middle of the aisle, with a camping … er, you know, a camping gas ring. And one of them said, 'Excuse me, miss. Have you got a light?'

© SANTILLANA

I: He didn't want to light a fire in the middle of the plane?
A: Yes, he did. They wanted to make a cup of tea.
I: Oh, no. Good job you stopped them.

I = Interviewer T = Travel agent

T: And another time, there was this old lady. She came in to buy a ticket for Spain. She said her and her husband used to go to Spain on holiday every year.
I: Uh-uh?
T: Anyway, she had this funny little thing on her knees, like a pot.
I: Mm-mm?
T: And she told me her husband had just died and this little pot was an urn with his ashes inside.
I: Oh, dear! Oh, was she taking her dead husband's ashes to Spain?
T: Yes, she wanted to scatter them in the sea where they used to go on holiday.
I: Oh, right!
T: Then she said, 'Well, I know my husband's dead but -er, do I need a passport for him?'
I: Oh, no! She wanted a passport for the ashes?
T: So, this man bought a ticket with us. And it was summer and all the airports were very busy. And on the day of his flight all the planes were delayed.
I: Mmm.
T: So, he was sitting on the plane, waiting for it to take off.
I: Uh-uh?
T: Well, he'd been sitting there about twenty minutes and then he -er, he had his mobile phone with him and he phoned me up.
I: Why did he phone you?
T: Good question. I was sitting here in the office and all of a sudden this angry voice on the phone shouts out, 'Well, we're twenty minutes late now. You sold me this ticket. When is this plane taking off?'
I: He didn't expect you to know that.
T: Yes. 'When is my plane taking off?' He shouted at me down the telephone.

Unit 2

Exercise 1b

I = Interviewer **C = Carol (child)**
A = Anna (teenager) **D = Danny (toddler)**
B = Bob (adult) **E = Emma (baby)**

I: So, what are your resolutions, Bob?
B: Well, first I'm going to lose weight and get fit.
I: Mmm-mm.
B: And then. I would like to work in another country for a while, learn another language, see something different. So I'm going to get a job abroad. I hope so, anyway.
I: Well, good luck!
B: Thanks.
I: What about you Anna?
A: I think, first I'm going to finish with my boyfriend.
I: Oh!
A: Yes. And then I'm going to stay in more at weekends and I want to study a lot more, because – I've decided – I'm going to pass all my maths exams this year.
I: OK. All the best. How about you?
C: Me, I'm going to save up for a new bike. I've got about £25 now and I'm saving all my pocket money.
I: Uh-uh!
C: And ... I really want to swim in the national junior team in a couple of years, so – my big resolution is, by the end of the year, I'm going to be the best swimmer in the class.
I: Well, I hope you manage it.
D: And I'm going to stop sucking my thumb.
I: Oh! You are!
D: Yes. Because my mummy says it's bad for me.
I: Oh, I see. Anything else.
D: Yes. I'm going to learn how to get dressed by myself 'cos my brother says I'm a baby.
I: Well, that's a really good idea.
E: Goo-goo, gee, kee ...
I: I think that means she's going to learn to talk. And I think she says she's going to make a lot of mess.

Exercise 6b

Child 1: And he's going to fall in the river. And then he's going to quickly catch all the fish, in his arms, like this. And he's going to put the fish quickly in the crocodile's mouth and then he's going to swim away because the crocodile is eating all the fish.
Child 2: I think he's going to jump up high in the air. And jump over the giant and then the giant is going to fall in the river and get eaten up.
Child 3: No, he's going to fall right in the river and splash! And the big, bad crocodile's going to go snap! And he's gone.
Child 4: No, no. I know. See, he's got a stick. And when he falls in the river, he's, he's going to go 'Wham!' and put the stick right in the crocodile's mouth, like this. And then the crocodile can't bite anybody? And then he'll swim away.

Exercise 8c

T = Teacher C = Children

T: So who can tell me the name of a really famous story? OK. Cinderella. Who can tell me the story of Cinderella? Right. You start.
C1: Well, Cinderella lives with her wicked step-mother. She's really horrible and cruel. She makes Cinderella do all the work and she never lets her have any new clothes. And she's got two daughters. The ugly sisters. They're horrible, too. They're really mean to Cinderella. They tell her she's stupid and no good at anything. They make her clean their shoes and cook their dinner. But really they're stupid and ugly. And Cinderella is nice and kind. She loves animals and they love her. She's really gentle and beautiful.
T: You carry on.
C2: So Cinderella does all the work, but even though she has nothing and everybody's mean to her, she's good-natured and she never gets angry. So one day they get an invitation to go to the king's palace. The prince is looking for a wife to marry so they invite everybody to a big party, er- what's it called?
C3: A ball.
C2: Yes. A big ball. So the stupid ugly sisters and step-mother think the prince might marry them, but he won't because they're so horrible and bad-tempered and he's really handsome and charming.
T: OK. You carry on.
C3: Well, the ugly sisters get ready for the ball but they don't let Cinderella go. They're nasty to her and boss her about. They say things like, 'Come on! Hurry up! Get my dress. Get my shoes, you stupid, lazy girl.' When they're ready they think they look really beautiful but they actually look ridiculous in their big dresses. They ask Cinderella, 'Well, how do we look? Do you think the prince will fall in love with us?' Cinderella knows they look really ugly, but she says, 'Oh, yes. You look really beautiful. You are lucky going to the ball. The prince is so good-looking and charming. I wish he would fall in love with me.' 'You! You stupid girl! How could a handsome, charming prince fall in love with an ugly, dirty girl like you?' her step-mother says. And off they go. Cinderella sits down and starts to cry.

Exercise 9b

T: Right. Who's going to carry on with the story? You carry on.
C4: So Cinderella sits there crying and the next minute there's a white light and there in the room is her fairy godmother. She's really kind and she says, 'Cinderella, don't cry. You are going to the ball.' Then she says, 'Fetch me six er – white mice and – er a ...
C5: A pineapple.
C4: No. A what's it called?
C6: A pumpkin.
C4: A pumpkin. So Cinderella gets the things and the fairy godmother waves her magic wand and suddenly they change into six white horses and a what's its name? A carriage. Then she waves her wand again and Cinderella's old dress changes into a beautiful white and gold dance dress.
T: Fine. You carry on.
C5: Then just before Cinderella goes the fairy godmother says, 'Just one thing. You must come back at midnight. Don't forget, at midnight.' So Cinderella goes to the ball. As soon as she enters, the prince wants to dance with her. And they dance and dance all night. The ugly sisters are really angry that the prince doesn't dance with them, but they don't know that it's Cinderella. Suddenly the clock strikes midnight and Cinderella remembers her promise. She runs out of the room and down the palace steps as the clock strikes midnight. As she runs down the steps one of her shoes, no er- what's it called?
C7: Glass slipper.

© SANTILLANA

C5: Yes. A glass slipper falls off. So the prince says he is going to look all round the town until he finds the person who the glass slipper fits.

T: OK. Your turn.

C6: So the next day he goes around the town with the glass slipper and all his servants er- blowing a trumpet, no er- what's that word?

C7: Trumpet?

C8: Fanfare.

C6: With a fanfare they arrive at every house. When they come to Cinderella's house the ugly sisters try to get their feet in the glass slipper, but they can't. Then the prince sees Cinderella and he asks her to try. The step-mother says, 'Oh, no! It can't be Cinderella She wasn't at the ball. Go away, girl.' But the prince's servant doesn't listen and he lets Cinderella try on the glass slipper. As soon as she puts her foot inside they can see it fits perfectly and the prince throws his arms round her. The next day the prince and Cinderella get married and they live happily ever after.

Exercise 10b

conversation 1

A: What kind of books do you like reading?

B: Er- Oh, lots of different kinds, but I like fiction – novels, short stories.

A: What kind of novels do you like?

B: Well, I like historical novels, detective stories … lots of things.

A: Science fiction?

B: Oh no. I'm not so keen on science fiction. I'd rather have a good detective or murder story.

conversation 2

A: What kind of books do you like best?

C: Biographies, I think. I like travel books, too? And I'm quite keen on books about politics and history, but I think I like biographies best.

A: How about novels, love stories, detective stories, things like that?

C: Oh no! I can't stand romantic novels, love stories, things like that.

conversation 3

A: Would you rather read fiction or non-fiction generally?

D: Non-fiction, really. I don't really read novels. I only read, you know, information er- guide books, computer magazines and so on.

Unit 3

Exercise 3

I = Interviewer J = John

I: You've run in hundreds of marathons in your time, John.

J: Yes. I've run marathon races for about ten years now. And I suppose I've done … oh hundreds. I don't know. I suppose I've run about two hundred.

I: Mmm. You're in your thirties now, aren't you?

J: Uh-huh. But there are runners of all ages. Some young, some old. I remember one race. It was in Scotland about two years ago. I was in this race and I met another runner. He must have been – I'm not sure. I suppose he was about seventy. And as he ran he made a little noise, like a steam engine.

I: Mmm?

J: A sort of 'cheeha-cheeha' little noise. Anyway, I passed him and was running OK. But then at about 11 miles into the race …

I: Mmm?

J: Well, I stopped. I couldn't run. My legs were gone. So I started to walk a bit. Then suddenly behind me I hear 'cheeha-cheeha'.

I: Oh.

J: And he passed me. This old man of seventy. Anyway, I finished next to last in that race. A long way behind the old man. Then, in the next race about two weeks later, I was running up this hill when I heard it again, 'cheeha-cheeha'!

I: Him again!

J: That's right. And I thought, I can't let him finish before me again. So I ran a bit faster and this time my legs were OK. In fact, I finished third that time.

I: Third? That's good. In front of the old man this time.

J: Yes, thank goodness. But it was the old man who made me run faster. I thought, I can't let him beat me again. So I should thank him really.

I: Yes.

J: Anyway, I've never seen him since.

I: No?

J: No. I've never seen him again, but I've often thought of him in races. Whenever I think of him, it makes me run just a little bit faster.

Exercise 8b

I = Interviewer J = John

I: When did this happen, John?

J: It was during the war. Let me see. November 1943. We were flying over the Indian Ocean when we got shot down. Well, my plane got hit and down it went – into the ocean. The whole plane was under water, going down fast. I looked round, but I couldn't get out through the door. The only way out was through a small look-out hole at the back of the plane. It was the gunner's look-out, so it wasn't very big. Well, I saw a small shaft of light through this look-out hole and I knew that was my only way out. So, I just swam to the hole and squeezed my way through. I was terrified. I can't remember much after that. I was floating in the sea I suppose for a couple of hours when I saw this boat come towards me. It was two sailors from one of the ships nearby. They had seen me and come to my rescue. Well, these two sailors put me in the boat and took me to a local military hospital.

I: Did you have many broken bones?

J: No, I just broke a couple of bones in my right arm. It was amazing really.

I: Then, when you were better your friends took you off to see how small the hole was that you had climbed through.

J: Yes. They took me to see my friend's plane. It was the same model as mine. And I looked at this small look-out hole at the back. I couldn't believe it. It was so small.

I: You were surprised how you'd got through?

J: Surprised? I was astonished. It was so small.

I: And you tried it again, didn't you?

J: Yes. I tried to squeeze through the look-out hole in my friend's plane.

I: And you couldn't?

J: No way! It was much too small. I could get my head through, but that was all. Nothing else. My shoulders and my body just wouldn't go through. It was impossible. I couldn't believe it!

Exercise 10b

A: Well, we were on holiday at the seaside. I was about twelve years old. Suddenly, I had a brilliant idea! I put some water into my bucket and I poured it over my cousin. My cousin was about fifteen at the time. He jumped up and yelled at me. I laughed and ran away, but I was a bit scared. Anyway, I ran towards the end of the beach. This wall was about the same height as me. It was about one metre fifty centimetres. Well, I jumped right over the wall. When I turned round and looked at the wall, I was shocked. I didn't know how I had jumped over it. I tried to jump it the next day, but I couldn't. We've been back to that place every year since then. I've always tried to jump over the wall, but I've never done it again. I've never jumped over that wall again to this day. It's the strangest experience I've ever had.

B: One day, the doctor told my father that he had gallstones. The doctor wanted to send him to hospital for an operation, but my father didn't want to go to hospital. He didn't like the idea of surgery. He decided to try and cure the gallstones himself. So he went on a special diet. He didn't eat anything for four weeks. He only drank water, or water with lemon. He knew that smoking was also bad for his gallstones so he stopped smoking, as well. Anyway, after a month he was cured. He has never had gallstones from that day to this and he has never had another cigarette in his life. I think it is the hardest thing he's ever done. But I really admire him for it.

Unit 4

Exercise 2c

I = Interviewer A = Guest

A: I was sitting in the hotel bedroom and it was terrible. Outside in the street, cars and taxis were hooting all day. A police siren was wailing and people were shouting under my bedroom window. Next door to my bedroom there was a TV on and it was blaring out all evening.

I: Oh, no.

A: And on top of all that, they had a dog in the room and it was barking and growling.

I: Oh, no. That must have been awful.

A: It was a terrible din. And upstairs. Well! Upstairs there was a children's disco.

I: Oh God!

A: And children were screaming and

© SANTILLANA

shouting and feet were thumping on the floor right over my head.

I: My God! What did you do?

A: I complained to the manager.

I: Yes.

A: Anyway, fortunately he changed my room and after that it was much better. But still not exactly quiet.

Exercise 3b

story 1

A: We were watching the late night film on TV. I was half-listening for the doorbell because my son was still out and I was expecting him home any minute. It was getting quite late and I was starting to get a bit worried.

story 2

A: Well, I was sunbathing, I was eating an ice-cream at the time. The sun wasshining and it was extremely hot. Hundreds of people were in the sea. They were swimming, sailing, surfing, wind-surfing … I was thinking about going back into the sea for another swim.

story 3

A: I was walking home one night. It was very dark. The moon was shining, but there were no street lamps on in the street so it was really dark and shadowy. Anyway, the street was deadly quiet and I was feeling a bit nervous.

Exercise 5a

I = Interviewer C = Christina

I: And you were about eighteen at the time?

C: Yes. I was living with my parents. I wasn't very happy. In fact, I wasn't speaking to my father at the time.

I: Oh?

C: Oh, we used to have lots of arguments and my dad was very strict. Oh, I suppose I was a bit wild, as well.

I: Mmm.

C: Anyway, so I was a student. I was studying for my final exams at school and I was planning to go to university. I was even thinking of going abroad for a year before I went to university. Anyway, that didn't happen because I got pregnant.

I: So, you didn't finish your exams or anything?

C: No. I left school straight away. My parents were really shocked and my dad threw me out.

I: Where did you go?

C: To stay with a friend. My mum helped me, though. I used to telephone her in the daytime when my dad was at work. So, then I got married after the baby was born.

I: Did your parents come to the wedding?

C: Oh, yes. They were OK when I told them I was going to get married.

I: And now, you've been married for how long?

C: Seven years now. My eldest boy is seven now.

I: And you've had two other children since then?

C: Yes, I've got a girl who's five and another boy, three.

I: And now? You're happy?

C: Yes, I am. Although I didn't choose to have any children at that time, I'm glad now that I've got my children. And, I'm happy I'm married.

I = Interviewer B = Birgit

I: You used to be a kindergarten teacher, Birgit?

B: That's right.

I: But you just decided you wanted a change?

B: Yes. I was working quite happily in the kindergarten. I was planning to get married to my boyfriend and I thought everything was fine. But then one day I just decided I wanted a complete change.

I: Just like that?

B: Yes. It was a sudden decision. I decided I wanted to be an air hostess. So I quit my job, I finished with my boyfriend and I got a job as an au pair in New York.

I: Why New York?

B: Well, I had to learn English before I could get a job as an air hostess, so I thought that was the best way. I got a job with a good family, met a lot a new people and I learned English. It all worked out OK. Then, before I left New York I applied for a job with Lufthansa.

I: So you came back to Germany after that?

B: Yes. And I did six months training with Lufthansa and then I started flying.

I: No regrets?

B: Oh, no! I go back and visit my friends in the kindergarten from time to time. And I enjoyed working in the kindergarten, working with children, but no,I'm glad I changed my job – and my life!

Exercise 5c

I: So how does your life compare now to how it used to be, Christina?

C: Before I had children?

I: Yes.

C: Oh. Now, I'm much busier than I was when I was a student. I don't have much free time any more. And, of course, moneywise – I'm much worse off financially. I don't have any money for myself now.

I: But you're not sorry that you had to leave school, lose your independence?

C: No. I think I'm much happier now than I was when I was living at home? I think my life is much more enjoyable now and I suppose I'm a nicer person than I used to be.

I: Really?

C: Yes. I think I'm kinder than I was before I had children. I don't know, maybe it's looking after other people and not just yourself. I mean life is much easier when you're living at home, spending your money on clothes, going out, and so on. You don't think about money, food, the cost of telephone bills, electricity bills, that sort of thing. I suppose you take things for granted.

I: Mmm. But now you're going to be a student again.

C: Yes. I'm going to university, after all, next year. Now the children are all at school I've passed all my exams and I'm ready to start in October.

I: So, everything's worked out OK after all.

C: Yes. Better than I expected.

I: So you don't want to turn the clock back?

B: Not at all. I think my life is much more exciting now than it used to be. I've been to so many different countries, met so many people. Things are much more interesting now.

I: What about money? Are you better-off now?

B: Erm. Slightly. Yes, I'm slightly better-off financially now than when I was a kindergarten teacher.

I: And would you say this job is easier?

B: Erm. Well, they're both difficult jobs really. But, as you can imagine, working with children all day can be quite difficult. I suppose being an air hostess is slightly easier. And staying in hotels is nice. No cooking, no cleaning. Anyway, I'm much happier in this job. And, no, I don't want to turn the clock back.

Exercise 8b

I = Interviewer E = Edison Ortega

I: So, you used to live in Chile? Was that in Santiago?

E: Yes. We used to live in a beautiful old house, right in the centre of Santiago. My parents were quite well-off so we had a good lifestyle.

I: Are your parents still there?

E: Yes. Just me and my brother left in 1973.

I: You left because of the military coup in Chile?

E: Yes. We were students at the time, me and my older brother. We were at university in Santiago. I was studying to be a journalist. I used to write a student magazine there. It was a socialist magazine so when the military coup happened I was really scared. I mean it was dangerous, at that time, to have, you know, socialist ideas.

I: Do you remember what you were doing when you heard the news that there was a military government?

E: Oh, yes. I remember it very well. I was in the university cafeteria. I was talking with a few friends. We'd heard something was happening and we were planning an article for the magazine. Of course, this article was against the military.

I: So what did you do when it finally happened?

E: Well. I stayed at home for a few days just to see what was really going on. And then I heard that some of my friends had been arrested by the police. So I didn't go back to university. I was beginning to be really frightened. Then my brother told me that a few of his friends were going to London. And I decided, the next day, to go with them. I packed a few things and left. It was a terrible time, saying goodbye to my parents, going to a strange country and all that.

I: But you didn't stay in London?

E: No. I had a friend in Scotland and I went there after a few weeks in London. I think I wanted to go somewhere quiet, somewhere peaceful, where I didn't see police cars every day. And I've lived here ever since, since 1974.

I: And now you're married with a family?

E: Yes. A lot has happened since then. I've got married, er- I've had two children, two boys. Er- I've re-trained as a mechanic and now I have my own garage here.

© SANTILLANA

I: And how do you find life here?
E: Oh. I like it. As you can see, it's very peaceful – much quieter than Santiago.
I: Have you been back to Santiago since you came here?
E: Yes. I went back two years ago.
I: And what was it like, then? Different?
E: Very different. Oh, now it's much more modern than when I left. More cosmopolitan, you know. It's much easier to buy anything you want? The atmosphere is a thousand times better. Of course, the military dictatorship is finished now.
I: And now? Do you think you and your family will go back to live there?
E: No. Not yet. I'm going to carry on with my business here. And I'm going to wait until the children finish school. And then, maybe. Maybe I'll go backwith Ann, my wife. I don't know. Anyway, I'm not going to go back for another ten years, at least. Well, holidays, maybe. But not to live.

Unit 5

Exercise 5b

I = Interviewer S = Sam J = Jim
K = Kim C = Chi

I: So where did you say you were from in the United States, Jim?
J: From New Jersey.
I: And your 35, that's right, isn't it?
J: That's it.

I: And you haven't got any children?
C: No. That's right. Not yet, anyway.
I: And how long have you been working for Swanky Modes as a designer?
C: Er- for about nine months now.

I: So you speak quite a lot of languages then. How did you learn them all?
S: Well, I lived in Spain for five years when I was at school so I'm bilingual in Spanish and English, really.
I: Oh, I see. Yes.
S: Then I found it quite easy to learn Italian and I spent six months there before I went to university so my Italian is very good, too.
I: Uh-uh.
S: And then I learned French at school and I was quite good at it so I'm not too bad at French, but my Spanish and Italian are much better.
I: That's excellent. I wish I could …

I: And do you speak any foreign languages at all?
J: No. I'm afraid not.
I: It doesn't matter for this job really …

I: And you find your job interesting at the moment?
K: Oh, yes. Very. I mean the children are really great and … well, we have a good time together really.
I: So, obviously you enjoy working with children?
K: Very much so.
I: But you haven't got children of your own.
K: No. And I'm free to travel anywhere at the moment.

I: And you've been in this job for about three months now, haven't you?

I: And you said you were twenty two didn't you?
C: That's right.

I: French?
K: No. I'm afraid not. A little Italian, but no French.
I: Right.

Exercise 9b

I = Interviewer K = Kim

I: OK. Kim. Tell us as much as you can about yourself in the next two minutes.
K: So, well, er- My name's Kim Sharp. Er- I'm nineteen and I come from Australia. Let me see, er- I finished school last year and I've been here in England for three months, working as a nanny. What else? Oh, yes. I like children and I want to train to be a teacher when I go back to Australia. Er- Let's think. Well, er- back in Australia people go swimming a lot and they play a lot of tennis. And, well, er- I like swimming and tennis too and scubadiving. What else can I say? Er- Oh, yes. I'm not very good at learning languages. I can speak a little Italian and Greek, but er- not very well. But I'm quite good at sport and, let's think, at sport and at maths and English. So, Let's see. What else? I er- want to stay in England another year or er- maybe ayear and a half and then go back to Australia. I er-, well, I like it here. It's different and I've learned a lot of different things. Er- I've made lots of new friends, but I don't want to stay here for ever because I miss my family and friends back home. Well. I think that's all.
I: That's just fine Kim. And now we're going to ask you a few questions.

Unit 6

Exercise 3b

A: So who are the world's biggest oil consumers?
B: Oh, no question. The United States. They consume about ten times as much as Britain or Canada. An enormous amount of oil.
A: And is there much difference between, say Britain and other European countries likeFrance?
B: No, not really. Britain consumes nearly as much as France and Italy. Spain, for example, consumes less than Britain. In fact, Italy consumes about twice as much as Spain, for example. But between Britain France and Italy there's not much difference. Let's see, er- I'd say France consumes slightly more than Britain and slightly less than Italy, but not much.
A: Germany?
B: Yes, well Germany consumes about as much as China. And, of course, China is a much bigger country. And you see Japan is much smaller than China, but in terms of oil, it consumes much more than China.

Exercise 6b

A: Hello and thank you for calling the Numerology Hotline. I'll just give you few simple instructions to follow so that you can get the information you want. Now, if you want to know how to calculate your personal numbers press 0 on your telephone and if you've already calculated your numbers and want this week's forecast press double 0. Do that now. Hello. I'm going to tell you how to calculate your personal numbers. Have a paper and pen handy. Ready? So, write down your date of birth in numbers only. For example, if you were born on the twentieth of September 1968, you'll write down 20, 9, 1968. Now add all these numbers together. So, for example for the twentieth of September 1968 you would add 20 plus nine, plus one, plus nine, plus six plus eight. If you add all those numbers together it will make 53. Then add the five and the three together and it will be 8. Do that for your own date of birth. Then for your second personal number just add the numbers of the date, not including the month and the year. So in our example that would be twenty, so two plus nought will be two. That's how to calculate your two personal numbers. If you get the same number each time it just means the forecast for your number will be doubly true. If you are ready to find out your forecast, press the number on your telephone that is the same as your first personal number. Are you ready? Press the number you want now.

Unit 7

Exercise 4b

I: Do you have any particular habits, you know, things you do if you're nervous or if you're reading something, like that?
B: Yes. I do.
I: What is it?
B: Biting my bottom lip.
I: Yes? Like this?
B: Like this. I put my teeth over my bottom lip and bite it. Sometimes it hurts after a while, but I still do it.
I: Do you do it when you're reading, watching TV? When?
B: Usually when I'm thinking or concentrating, like doing homework, doing an exam, things like that.

I: What are your particular habits, then?
C: Oh er-, yes. Twisting my hair round my finger.
I: Well, you've got long hair, haven't you? I can't do that.
C: No. Yes, I do it like this, round and round my finger.
I: All the time?
C: Well … usually when I am listening to someone, or yes, I suppose when I'm really interested in something. Look? I've started to do it now.

I: Jack?
D: Yes. Mine's coughing. I cough, like this.
I: But you haven't really got a cough?
D: Oh no. It isn't like a normal cough. I do it because I'm nervous or worried about something.

© SANTILLANA

I: What about you, Sue?
E: Me, well one of my bad habits is tapping my feet.
I: What? When you're angry or something?
E: That's right. I can feel myself getting angry and my feet start going … tapping tapping … like this. Or sometimes if I'm getting impatient. You know if someone is a bit stupid in class and I get impatient with them. My feet start tapping.
I: Or if someone's late, or something like that?
E: Yes. If I'm angry.

I: What about you, Sam?
F: I'm afraid its biting my nails, in my case. I've done it since I was a child.
I: What? When you're nervous, or …?
F: No, not nervous. I think it's mostly when I'm bored actually.

Exercise 6b

T = Teacher C = Children

T: Of course the simplest way to communicate with someone is to speak to them. But what happens if they're too far away and can't hear. The North American Indians, for example, had a very good way of sending messages. What was it?
C: Smoke signals.
T: That's right. The North American Indians spoke different languages so it was very useful to send messages by smoke signals from one tribe to another because everyone could understand them. And, of course, they could be seen from a long way away. Then there have been several ways of sending messages in code, by using sounds to spell out letters of the alphabet. Does anyone know what system ships use to send messages across the sea?
C: Is it the Morse Code?
T: Yes. The Morse Code. You can send bleeps of sound by the radio, using long and short sounds to make letters of the alphabet. And then other people have used sound, too, in a different way. Have you ever heard about drum language?
C: Sending messages by drum beats? They used to do that in parts of Africa.
T: That's right. People could send messages over several miles, very fast, by beating different sounds on drums. Now, of course we can use modern technology.
C: Like fax machines.
T: Fax machines, and …
C: Telephones, computers.
T: Yes. Now we have so much technology for sending messages across the world. But of course there are people who can't see, blind people who can't read letters on the page, they have to feel the letters.
C: That's Braille. I've seen some Braille books in the library.
T: Exactly. There's the Braille alphabet for the blind and there's sign language.
C: For people who are deaf or dumb.
T: That's right. If people are deaf and dumb and can't hear anything and can't speak, they need a special way of communicating with sign language.

Exercise 8b

A: We hadn't seen each other for three years. She was sitting in the restaurant when I walked in, behind her, very quietly. Then I tapped her on the shoulder. When she turned round she looked at me for a second and then her jaw dropped.
B: Was she very surprised?
A: Oh, yes. Very surprised indeed. I mean she was absolutely amazed.

Exercise 8c

conversation 1

A: So, I was about 40 minutes late. When I got there she was standing outside the cinema. She was standing there with her hands on her hips, tapping her foot.
B: Was she very annoyed?
A: Oh, God, yes. Very annoyed indeed. I mean she was really furious.

conversation 2

A: So, I gave him the present next morning. When he opened it he had a great big smile on his face.
B: Was he really pleased?
A: Oh, yes. He was absolutely delighted.

conversation 3

A: I mean, he just walked into the living room, threw off his shoes and went straight upstairs to bed.
B: Was he very tired?
A: Oh, yes. He was really exhausted.

conversation 4

A: We were walking through the forest and it was completely dark. We had no light, no map or anything. Honestly we didn't know which way to go.
B: Was it very frightening?
A: Very frightening indeed. It was absolutely terrifying.

conversation 5

A: It was a great film. We didn't move at all, from the first few minutes until the very end. We just sat with our eyes glued to the screen the whole time.
B: So, it was very interesting.
A: Oh, yes. Very. It was absolutely fascinating.

Unit 8

Exercise 3b

I = Interviewer

I: Do you have any pet hates, Tony?
A: Well, one of my pet hates is people who talk too much. I can't stand people that never stop talking. Like my aunty Theresa.
B: Me, too. But one of my pet hates is restaurants where people come up to your table singing, you know, playing a guitar and singing to you while you eat. Oh, I hate that.
I: What about you Kim?
C: Me, oh I can't stand the moment when the alarm rings. You're lying in bed, all nice and warm and then brrr-rr and you think, Oh no. I really hate that moment when the alarm goes off.
D: I really dislike the moment when an exam starts. The room's all silent. Everyone's really nervous and you all sit there with your pens ready. Ugh! Horrible!
E: Well, one of my pet hates is people whose nails are all dirty and broken. I think that looks really disgusting. Scruffy hair and scruffy clothes are not too bad, but I can't stand dirty nails.
I: How about you Angie?
F: Oh, for me its violent films. I hate films which are too violent. I just can't watch and usually I have to leave the cinema if it's a film that's really violent.
G: My pet hate is machines that don't work properly. Especially vending machines. You know, you put your money in, your money disappears and then there's this strange noise and you know that the machine just isn't working. You've lost your money and all you want is a cup of coffee. That drives me mad. And sometimes at work when the photocopier or the computer breaks down. God! I feel like kicking it – I do sometimes.
G: … and then it works.
G: That's right. Infuriating, isn't it? I hate any machine that doesn't work properly.
H: For me, it's people who look really snobbish. You know. They walk round with their noses in the air. I really dislike people like that.
I: What about you, Ian? Have you got any pet hates?
J: I think that my pet hate is any place where thousands of people go for their holiday. I can't stand beaches, for example, where hundreds of people are sunbathing, playing loud music, shouting on the beach, that kind of thing. Or amusement arcades where hundreds of people sit for hours playing the machines. I hate those kind of places.

Exercise 6a

P = Policeman W = Witness

W: Well, I don't know. He looked a bit dirty, really.
P: Well, er- how tall was he – approximately?
W: Oh, I'm not sure. Not very big. Smallish I suppose.
P: Middle-aged, young?
W: Well, youngish.
P: Was he white?
W: Yes. White. I think he had blue eyes.
P: What about his hair?
W: Oh, yes. It was horrible. Dirty, you know, long and greasy.
P: What colour?
W: I think it was blond. Yes. It was and he had it in a ponytail.
P: Can you remember anything about his face?
W: Well, he had a thin, pale face. And his nose was thin, too. You know, kind of long and pointed. Oh, yes. I remember now, he wore glasses. And!
P: Yes?
W: He had a mole on his cheek.
P: Right. Thanks. Now let's see I've got it all down. He was white, male, youngish. Er- what, late twenties, thirties?
W: Yes, he was in his late twenties or early thirties.
P: And he was slight in build with a pale complexion. He had blue eyes and he

© SANTILLANA

wore glasses. His hair was blond, long and greasy and he wore it in a ponytail. He had a thin face and a long pointed nose. You also remember he had a mole on his cheek. Is that about everything?

W: Yes, I think so. And his general appearance was very scruffy.

P: Well, thanks a lot for your help.

Unit 9

Exercise 3a

I = Interviewer B = Beth

I: You were attacked once Beth, weren't you?

B: Mmm-mm.

I: Can you tell us about it?

B: Yes. Well, I took a taxi home one night after a party at my friend's house. The taxi dropped me off at my front door. I just got my key out and as I was putting my key in the door someone tapped me on the shoulder. For a second I just thought it was my brother but when I turned round I came face-to-face with a man I'd never seen before. He grabbed my throat as if he was trying to strangle me. I don't know how I did it, but I twisted round and elbowed him in the stomach – really hard.

I: Did he let go, then?

B: Yeah! He let go for a second and I screamed and screamed. Just then someone put a light on in the house opposite and my attacker, he ran off.

I: Did you call the police?

B: Well, someone called the police and they came a few minutes later.

I: Did they catch him?

B: No. They drove me round to see if we could find him, but he'd disappeared. The police were very good, though. They really tried to find him. They said I'd done really well. A police woman came the next day to see if I was OK. She gave me a bit of advice. She said, 'If I were you I'd fix a light over your front door, so you can see better at night.' And she said 'In future, I wouldn't let the taxi go before you're inside the house.' She was really nice.

Exercise 7a

I: What do you think about crime these days?

A: Well, in my opinion people watch too much television. They see all this violence and crime and they copy what they see on television. That's what I think.

B: If you ask me, the police are at fault. They are not interested in small crimes like burglary and pickpocketing. So the police don't follow things up enough. People commit crimes and then nothing happens to them.

C: If you want to know what I think, I think it's terrible. Most crimes are committed by young people, teenagers who should be in school. I can't understand it, we didn't do things like that. It's awful, young people today don't seem to know what's right and wrong.

D: As far as I'm concerned I blame unemployment. People today don't see any future. A lot of people have no job, no money and so they turn to crime. I don't think it's right what they do, but I just think people have no hope, no hope for the future.

E: Well, in my view parents are to blame. Parents don't teach their children the difference between right and wrong properly. That's how I see it.

Unit 10

Exercise 1a

N = Narrator

N: Here is the story of the Gingerbread Boy. Once upon a time, there was a little old woman and a little old man who lived all alone in a little old house. They had no children at all. So, one day the little old woman made a boy out of gingerbread. She made him a chocolate jacket with seeds for buttons. His mouth was made of pink sugar and his eyes were two raisins.
The little old woman put the Gingerbread Boy on a tray and put him into the oven to bake. She thought, 'Now I'll have a little boy of my own.' When it was time for the Gingerbread Boy to be ready, she opened the oven door and pulled out the tray …
The little old woman and the little old man ran after him as fast as they could. But the Gingerbread Boy just laughed and shouted, 'Run, run as fast as you can! You can't catch me, I'm the Gingerbread Man!' And they couldn't catch him. The Gingerbread Boy ran on until he came to a cow by the roadside. 'Stop, little Gingerbread Boy,' said the cow, 'I want to eat you.' The Gingerbread Boy laughed and said, 'I have run away form a little old woman and a little old man. And I can run away from you, I can. You can't catch me, I'm the Gingerbread Man.' The Gingerbread Boy ran on until he came to a horse in a field …
But the Gingerbread Boy just laughed and said, 'I have run away from a little old woman, a little old man and a cow. And I can run away from you, I can. You can't catch me, I'm the Gingerbread Man.' And the horse couldn't catch him. After a while the Gingerbread Boy came to a gate with a flock of birds sitting on it. When the birds smelled the Gingerbread Boy they said to him, 'Don't run away! You look very good to eat.' But the Gingerbread Boy ran faster than ever and as he ran, he called out, …
By this time, the Gingerbread Boy was so proud he didn't think anyone could catch him. Quite soon he saw a fox coming from behind a tree. The fox looked at him and began to run. But the Gingerbread Boy shouted to the fox, … 'Run, run as fast as you can. You can't catch me, I'm the Gingerbread Man.' 'Ho-ho!' laughed the fox, 'I wouldn't catch you even if I could. I don't want to disturb you at all.' At that moment the Gingerbread Boy came to a river. He could not swim across it so the fox kindly offered to help him. 'Jump on my tail and I'll take you across,' smiled the fox. So the Gingerbread Boy jumped on the fox's tail. Just when they were in the middle of the river the fox said, 'You are too heavy for my tail. I think you had better jump on my back or you might sink under the water.' So the Gingerbread Boy jumped on the fox's back. A few metres further on, the fox turned his head round and said, …
So the Gingerbread Boy jumped on his nose. The minute the fox reached the other side of the river, he threw his head back and – Snap – 'Dear me!' said the Gingerbread Boy, 'I am a quarter gone!' The next minute he said, 'Oh dear! Now I am half gone.' The next minute he said, 'My goodness gracious, I am three quarters gone.'

Exercise 3b

I = Interviewer J = John

I: Now I know you believe that we humans are not really so superior. We think we're very clever, but in fact, we're not as clever as we think.

J: That's right. Let's take one example. We have our Olympic games and every time someone runs faster than before. But what's the fastest we can run? About 100 metres in 10 seconds, that's about 30 kilometres an hour. Well, many animals can run faster than that. A cheetah, for example can run about 100 kilometres an hour.

I: But that's just running.

J: No. We humans are not very good at many things. We're not very good at seeing in the dark. Cat's are able to see in the dark very well. We think we're experts at music, but we're unable to hear very high-pitched sounds. Look at dogs they can hear many more sounds than we can. I mean, we're not very clever at all. We have to live in nice warm houses, we need our cars to take us everywhere. I sometimes think we're going to lose the ability to walk in a few hundred years time, we use our cars so much. Can you imagine humans living like penguins in freezing cold weather or walking hundreds of miles, like so many animals do. No, I'm afraid we're not very strong. We wouldn't be able to survive without our restaurants, supermarkets, microwave ovens our freezers. And look at the rubbish we make. Because we have to have all our food prepared and our houses so warm, we leave our rubbish everywhere. You don't find animals polluting the world, leaving their rubbish behind them wherever they go. It's humans who pollute the Earth. We think we're clever, but who's going to clear up all this rubbish we make? Everybody knows we're destroying the world – and we're destroying animals, too. We must stop thinking we're so clever when obviously we're not.

Exercise 3c

I: And you believe that we've lost a lot of our abilities in the last few hundred years.

J: Certainly. Look at what we used to do. In the past we were able to catch our

© SANTILLANA

own food or grow food for our families. Now we don't know how to do that any more. Half the world hasn't got enough food and the other half buys everything in the supermarket. And so many other things. I mean, in the past humans could travel for days on foot, whereas now, look at us, we have to drive everywhere. At one time we had to build our own homes, our own houses, but now we just buy one and move in.

I: But do you really think we are worse as people now.

J: Yes! Definitely. Look at us, every evening in front of the television, nobody talking, nobody playing music, telling stories. At one time we had the ability to entertain ourselves, but now we're lost without TV or videos. And what do we spend our time doing? Rushing off to work, learning a lot of useless information. Most of the information is no use anyway. We didn't have to use and understand so much information in the past so we could spend more time relaxing, painting, reading – doing things which are better for us. And, of course, in the past we needed nature; we had to respect nature, now, on the other hand we think we can control nature. But that's rubbish. We can't! We're just destroying ourselves.

Exercise 8a

I = Interviewer

I: What do you think about interpreting dreams? You know, if we look at our dreams we can learn a lot about our secret feelings and so on? Do you think it's true? Do you believe in it?

A: Well, yes and no. I mean I do and I don't. I mean, I believe dreams have a meaning, but I don't believe they predict the future.

I: What do you believe?

B: As far as I'm concerned, it's a load of rubbish. We have to understand reality not dreams.

I: So you don't believe in it at all?

B: No. I mean, yes, of course we dream, I know that and maybe it all means something important but I don't think dreams tell us much about ourselves.

I: You disagree, don't you?

C: Yes. I definitely believe in it. Interpreting our dreams helps us to understand ourselves better. I definitely believe that's true. Sometimes we're not very honest with ourselves and we can see the truth about ourselves in our dreams.

D: I haven't time for all that nonsense. Life's too short to worry about things like dreams. Just get on with life. That's what I say. We spend too much time thinking about what's really in our minds, our real feelings and all that. What's it all for, I ask myself. Are we any better off in the end?

I: What about you?

E: Let's say I believe in it to some extent. I think it's all very interesting, but I don't take it too seriously.

Unit 11

Exercise 2b

I = Interviewer A = Bank manageress

I: So you've seen one or two robberies in your time here?

A: Oh, yes. One very serious one. But my favourite robbery …

I: Your favourite?

A: Well, yes. It was my favourite because it didn't succeed and, in fact, it was ridiculous how it happened.

I: What happened exactly?

A: Well, it was Friday afternoon, just a few minutes before closing time and the bank was empty when suddenly this man came in. He rushed through the doors. He was quite young really, but we couldn't see his face. It was covered with a red scarf. You know, tied across his mouth. Well, he rushed in holding a gun and he shouted to the cashier, 'Give me the money! Come on, I want the money in the till!' Well, she was terrified …

I: The cashier?

A: Yes. And she tried to explain that we didn't have much money in the till. But he didn't want to listen. I suppose he was in a hurry. So he shouted again, 'Just hand over the money.' So I stepped in and said, 'Most of the money has been taken away. Every Friday morning the money is taken out of the till and we haven't got much left by Friday afternoon.' Anyway I gave him what was in the till. Of course there was much more in the safe at the back, but I wasn't going to offer him that, was I?

I: No.

A: So he grabbed the money I gave him and ran.

I: Out?

A: Well no. That was the funny thing. He ran to the door and he pushed and pushed, but it wouldn't open. He just kept pushing and pushing on the door. I think he thought we'd locked him in, you know, electronically.

I: And you hadn't?

A: No. You see you have to pull the door, not push. It was even written right across the door, 'Pull' but he was in such a panic he didn't think about pulling the door. When he saw that he couldn't open it by pushing he just sat down.

I: By the door?

A: Yes. His gun hadn't been a real one, you see. And he thought we'd locked him in. So he just sat down with his head on his knees. We called the police. In fact, someone in the street had called the police earlier because they'd seen something through the door. And anyway, the police came and he was arrested. That was that.

I: Not a very clever robber really, was he?

A: No, fortunately.

Exercise 6a

A: These are two stories I read about. I don't know whether to believe them or not. But anyway, the first one took place in January 1970. A Mrs Doreen Jackson was having a driving lesson. This was in Cheltenham, in England. She was with her driving instructor when suddenly she changed gear and came to a stop. The driving instructor was really surprised. Mrs Jackson explained that she had stopped so quickly to avoid a woman who had stepped in front of the car. The driving instructor had seen nothing and he thought she was just making excuses for bad driving so he said, 'Oh yeah? And I saw a group of pink elephants.' But Mrs Jackson was certain she had seen a tall woman in black, old-fashioned clothes, holding her hand up to her face. It seems that a woman like this had been seen on many occasions on this road. People had described a tall woman in black clothes, sometimes holding a handkerchief to her face. Lots of people had seen such a woman who then just disappeared. It seems that a woman called Imogen Swinhoe had died nearby in 1878 and this woman was thought to be her ghost.

Exercise 6b

A: The other story was from about the same time. It happened in 1968 in the south of England. A Mr P. J. Chase was waiting for the bus. He was just looking up and down the street daydreaming when suddenly he noticed two small, old-fashioned cottages. One of the cottages had a sign on the wall with the date 1837. When he mentioned this to a colleague, who was a local man, his colleague was certain that there were no such cottages and that in that place were two modern brick houses. When Mr Chase went back to check he saw that his colleague had been right. The site was occupied by two red brick modern houses, not the cottages which he thought he had seen. When some of the local people who had lived around there a long time were asked about the site, they said that there had been two cottages there at one time, but they had been demolished several years ago.

Unit 12

Exercise 1b

A: I know this one. This is a person, isn't it?

B: That's right. Can you see? It looks like the legs and body of a person, doesn't it? A lot of these Japanese characters are like small pictures.

C: So, is number two another person, but with his arms out?

B: Yes.

C: I think this is 'big', isn't it?

B: Exactly.

A: Oh yes. Look! It's a person with his arms out to show something is big.

B: That's it. Number two is 'big'. Can you guess this one? Think what it looks like.

C: Number three?

B: Yes.

D: Water?

A: Yes. This looks like a river, doesn't it?

D: Mmm.

B: It is. It means 'river'. What about number four?

C: I'm not sure.

A: Mmm?

© SANTILLANA

B: OK. Try number five. Do you think it looks more like a mountain, a tree or a forest?

D: A tree, I suppose.

B: Uh-huh. Number five is a tree. So look carefully at number six.

D: Oh yes. It has the same symbol as number five, but there are three of them. So, if that was a tree, this would be a forest, wouldn't it?

B: Right again. See? It's not really so difficult, is it?

A: So number six is a forest. Yes, I see it.

C: So this must be a mountain, mustn't it?

D Yes.

A: Number four is a mountain, yes. It has three points like the peaks of a mountain.

B: Good. Do you want to try a few more?

Exercise 4a

I = Interviewer L = Linguist

I: So how exactly do we learn to talk? I mean when we are babies?

L: Well. Let's start with the sounds. There's a theory that babies all over the world make the same sounds first. You know …

I: Ga-ga-goo-goo-brr-brr-ma-ma …

L: Yes! That's exactly it. It sounds like that, doesn't it? It doesn't matter what language the parents speak at first.

I: They all make more or less the same sounds?

L: Yes. But then slowly they stop making certain sounds.

I: Which ones?

L: Well, if they don't hear a particular sound because that sound is not in the language their parents speak, then babies forget it.

I: You mean, for example, the rr-rrr-rr sound. We don't really have that in English, do we? But you mean, little babies can do it before they learn to speak?

L: Exactly. But if their parents speak English, then they don't hear that sound so they stop doing it and they, we, forget how to do it.

I: That's true. We can't really do that very well, can we?

L: That's right. And they, babies, begin to make only the sounds they hear in their parents' language.

I: And what about words? They have to get sounds from words, don't they?

L: Well. You remember when you made your baby sound just now? You said, something like 'Ga-ga-boo-boo br-brr-ma-ma …' Can you hear it?

I: Ma-ma?

L: Yes. Babies are making all these sounds, just like that, and then in the middle they might say, 'Ma-ma'. And what happens?

I: The mother jumps up and down and says, 'Did you hear him?' He said, 'Ma-ma. Ma-ma. Did you hear him?'

L: Exactly. And she's really pleased, isn't she? So the baby says it again because he knows his mother loves it.

Exercise 4c

I = Interviewer M = Mother
L = Linguist C = Child

I: … and simple sentences?

L: Yes, like, 'Me want more juice', 'That my car', simple things like that.

I: But they make mistakes, don't they? You know, 'That my car', instead of 'That's my car'.

L: Oh yes. And things like, 'I drinked my juice', not 'I drank my juice'.

I: Yes. That's right.

L: That's very important. Because babies don't just copy, you know, imitate what they hear, they are very logical. So, if we say 'walked' and 'washed' in the past tense, why not 'drinked' instead of 'drank'. It's very logical, isn't it?

I: Yes.

L: But that's not all. Let me play you an example of a mother talking to her child and you'll hear something very interesting.

I: OK.

M: Have you finished?

C: Yes. No.

M: Come on now. Finish your dinner. Do you want an apple? What are you doing?

M: No. Don't do that. Here, wipe your mouth.

C: Dinner all gone.

M: Don't put your apple in the water.

C: Apples. Apples.

M: Have you finished?

L: Now. Let me ask you. What kind of language was the mother using there?

I: Er- I'm not quite sure what you mean.

L: Well, she asked him if he had finished his dinner, whether he wanted an apple. She asked him what he was doing when he dropped his plate.

I: You mean asking a lot of questions?

L: Yes. And giving instructions.

I: Mmm-mm. She told him not to do that when he dropped his plate and she told him to wipe his mouth and er- …

L: Exactly. And that's what small children hear most – questions and instructions. But! When children first speak, they don't usually ask a lot of questions or give instructions. They make statements like: 'That my car.' 'My dinner all gone.' And that's what I find so interesting. When we learn a language we don't just imitate, we use our own logic to make up our own language.

I: Even if we sometimes make mistakes in what we say.

L: Exactly. We make logical mistakes.

Exercise 7a

A: So, when we think that 2,000 years ago English did not exist and now it's become an international, a world language – that's a very strange accident of history, isn't it? Let's say it all began with the old British Empire, with its colonies all over the world, from Australia to Hong Kong and Singapore and India, Nigeria and Ghana in West Africa, Canada and, of course, the most famous of all, the United States. It's true, other countries also had colonies too, like France, Spain, Germany, Portugal, Holland and Italy. And naturally there are millions of French, Spanish and Portuguese speakers in the world today – not to mention the millions who all speak Arabic from the old Islamic empires. So, why aren't we all busy learning, say, Portuguese or Arabic today? I suppose one reason has to be the enormous power and influence of the United States. With the rise in technology and communications systems, so much information has come out of the United States in the last century that the world has gradually adopted English as its lingua franca, its international language. There were attempts to create an international language in the past. Even a hundred years ago, people realised the importance of having one language for international communication. But the idea was always to have a created language, an artificial language, like Esperanto, but this idea never really succeeded. Maybe language is such a natural, human thing that we can never really accept an artificial language. Anyway, it looks like there's no going back now, doesn't it? I suppose it's going to be English for the next century, at any rate. But who knows, it could be a different language in another hundred or two hundred years. History can be a very funny business. To give you an example – in the United States, those early European settlers whose families had recently arrived from Holland, Britain, Germany and so on, had to decide what language they would use as their official language at that time. They took a vote and, do you, know that it was a very close vote between English and Dutch. Just think, if the voting had been a little different we could all be learning Dutch right now and not English. Funny to think of, isn't it? Language is a strange thing and it's very often difficult to control. Just look at another example. Probably the most famous word in the world. What would you say it was? Yes. I think it's probably those two letters. OK. Do you know the origin of that word? The story goes that the seventh President of the United States, Andrew Jackson, was not very well-educated and that he wasn't very good at spelling. OK in the American Army was a quick way of saying 'All Correct'. President Jackson thought 'all' was spelt 'o-l-l' and that correct was spelt with a 'k', so OK was short for 'All Correct'. I tell you, language is a very strange business.

© SANTILLANA

Additional material

Unit 1 Exercise 3

What's Australia like?

Partner B reads this text. Partner A reads the text on page 7. Ask and answer questions to complete the text.

Australia is the world's sixth largest country. Although it is large in size, it has a very small population of about 16.5 million. About 90% of the people live in ______. The largest city is Sydney with a population of over ______, but the capital is Canberra with only about ______ people.

The climate is varied: in the north it is tropical with summer rains, parts of the south and west are ______, while in the southeast there are cool, wet winters and ______ summers. Australia is rich in metals, oil and coal and the main farming produce is ______ and dairy produce such as butter, milk and cheese.

The first people in Australia were Aborigines who came from Asia ______ years ago. Now there are only about 100,000 Australian Aborigines and approximately ______ of the population is of British origin. The official language is English and the currency is the ______.

Exercise 12 Role play

Act out a conversation in a travel agent's office with a partner. Partner B is the travel agent. Partner A is the passenger and reads the information on page 15. Only partner B reads this.

The Philippines

Passport/Visa Requirements:

A valid passport is required by all.

Visas are not required by tourists provided they stay no longer than 21 days and they have passports valid for at least one year and travel tickets showing onward journeys. A visa is necessary for stays exceeding 21 days.

Population: 56 million

Capital: Manila

Transport: Bus and taxi

Language: Tagalog, English and Spanish

Currency: Pesos. 100 centavos = 1 peso

You need to know:

1 how many passengers are travelling and the ages of any children
2 how long they are planning to travel
3 how many stopovers they are making in the USA.
4 how long they are staying in Manila

Review units 3-4 Exercise 1

Biography of a president

In pairs, ask and answer questions to complete the information on Nelson Mandela. Partner B reads this information. Partner A reads the information on page 48.

Full name:	______ Rolihlahla ______
Date of birth:	18th July, ______
Place of birth:	______
Education:	University of ______. He was expelled for political activities.
First job:	______.
Entered politics:	in ______ as a member of the Youth League. He campaigned for ______.
	became head of the African National Congress in 1991
Married:	married ______ in 1958
Imprisoned:	on Robben Island in 1964. In ______, he was put under house arrest.
Released:	in 1991, after world-wide campaigns for his release
Present job:	______ since May 1994

© SANTILLANA

Unit 5 Exercise 3

The Little old lady from Cricket Creek

These are the missing paragraphs for the story on page 51. The paragraphs are in a jumbled order. Read the paragraphs and put them into the correct place in the text.

A

It turned out to be more like ninety. She handled the typewriter like a machine gun. Art almost got a sore neck watching the keys fly. Mabel handed me three pages. I couldn't find a single error.

'Well, what do you think?' Art asked.

'She's the best typist in the building.'

He shrugged. 'Let's hire ourselves a little old lady from Cricket Creek.'

B

Art stared at me. 'Do you remember anything on the application? Anything?'

'Art! It was six months ago!' I paused for a moment. I can remember *one thing*. Just one.'

'What?'

'She came from Cricket Creek. I wonder if there *is* a Cricket Creek.'

We checked.

There wasn't.

C

Mabel shrugged her tiny shoulders. 'Young man, have you ever lived up North? It's another world. Cold and foggy. I told Harry – that's my husband who died recently, God rest his soul – that we had to come down here. Of course you've never been in Cricket Creek,' she added. I don't think Art had ever heard of Cricket Creek before. Mabel smiled brightly at him, nodding her head.

D

Six months after we hired her, Art walked slowly into my office.

'What's the matter with you?' I asked.

'The cash mail,' he groaned.

We receive a lot of cash mail from our customers. Once a week, on Friday, we take it to the bank. It was Friday.

'What about the cash mail, Art? Come on, what's the matter?'

He looked at me blinking. 'Harvey was taking it to the bank. He called ten minutes ago. He was robbed. Knocked out. And guess who did it?'

'Who?'

'Mabel. Mabel Jumpstone. Our little old lady.'

E

Mrs Jumpstone came shuffling into the office, smiling and nodding her head like an old grey mare. She had on an old black outfit and a purple hat with pink plastic flowers.

She sat down and shouted 'Hello there!'

I looked at Art who was leaning forward in his chair, his mouth open, his eyes round.

'Er ... Mrs Jumpstone,' I began.

'Mabel. Please.'

'OK, Mabel. This is Mr Bowen, my associate.' I waved a hand at Art who muttered something.

Unit 11 Exercise 1

Bad timing

This is the ending of the story *Nightmare in Yellow* on page 116.

Before they could see that his wife was dead and that he was holding her up, all the assembled birthday party guests shouted 'SURPRISE!'

Review units 11-12 Exercise 1

The most famous statue in the world

Partner B reads this text. Partner A reads the text on page 136. Ask and answer questions to complete the text.

THE STATUE OF LIBERTY, situated on Liberty Island in New York Harbour, is one of the world's most famous monuments. The statue was originally designed by Auguste Bartholdi in the 1860s. She was made from _____ and Bartholdi was given advice on _____ by Gustav Eiffel - the creator of the famous _____. The statue is 46 metres high, it weighs 225 tons and each eye is 75 centimetres wide. The statue itself was paid for by the _____ and it was only the pedestal that was funded by the Americans. In fact, the statue had been planned for nearly 20 years before the Americans came up with the money for the pedestal. Everything was finally completed in _____.

The Statue of Liberty can be reached by ferry from Battery Park, every _____ from 10.00am to 4.00pm. The tickets are sold in the _____. The American Museum of Immigration is housed inside the statue and the story of the immigrants to America, who helped to create a nation, is told by slide shows and photographs. The Statue of Liberty was restored in _____ for her _____.

Glossary of dictionary terms

ADJ CLASSIF	Classifying adjective. These are adjectives which cannot have adverbs like *very, more* or *rather* in front of them. You cannot say, *His wife is more* ***dead*** *than yesterday*.
ADJ QUALIT	Qualitative adjective. These adjectives describe a quality and can have adverbs like *very, more* or *rather* in front of them. *Funny* is an example... *a very* ***funny*** film.
ADV	Adverb
ATTRIB	Indicates an adjective which is used in front of a noun.
CONVENTION	Describes words and phrases which are used in standard expressions.
NO CONT	Indicates when a verb is not normally used in the continuous form.
ONLY CONT	Indicates when a verb is only used in the continuous form.
N-COUNT	Countable noun
N-UNCOUNT	Uncountable noun
PASS	Refers to the passive form of the verb.
PHR	Refers to a phrase or expression.
PHRASAL VERB	Phrasal verb
PRED	Shows when an adjective is used after a verb.
PREP	Preposition
USU	Shows how a word is usually used.
V	Intransitive verb (does not need an object)
V+O	Transitive verb (needs an object)
V+REPORT-CL/QUOTE	Indicates that a verb can be used in a reporting clause or quotation.
WH	Indicates a 'wh' question word.
⇑	This symbol shows that the following word has a more general meaning similar to the entry word.
=	This symbol shows a synonym to the entry word.
≠	This symbol shows an antonym to the entry word.
▶	This symbol introduces a slight change in the way a word is used.
◊	This symbol indicates a derived word formed by the addition of a suffix.

Irregular verbs

Infinitive	**Simple past**	**Past participle**
be	was/were	been
become	became	become
begin	began	begun
break	broke	broken
burn	burnt	burnt
buy	bought	bought
catch	caught	caught
choose	chose	chosen
come	came	come
cost	cost	cost
cut	cut	cut
do	did	done
draw	drew	drawn
dream	dreamt	dreamt
drink	drank	drunk
drive	drove	driven
eat	ate	eaten
fall	fell	fallen
feel	felt	felt
find	found	found
forget	forgot	forgotten
get	got	got
give	gave	given
go	went	gone
have	had	had
hear	heard	heard
hit	hit	hit
hold	held	held
keep	kept	kept
know	knew	known
leave	left	left
lend	lent	lent
let	let	let
lie	lay	lain
make	made	made
mean	meant	meant
meet	met	met
pay	paid	paid
put	put	put
read /ri:d/	read /red/	read /red/
ring	rang	rung
run	ran	run
say	said	said
see	saw	seen
sell	sold	sold
send	sent	sent
show	showed	shown
shut	shut	shut
sing	sang	sung
sit	sat	sat
sleep	slept	slept
smell	smelt	smelt
speak	spoke	spoken
spell	spelt	spelt
spend	spent	spent
stand	stood	stood
steal	stole	stolen
swim	swam	swum
take	took	taken
teach	taught	taught
tell	told	told
think	thought	thought
throw	threw	thrown
understand	understood	understood
wake	woke	woken
wear	wore	worn
win	won	won
write	wrote	written

© SANTILLANA